Psychoses and Pervasive Developmental Disorders in Childhood and Adolescence

American Academy of Child and Adolescent Psychiatry
and
American Psychiatric Press, Inc.

Psychoses and Pervasive Developmental Disorders in Childhood and Adolescence

Edited by
Fred R. Volkmar, M.D.

Washington, DC
London, England

Copyright © 1996 American Academy of Child and Adolescent Psychiatry
ALL RIGHTS RESERVED
Manufactured in the United States of America on acid-free paper
99 98 97 96   4 3 2 1
First Edition

American Psychiatric Press, Inc.
1400 K Street, N.W., Washington, DC   20005

Library of Congress Cataloging-in-Publication Data
Psychoses and pervasive developmental disorders in childhood and
   adolescence / edited by Fred R. Volkmar.
      p.   cm.
   Includes bibliographical references and index.
   ISBN 1-882103-01-7 (alk. paper)
   1. Psychoses in children.   2. Psychoses in adolescence
3. Developmental disabilities.   I. Volkmar, Fred R.
   [DNLM: 1. Child Development Disorders, Pervasive.   2. Affective
Disorders, Psychotic—in adolescence.   3. Affective Disorders,
Psychotic—in infancy & childhood.   WS 350 P9705 1996]
RJ506.P69P786
618.92′89—dc20
DNLM/DLC
for Library of Congress   95-38068
                                                                        CIP

British Library Cataloguing in Publication Data
A CIP record is available from the British Library.

Contents

Fred R. Volkmar, M.D.

Donald J. Cohen, M.D., and Fred R. Volkmar, M.D.

Contributors

Robert Begtrup, M.D.
Associate Clinical Professor, Division of Child and Adolescent
Psychiatry, School of Medicine, Vanderbilt University, Nashville,
Tennessee

Donald J. Cohen, M.D.
Professor, Child Study Center, Yale University, New Haven,
Connecticut

Ami Klin, Ph.D.
Assistant Professor, Child Study Center, Yale University, New Haven,
Connecticut

Joseph LaBarbera, Ph.D.
Associate Professor, Division of Child and Adolescent Psychiatry,
School of Medicine, Vanderbilt University, Nashville, Tennessee

Melvin Lewis, M.B.B.S., F.R.C.Psych., D.C.H.
Professor of Child Psychiatry and Pediatrics, Child Study Center, Yale
University, New Haven, Connecticut

Wendy D. Marans, M.S.
Associate Research Scientist, Child Study Center, Yale University, New Haven, Connecticut

Christopher J. McDougle, M.D.
Assistant Professor, Child Study Center, Yale University, New Haven, Connecticut

William Mitchell, M.D.
Clinical Assistant Professor, Division of Child and Adolescent Psychiatry, School of Medicine, Vanderbilt University, Nashville, Tennessee

Barry Nurcombe, M.D.
Professor, Division of Child and Adolescent Psychiatry, School of Medicine, Vanderbilt University, Nashville, Tennessee

John Pruitt, M.D.
Fellow, Division of Child and Adolescent Psychiatry, School of Medicine, Vanderbilt University, Nashville, Tennessee

Peter Szatmari, M.D.
Professor, McMaster University Department of Psychiatry, Chedoke-McMaster Hospitals, Hamilton, Ontario, Canada

Michael Tramontana, Ph.D.
Associate Professor, Division of Child and Adolescent Psychiatry, School of Medicine, Vanderbilt University, Nashville, Tennessee

Rameshwari V. Tumuluru, M.D.
Assistant Professor, Department of Psychiatry, Ohio State University, Columbus, Ohio

Fred R. Volkmar, M.D.
Associate Professor, Child Study Center, Yale University, New Haven, Connecticut

Elizabeth B. Weller, M.D.
Professor, Department of Psychiatry, Ohio State University, Columbus, Ohio

Ronald A. Weller, M.D.
Professor, Department of Psychiatry, Ohio State University,
Columbus, Ohio

John Scott Werry, M.D.
Professor Emeritus of Psychiatry, University of Auckland, Auckland,
New Zealand

Shahnour Yaylayan, M.D.
Private Practice, Child and Adolescent Psychiatry, Columbus, Ohio

Preface

Interest in the psychoses and pervasive developmental disorders of childhood and adolescence has increased markedly in recent years. The renewed interest in these conditions was particularly stimulated by the major changes in classification introduced by DSM-III (American Psychiatric Association 1980). It is likely that DSM-IV (American Psychiatric Association 1994) will have a similar impact on the field. This is not a new phenomenon: changes in fundamental diagnostic concepts and their impact on both clinical work and research can be traced back well into the nineteenth century; for example, Maudsley's (1867) description of childhood "insanity" and Kraepelin's description of dementia praecox (Kraepelin 1919). Interest in these conditions arose on both the theoretical and the practical levels: in terms of our theoretical understanding of the nature of early childhood development and the role of experience on the one hand, and on the other, the need to care for severely disabled children and adolescents. Work in the growing field of developmental psychology on normative developmental processes and on intellectual assessment and mental handicap provided yet other lines of work relevant to the understanding of serious psychi-

atric conditions. Unfortunately, both disciplinary and theoretical disagreements made integration of these various lines of work difficult.

At the beginning of the twentieth century, clinicians grappled with
the particular challenges posed by the diagnosis and assessment of children with severe disturbance; several diagnostic concepts with a unique
childhood onset were proposed, such as dementia praecossima (DeSanctis 1906) and dementia infantilis (1908, 1930/1969). On the other hand,
others advocated an apparently more straightforward and parsimonious
approach: the "downward" extrapolation of diagnostic concepts derived
from work with adults. Within this tradition the term *childhood schizophrenia* came to encompass all forms of severe psychiatric disturbance
with an onset in childhood. The battle of "lumpers" versus "splitters"
has continued to the present and is exemplified in the marked differences
between the diagnostic systems of DSM-III-R (American Psychiatric Association 1987) and DSM-IV (American Psychiatric Association 1994)
(see Rutter and Schopler 1992 for a discussion).

For childhood-onset conditions, the assumption of general continuity between adult and childhood schizophrenia proved unsatisfactory
in several ways. Schizophrenia, if strictly defined, was relatively less common in children than in adults (Eisenberg 1957; Potter 1933). The assumption of general continuity in syndrome expression glossed over the
major developmental discontinuities in psychological functioning between children and adults: the notion of "psychosis" in children failed
to recognize the important developmental aspects of children's percep-
tions of reality (see King 1994). Although various alternative diagnostic
concepts had been provided, it was the appearance in 1943 of Leo Kanner's classic description of the syndrome of early infantile autism that
proved to be a watershed event for the emerging field of child psychiatry.
Kanner's description was and remains a remarkably lucid, developmentally and phenomenologically based clinical description. Although important advances have been made in our understanding of this disorder,
resulting in modifications to Kanner's original impressions, his description of the condition stands, five decades later, as a truly remarkable and
indeed a central event. Controversy about the continuity of autism and
childhood schizophrenia continued for nearly two decades following
Kanner's (1943) report and was reflected in DSM-I (American Psychiatric Association 1952) and DSM-II (American Psychiatric Association

1968), in which only childhood schizophrenia was officially recognized as a diagnostic concept.

During the 1960s and 1970s a growing body of evidence began to support the distinctiveness of autism from childhood schizophrenia (see Volkmar 1994). This evidence included differences in aspects of clinical phenomenology, such as onset, specific clinical features, family history, natural history, and so forth (Kolvin 1971; Rutter 1970, 1972). At the same time there was a growing awareness that other assumptions about childhood psychopathology should also be questioned. For example, the notion that children were somehow "protected" from depression and other forms of affective illness appeared to be mistaken (see Chapter 2), and an awareness of important developmental correlates of reality testing raised basic theoretical issues about the notion of childhood "psychosis" (see Chapter 1). The growing body of work on serious psychopathological conditions of childhood onset resulted in major modifications in DSM-III.

DSM-III explicitly recognized the continuities and discontinuities of severe psychiatric disturbance over the course of development. It also adopted a multiaxial approach, which proved particularly relevant to childhood- and adolescent-onset conditions and provided much more specific definitions of conditions included within it (Rutter et al. 1975). Advances of the previous two decades were acknowledged by recognizing autism as an official diagnostic category. Changes in syndrome descriptions were made in recognition of the emerging literature on such conditions as childhood schizophrenia and affective illness. The emphasis on a phenomenologically and theoretically based system proved to be a truly remarkable stimulus to subsequent research. In DSM-III and its successors, both the continuities and the discontinuities of psychiatric disturbance in children and adults were emphasized. The term *childhood schizophrenia* disappeared from the "official" psychiatric lexicon, and an attempt was made to apply the diagnostic criteria for schizophrenia to both children and adults with the disorder. These efforts resulted in major shifts in research and clinical service. The changing definition of schizophrenia meant, for example, that this childhood condition was much less common than autism (King 1994). Greater precision in the diagnosis of autism stimulated interest in rather similar, but apparently even less frequently occurring, conditions, such as those described by

Heller (1908), Asperger (1944), and Rett (1966).

The growing body of work based on DSM-III and DSM-III-R re-sulted in further refinements of diagnostic concepts. As a result, DSM-IV includes additional disorders; for example, within the pervasive devel-opmental class various diagnostic concepts are included in addition to autism. Research on these conditions (see Klin 1994; Tsai 1994; Volkmar 1994) is not as extensive as that relative to autism but does suggest to varying degrees the validity of these conditions, apart from strictly di-agnosed autism (Klin 1994; Volkmar et al. 1994).

Although DSM-IV and ICD-10 (World Health Organization 1992) represent the most recent attempts at a truly comprehensive psychiatric taxonomy, it is important to note that major limitations still exist in our understanding of the severe psychiatric disturbances of childhood onset. For example, although the general view has supported the approach of DSM-III, DSM-III-R, and now DSM-IV to the diagnosis of schizophre-nia in childhood, some investigators (e.g., Cantor 1988) have argued that the earlier and rather broader view of that diagnostic concept was too readily abandoned. They have pointed out inconsistencies and limita-tions in current criteria and rightly note important areas of diagnostic uncertainty.

Similar problems exist regarding the specification of the "subthresh-old" conditions in DSM-IV, particularly pervasive developmental disor-der not otherwise specified (PDD NOS). Although various attempts have been made to delineate subgroups within this broad category, none of these attempts has, as yet, achieved widespread acceptance (Towbin 1994). Somewhat paradoxically, the group of children with this disorder, undoubtedly much more common than those with strictly diagnosed autism, are only very rarely studied systematically (see Towbin 1994). As noted in Chapters 4 and 5, the classification of disorders of children who exhibit apparent borderline conditions and relatively more isolated hallucinatory phenomena has been similarly problematic.

This volume provides an overview of the conditions traditionally considered the "childhood psychoses" and now more properly called the psychoses and pervasive developmental disorders of childhood and ado-lescence. The stimulus for this book was a training institute held in 1990 as part of the annual meeting of the American Academy of Child and Adolescent Psychiatry, in Chicago, Illinois. The interest in this topic and the changes in DSM-IV categories and criteria that were pending at that time suggested the potential usefulness of a volume on this topic designed specifically for clinicians interested in the care of children with these disorders.

The authors are most grateful to the staff of the American Academy of Child and Adolescent Psychiatry for their support of the original institute and the production of this volume. The particular support of Virginia Q. Anthony and Laurie Loy is acknowledged, as are the efforts of Owen Lewis, M.D., and other members of the Institute Subcommittee. We are also grateful for the suggestions of Dr. Barry Nurcombe and other members of the publication committee, which enlarged the scope of the institute and this volume. The support of the staff of the American Psychiatric Press is also gratefully acknowledged, as is the permission to reprint portions of DSM-IV criteria for these conditions.

Fred R. Volkmar, M.D.

References

American Psychiatric Association: Diagnostic and Statistical Manual: Mental Disorders. Washington, DC, American Psychiatric Association, 1952

American Psychiatric Association: Diagnostic and Statistical Manual of Mental Disorders, 2nd Edition. Washington, DC, American Psychiatric Association, 1968

American Psychiatric Association: Diagnostic and Statistical Manual of Mental Disorders, 3rd Edition. Washington, DC, American Psychiatric Association, 1980

American Psychiatric Association: Diagnostic and Statistical Manual of Mental Disorders, 3rd Edition, Revised. Washington, DC, American Psychiatric Association, 1987

American Psychiatric Association: Diagnostic and Statistical Manual of Mental Disorders, 4th Edition. Washington, DC, American Psychiatric Association, 1994

Asperger H: Die "autistichen Psychopathen" im Kindersalter. Archiv für Psychiatrie und Nervenkrankheiten 117:76–136, 1944

Cantor S: Childhood Schizophrenia. New York, Guilford, 1988

DeSanctis S: Sopra aclune varieta della demenzi precocce. Revista Sperimental de Feniatria E. di Medicina Legale 32:141–165, 1906

Eisenberg L: The course of childhood schizophrenia. Archives of Neurology and Psychiatry 78:69–83, 1957

Heller T: Dementia infantilis. Zeitschrift für die Erforschung und Behandlung des Jugendlichen Schwachsins 2:141–165, 1908

Heller T: Uber Dementia infantilis. Zeitschrift für Kinderforschung 37:661–667, 1930. Reprinted in Howells JG (ed and translator): Modern Perspectives in International Child Psychiatry. Edinburgh, Oliver and Boyd, 1969

Kanner L: Autistic disturbances of affective contact. Nervous Child 2: 217–250, 1943

King R: Childhood-onset schizophrenia. Child and Adolescent Psychiatry Clinics of North America 3:1–13, 1994

Klin A: Asperger syndrome. Child and Adolescent Psychiatry Clinics of North America 3:131–148, 1994

Kolvin I: Studies in childhood psychoses, I: Diagnostic criteria and classification. Br J Psychiatry 118:381–384, 1971

Kraepelin E: Dementia praecox and paraphrenia. Edinburgh, Churchill Livingstone, 1919

Maudsley H: The physiology and pathology of the mind. London, Macmillan, 1867

Potter HW: Schizophrenia in children. Am J Psychiatry 89:1253–1270, 1933

Rett A: Uber ein eigenartiges hirntophisces Syndrome bei Hyperammonie im Kindersalter. Wein Medizinische Wochenschrift 118:723–726, 1966

Rutter M: Autistic children: infancy to adulthood. Seminars in Psychiatry 2: 435–450, 1970

Rutter M: Childhood schizophrenia reconsidered. Journal of Autism and Childhood Schizophrenia 2:315–338, 1972

Rutter M, Schopler E: Classification of pervasive developmental disorders: some concepts and practical considerations. J Autism Dev Disord 22:459–482, 1992

Rutter M, Shaffer D, Shepherd M: A Multiaxial Classification of Child Psychiatric Disorders. Geneva, World Health Organization, 1975

Towbin K: Pervasive developmental disorder not otherwise specified: a review and guidelines for clinical care. Child and Adolescent Psychiatry Clinics of North America 3:149–160, 1994

Tsai L: Rett syndrome. Child and Adolescent Psychiatry Clinics of North America 3:105–118, 1994

Volkmar F: Childhood disintegrative disorder. Child and Adolescent Psychiatry Clinics of North America 3:119–129, 1994

Volkmar F, Klin A, Siegel B, et al: DSM-IV Autism/Pervasive Developmental Disorders Field Trial. Am J Psychiatry 151:1361–1367, 1994

World Health Organization: The ICD-10 Classification of Mental and Behavioural Disorders: Clinical Descriptions and Diagnostic Guidelines. Geneva, World Health Organization, 1992

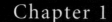

Chapter 1

Childhood Schizophrenia

John Scott Werry, M.D.

Introduction

Schizophrenia is a serious psychiatric illness marked primarily by disorders of thinking, perception, emotion, and motivation that disrupt normal function. It is the one that most readily typifies the lay conception of insanity or madness. It can begin in the preschool period and in old age, but it is primarily a disorder of late adolescence and early adulthood. Because it begins so early in life and often results in chronic disability, it is responsible for the major cost of public psychiatric services in most countries. The hidden cost in terms of lost productivity and burdens on families is even higher (McGuire 1990).

Although most adolescents with schizophrenia are probably admitted to adult psychiatric wards and services (even in as affluent a city as Sydney, Australia), the World Health Organization (WHO) policy is that adolescents should not be put in adult wards of any kind. Thus, there is a compelling need for child and adolescent psychiatrists and mental health professionals to interest themselves in this disorder. Some attention to the history of the study of schizophrenia will aid in understanding the above points.

Historical Review

There seems little doubt that schizophrenia is a disorder of great antiquity but also that there was some kind of significant increase in the frequency of the disorder in the nineteenth century. Though some of this increase was due to the humanitarian reforms of the late eighteenth and early nineteenth centuries, which moved the insane from street and jails to hospitals, it has been suggested that the huge programs established to build mental hospitals in most western countries from 1850 to 1900 cannot be explained solely by social concern. Further, the prevalence seems to be declining in some countries (Torrey 1987), just as it surged 150 years ago.

Although most studies have shown that schizophrenia is found in all races, regions, and countries, there are significant variations in prevalence (Harrison 1990). In fact, the oral history of certain ethnic groups isolated from contact with the rest of the world, such as the New Zealand Maori, shows that schizophrenia was virtually unknown until the arrival of Europeans. If this is correct, the model that fits the facts best is that of a viral disorder, though such a concept is still controversial (Meltzer 1987).

Schizophrenia as it is understood today unites a wide variety of different kinds of psychoses and is considered separate from manic-depressive disorder. Schizophrenia was first defined operationally by Kraepelin toward the end of the nineteenth century. He called it dementia praecox, or dementia occurring in young persons, because he saw it as a necessarily progressive disorder. He also defined the primary symptomatology (delusions, hallucinations, etc.), although he thought it primarily a "disorder of the will."

In 1911, Eugen Bleuler introduced the term *schizophrenia* to underline the coexistence of contradictory impulses or thoughts (ambivalence) as a primary feature. However, Bleuler's main contributions were other than terminology. Under the influence of Freud, he introduced the notion of reaction, in which symptoms were seen as shaped by the person's dynamics rather than wholly by the disease process as Kraepelin saw them. Second, Bleuler referred to "the schizophrenias," believing that it was not one but several disorders (i.e., phenotypic). Finally, he did not accept that the prognosis was inexorably poor or that treatment was unavailing. He was a great believer in occupational therapy or work as a keystone of treatment and thus anticipated by many years (as indeed did the great reformers of the late eighteenth century) the notion of institutionalization and custodial care as the cause of much disability in schizophrenia. Bleuler worked in the same Zurich hospital for many years and was succeeded by his son Manfred. Much of what we know or assume about schizophrenia stems from their study of the same patients over many years. Their work is one of the great examples in the history of medicine of how much can be accomplished by "mere" clinical observation, even where etiology is quite unknown and the contribution of cellular pathology of little help.

Kraepelin remained influential—notably in German psychiatry under Kurt Schneider, who developed and named the concept of first-ranked symptoms embodied in DSM-IV. This concept was brought to the United Kingdom by researchers such as Myer-Gross, who escaped Nazi Germany. His work at the Institute of Psychiatry in London—the main training center for much of the old British Empire—and his classic textbook coauthored with Slater and Roth, were influential in maintaining the purist concept of schizophrenia in much of the English-speaking world, as well as in Africa and Asia.

However, in the United States, Bleuler's concept of reaction was taken to extreme limits. The qualitative notion of a disorder defined by unique symptoms such as delusions or hallucinations was replaced by a quantitative notion in which severity is defined by the concept of borderline states. In child psychiatry, psychotic disorders were all included in DSM-II (American Psychiatric Association 1968) under the single rubric of childhood schizophrenia (although interestingly, a British group was primarily responsible for this disaster—see below). This concept reached its absurd end in the antipsychiatric movement of the 1960s and 1970s, which was led by psychiatrists such as Szasz and Laing who wanted to deny the concept of illness altogether. Fortunately, a counter-revolution in psychiatry was brewing in the midwestern city of St. Louis.

It is well known that the so-called Feigner criteria were begun in the 1960s and 1970s at Washington University, St. Louis, and went on to take the world by storm in DSM-III (American Psychiatric Association 1980). What is probably less well known is the isolation and ostracism suffered by the St. Louis group of Robins, Guze, Winokur, Feigner, and others when they first began their work in psychiatric taxonomy. I visited this fine department in 1967 and was told sadly that no one was ever invited to speak in the United States—only London seemed interested. How things can change!

There is still no universally accepted definition of schizophrenia, and each one produces different samples of patients with different symptoms, correlates, and prognosis (Andreasen 1987; Angst 1988). The two definitions that probably come closest to being universally accepted are those provided by DSM and ICD-10 (World Health Organization 1992). The DSM definition is probably the most restrictive; it closely resembles Kraepelin's dementia praecox with poor outcome. The ICD-10 definition allows considerably more clinical judgment, more elastic boundaries, and hence more variation in symptomatology, severity, and outcome.

Although it might be felt that the sickness concept of schizophrenia reigns supreme, the most prevalent view of schizophrenia among laypersons—even those who are well educated and who shape public opinion—is the view typified by Shakespeare's Lady Macbeth or Ophelia: someone with an illness perhaps, but an illness of the mind or soul and not of the body; an illness evoked, not by biochemistry or heredity, but by intolerable sin, loss, or stress.

Other Historical Aspects

The management of schizophrenia and of attitudes to schizophrenia are also of interest, although many of these attitudes are enmeshed in those held toward the mentally ill in general. History has been marked by oscillations between concepts of sin and sickness and of psychogenesis and biogenesis. Whereas Greek physicians saw insanity as an illness due to disturbances of body humors, in Europe in the Middle Ages the Christian church declared it a sign of sin. Witches burned at the stake no doubt included women with schizophrenia. The medical profession resisted this and had its own martyrs burnt at the stake as a result. However, although a few enlightened communities like Gheel, in Europe, still cared for their mentally ill in humane ways, the decline of the Inquisition in Europe and Puritan zeal in the United States did little to help the mentally ill. Such people languished in jails or in so-called hospitals such as Bedlam, where the fashionable might seek an afternoon's entertainment by visiting to watch the antics of the patients.

By the late eighteenth century, the Age of Enlightenment had produced humanitarian reformers, with the result that Pinel in France, Tuke in York, and Rush in Philadelphia developed the *moral treatment of the insane,* which despite its theological title was basically open-door normalization management. In the United States, Dorothea Dix, the nursing heroine of the Civil War, pushed for the development of proper psychiatric hospitals, to be located in the countryside where the bucolic atmosphere and freedom from the stresses of modern (i.e., city) life would allow the mind to heal. However, by the end of the nineteenth century, harsh economic times resulted in overcrowding of the psychiatric hospitals; what had at first been places of sanctuary, appropriately called asylums, now became the huge custodial warehouses that would predominate until the 1960s.

Two dramatic changes occurred shortly after World War II. The first was the rediscovery of the moral treatment of the insane in Nottingham, England, around 1950, that led to the open-door policy and ultimately to community care. The second was the serendipitous discovery in France of the antipsychotic properties of chlorpromazine, synthesized in the search for better antihistamines to allow reductions of body temperature during cardiac surgery and thus prolong the possible operating time before the advent of bypass techniques. Chlorpromazine treatment did more than just help those with schizophrenia; it laid the foundations for the basic medical science study of schizophrenia, catalyzed the return of psychiatry to medicine, facilitated a revolution in medical taxonomy, and produced a technology for evaluation of treatment efficacy and safety for psychiatry. A cynic might also add that it made certain pharmaceutical houses very wealthy.

Another theme that typifies the history of schizophrenia, or more properly that of medicine as a whole, is oscillations between therapeutic optimism and nihilism. Pinel, Tuke, and Rush gave us optimism; Kraepelin (as well as hard economic times) destroyed it. Bleuler and psychoanalysis rekindled optimism, and so did Duncan McMillan, pioneer of the open-door policy; Goffman, with his studies of institutionalization; and the controlled studies of community care in Wisconsin, Los Angeles, and Sydney (see Goldberg 1991). However, perhaps nothing rekindled optimism so much as chlorpromazine and its offspring, biochemical psychiatry. Yet as we move toward the twenty-first century, a note of pessimism is returning. Community care is not a panacea. There is talk again of the need for asylum (Wing 1990), humane care seems to be in jeopardy every time a former psychiatric patient commits some hideous crime, and previously generous governments have become niggardly and promote individualism and self-interest as the supreme value. Even biochemistry is gloomy—antipsychotic drugs do not, in fact, cure schizophrenia as was first thought (Kane 1987), and the disease runs its inexorable course over 10 years or more (McGlashan 1988). Molecular geneticists speak of the unbelievable complexities of discovering what any genetic base of schizophrenia might be (Gottesman et al. 1987). Enemies abound—Scientologists seem to have the ear of the media; states intervene in proven, safe treatments like electroconvulsive therapy; and psychiatrists are no longer immune from the danger of frivolous malpractice suits.

The problem is to keep a sense of balance. Although most psychiatrists probably now believe that schizophrenia is a true disease of the brain, psychosocial factors are important in provoking relapses, in determining the level of disability, and in dealing with the patient as opposed to the disease. Although antipsychotic drugs are no panacea, they do enable many patients to lead more comfortable lives and enable their families to share the burden of care. Nowhere in medicine is there a greater challenge to sustain compassion, to give patients and families accurate information, to eschew the need for certainty, to understand the concept of probabilities in such matters as dangerousness and suicidality, to balance biology and psychosocial concepts in care, and to give enough treatment without resorting to the historically shameful yet repetitive overzealous intervention that lays waste the principle of primum non nocere.

History of Childhood Schizophrenia

The history of childhood schizophrenia has been discussed in detail in a classic paper by Eisenberg (1957) and somewhat more briefly elsewhere (Beitchman 1985; Kydd and Werry 1981; Werry 1979). Eisenberg (1957) pointed out that Kraepelin had noted that schizophrenia could begin in children and that there was some systematic study before World War II.

One of these papers, by Bradley and Bowen (see Kydd and Werry 1981; Werry 1979), is a scientific classic that, had it been emulated, might have advanced nosology in child psychiatry 50 years ahead of its time. Unfortunately, this was not to be.

In 1942 Kanner described infantile autism (see Chapter 6), yet by the 1960s, Bender and Fish at Bellevue were suggesting that any differences between autism and schizophrenia (and indeed some conduct disorders as well) were developmentally, not etiologically, determined. Elasticity of diagnosis of childhood schizophrenia reached its peak in 1963 in the British Nine (Diagnostic) Points (see Kydd and Werry 1981), which described a child psychotic phenotype so broad that it encompassed almost any severe abnormality of development and, worse, gave it the title of childhood schizophrenia. Somewhat unusually, the United States seemed to embrace this alien concept with enthusiasm so that in 1968 it was codified in DSM-II. As a result, most research on childhood schizophrenia from about 1960 to 1980 is actually about autism. When cases of schizophrenia were included, as they sometimes clearly were, it is impossible to disentangle the findings applying to autism from those applying to schizophrenia and from those applying to other pervasive developmental disorders.

In the late 1950s, Anthony in the United Kingdom and Kanner and Eisenberg in the United States (see Werry 1979) suggested that psychoses should be classified by age at onset. Although the first systematic study, carried out in Japan by Makita (1966), showed that early-onset psychosis (autism) was quite different symptomatologically from later-onset psychosis (schizophrenia), it was Rutter's (1972) proselytization of the much better studies by Kolvin (1971) that led to the final reseparation of schizophrenia and its reinclusion within adult-type schizophrenia in DSM-III (American Psychiatric Association 1980) and ICD-9 (World Health Organization 1978). After the work of Makita and Kolvin, emphasis in diagnosis has shifted away from age at onset to whether primary schizophrenic symptomatology is present, although age at onset can still be a helpful guide.

After Makita and Kolvin, apart from one classic follow-up study by Eggers (1978) there was almost no research on schizophrenia in children until the 1980s and—interestingly, given that it is much more common—even less on schizophrenia in adolescents.

Schizophrenia in Children and Adolescents: Current Status

In reviews of all studies that used diagnostic criteria similar to current criteria in DSM or ICD, Werry (1992a, 1992b) could find only seven in English since 1960 (four from the United States, one from the United Kingdom, one from West Germany, and one from New Zealand) that yielded comprehensive, usable data, and four others that offered partial information. The greatest deficiency was in adolescent schizophrenia. This means that the database on child and adolescent (early-onset) schizophrenia (EOS) is very limited. However, such data as there are seem strongly to support the ICD and DSM positions that EOS is but a variant of schizophrenia in general (Beitchman 1985; Russell 1992; Werry 1992a, 1992b). Therefore, this review will operate from this premise, laying a foundation on what is known about schizophrenia and then emphasizing any differences or deficiencies in knowledge in EOS.

At present there are active research groups in EOS in only a few centers, such as Bellevue Hospital, Yale University, the University of California at Los Angeles (UCLA), the National Institute of Mental Health (NIMH), Albuquerque, and Seattle, in the United States, Mannheim, Germany, and New Zealand; and most of these are researching adults as well as children. Given the size of the problem, especially in adolescence, and the severity of the disorder, this is far too little research. As a result, certain ideas—for example, that the disorder is more severe in children and that children do not respond as well to antipsychotic drugs—abound but are almost certainly untrue (Campbell et al. 1993; McClellan and Werry 1991; Werry et al. 1991a, 1991b). Developmental effects on symptomatology are only just beginning to be researched and studies of behavioral and family interventions of the type seemingly effective in adults have not even been attempted. Further, confusion between bipolar mood disorder with psychosis and schizophrenia is maximal at younger ages (Werry et al. 1991a, 1991b), and therefore it is plausible to suggest that many children and adolescents are being misdiagnosed and hence mistreated. But probably the biggest problem of all is the fact that, because of the lack of interest in schizophrenia among child and adolescent psychiatrists, young persons are being dealt with by adult facilities. This is a denial of a basic right. Few adult units have schools attached, know how to deal with families, or understand special developmental needs.

For example, one 14-year-old disinhibited psychotic girl in Auckland, New Zealand, with a possible history of sexual abuse was allowed unescorted parole with an adult male patient because that was the policy of "normalization" on the adult ward.

In summary then, schizophrenia in the 1990s presents a challenge to child and adolescent psychiatry—clinically, humanely, and scientifically. On the positive side, NIMH, in prosecuting the Academy of Medicine Plan for fostering research in child and adolescent psychiatric disorders, has established a section in its extramural child branch to facilitate research in schizophrenia; and the *Schizophrenia Bulletin* (Asarnow and Asarnow 1994) has recently published a special section on childhood-onset schizophrenia.

Definition

Child and Adolescent (Early-Onset) Schizophrenia

It has been argued elsewhere (Werry et al. 1991b) that child and adolescent schizophrenia should be referred to as *early onset* and that schizophrenia occurring before age 13 should be referred to as *very early onset* (VEOS)." These terms will be used here. The term *prepubertal* should not be tied to an age (as it is at present) because the onset of puberty is highly variable and defined by body changes, not any particular age. However, at the current moment the diagnostic criteria for schizophrenia or, in the case of EOS, the diagnostic criteria for adult schizophrenia are similar across the entire life span.

ICD-10 and DSM Criteria

There are a number of different ways of diagnosing schizophrenia, all of which yield somewhat different patient groups (Andreasen 1987; Angst 1988; Westermeyer and Harrow 1988). The needs of the practitioner in diagnosis differ from those of the researcher, but both need some criteria to work by. For most purposes, either DSM or ICD will fulfill these needs, and both have the advantage of widespread use. Both are similar in that the diagnosis is made primarily on symptomatology and other clinical features such as duration without reference to any posited etiological features (e.g., stress, dynamics, or family factors). Both also rely on Schneiderian first-ranked symptoms (despite the fact that these have, until recently, not been subject to any formal analysis of their sensitivity and specificity). The main differences lie in the explicitness (and, some might say, the rigidity) and the 6-month-duration DSM criteria, so that the ICD-10 definition would be predicted to bring in more doubtful or borderline cases.

Diagnostic criteria for schizophrenia in DSM-IV (American Psychiatric Association 1994) are presented in Table 1–1. It is important to remember that when this diagnosis is considered in children, consideration should be given to developmental factors and, particularly for the clinician less familiar with this diagnosis, the text of DSM-IV should be carefully reviewed.

The main difference in these criteria from DSM-III-R (American Psychiatric Association 1987) is that the descriptions of symptoms in criterion A (characteristic symptoms) and criterion D (duration), which include the prodromal and residual phase symptoms, have been made a great deal simpler and more spartan. Most descriptive terms are now to be found in the text, not in the criteria. This seems likely to increase overdiagnosis in children unless careful attention is also paid to the definitions of symptoms in the text, since some of the symptoms (hallucinations, disorganized speech, grossly disorganized behavior) in this age group are quite commonly nonpsychotic. The number of symptoms needed in criterion A has been simplified to two (one if the delusions are bizarre or if the hallucinations are Schneiderian or first ranked in type) without the combinations of subgroup menus found in DSM-III-R. Again, this probably increases the risk of overdiagnosis in children because children's fantasies may be mistaken for bizarre delusions.

The reference to absence of an organic cause has been expanded to include specific mention of substance abuse (elsewhere, drug-induced disorder is allowed a duration of 1 month). This is likely to cause initial underdiagnosis of schizophrenia in adolescence when cannabis and other abuse is common. Careful attention needs to be given to whether the cannabis is being used primarily as self-treatment of schizophrenic symptoms, especially prodromal ones, or whether it induces them. Antipsychotic medication may also reduce symptoms and further add to the misdiagnosis of schizophrenia as being drug-induced.

The exclusion criterion of autism is tightened by specifying that the prominent hallucinations or delusions must be present for at least a month.

The main difference between the DSM-IV criteria and those in ICD-10 is that the latter system tends to be more narrative and less operational. However, somewhat paradoxically in view of the changes in DSM-IV, a menu of nine detailed symptoms or symptom areas similar to the five

---

Table 1–1.   DSM-IV diagnostic criteria for schizophrenia

A. *Characteristic symptoms:* Two (or more) of the following, each present for a significant portion of time during a 1-month period (or less if successfully treated):

  (1) delusions
  (2) hallucinations
  (3) disorganized speech (e.g., frequent derailment or incoherence)
  (4) grossly disorganized or catatonic behavior
  (5) negative symptoms, i.e., affective flattening, alogia, or avolition

  Note: Only one Criterion A symptom is required if delusions are bizarre or hallucinations consist of a voice keeping up a running commentary on the person's behavior or thoughts, or two or more voices conversing with each other.

B. *Social/occupational dysfunction:* For a significant portion of the time since the onset of the disturbance, one or more major areas of functioning such as work, interpersonal relations, or self-care are markedly below the level achieved prior to the onset (or when the onset is in childhood or adolescence, failure to achieve expected level of interpersonal, academic, or occupational achievement).

C. *Duration:* Continuous signs of the disturbance persist for at least 6 months. This 6-month period must include at least 1 month of symptoms (or less if successfully treated) that meet Criterion A (i.e., active-phase symptoms) and may include periods of prodromal or residual symptoms. During these prodromal or residual periods, the signs of the disturbance may be manifested by only negative symptoms or two or more symptoms listed in Criterion A present in an attenuated form (e.g., odd beliefs, unusual perceptual experiences).

D. *Schizoaffective and mood disorder exclusion:* Schizoaffective disorder and mood disorder with psychotic features have been ruled out because either (1) no major depressive, manic, or mixed episodes have occurred concurrently with the active-phase symptoms; or (2) if mood episodes have occurred during active-phase symptoms, their total duration has been brief relative to the duration of the active and residual periods.

E. *Substance/general medical condition exclusion:* The disturbance is not due to the direct physiological effects of a substance (e.g., a drug of abuse, a medication) or a general medical condition

(continued)

in DSM-IV are listed, and one from the first four may suffice, but ordinarily two of the nine are needed. The other main difference is that a duration of a month of active symptoms from the nine is required, with no concessions to prodromal or to residual phases. The same exclusions for mood and organic disorders obtain, but they are textual, not explicated, criteria. ICD has tended to generate more diagnoses of schizophrenia than has DSM-III or DSM-III-R, which is regarded by many as a reversion to dementia praecox.

ICD-10 makes no mention of children and adolescents and does not indicate that the disorder may occur before adulthood. As noted, DSM-IV does make a reference in the criteria with respect to autism, and in the text it indicates a few developmental differences in symptoms (e.g., less structured delusions and more visual hallucinations) and differential diagnoses from other childhood disorders (communication disorders and attention-deficit/hyperactivity disorder [ADHD]). On the whole, however, neither system can be considered as paying sufficient attention to schizophrenia in children and adolescents.

Table 1–1. DSM-IV diagnostic criteria for schizophrenia *(continued)*

F. *Relationship to a pervasive developmental disorder:* If there is a history of autistic disorder or another pervasive developmental disorder, the additional diagnosis of schizophrenia is made only if prominent delusions or hallucinations are also present for at least a month (or less if successfully treated).

Classification of longitudinal course (can be applied only after at least 1 year has elapsed since the initial onset of active-phase symptoms):
  Episodic with interepisode residual symptoms (episodes are defined by the reemergence of prominent psychotic symptoms); *also specify if:* with prominent negative symptoms
  Episodic with no interepisode residual symptoms
  Continuous (prominent psychotic symptoms are present throughout the period of observation); *also specify if:* **with prominent negative symptoms**
  Single episode in partial remission; *also specify if:* **with prominent negative symptoms**
  Single episode in full remission
  Other or unspecified pattern

Source. American Psychiatric Association: Diagnostic and Statistical Manual of Mental Disorders, 4th Edition. Washington, DC, American Psychiatric Association, 1994, pp. 285–286. Used with permission.

Core Indicators

There are five core indicators of schizophrenia in children and adolescents: psychotic symptoms; change in adaptive function; 6-month duration; elimination of schizoaffective disorder, psychotic mood disorder, or organic causes (e.g., drug intoxication); and autism.

1. *Psychotic symptoms.* These can be delusions, prominent and persistent hallucinations, incoherence or loosening of associations, catatonic behavior, and flat or inappropriate affect. All have to be of a particular type and in allowable numbers and combinations. Symptoms must have been present for 1 month in DSM-IV and 2 in ICD-10. With the exception of flat affect, the psychotic symptoms are known as positive symptoms to differentiate them from those that represent deficits of function (negative symptoms), such as lack of motivation, impoverishment of thought, and inattention (Andreasen 1987; Kay 1991).
2. *Change in adaptive function.* There is a clear deterioration or, in children, failure to achieve the level expected for age and intelligence.
3. *Six-month duration.* This can include any prodromal or residual phase. ICD does not require this but does require a week longer of psychotic symptoms than DSM.
4. *Elimination of schizoaffective disorder, psychotic mood disorder, or organic causes (e.g., drug intoxication).* This is an ordering of priorities in diagnosis and makes schizophrenia even more restrictive as a kind of residual category. ICD has no such exclusions.
5. *Autism.* DSM-IV also has a special exclusion category stating that if autism has been diagnosed previously, hallucinations and delusions must now be a prominent and durable part of the symptoms.

Subtypes

The classical subtypes (McGlashan and Fenton 1991) defined by the most prominent symptomatology are still used.

1. Paranoid subtype, marked by delusions referring to the self.
2. Catatonic subtype, marked by stereotyped motor behaviors, negativism, or both.

3. Disorganized (hebephrenic) subtype, marked by gross thought disorder and silly affect.
4. Undifferentiated subtype, in which most features are present and no one feature predominates.
5. Residual subtype, in which a variety of symptoms (some positive but most negative) and/or eccentric/maladaptive behaviors insufficient in themselves to diagnose the full active syndrome follow an acute episode by a variable interval.
6. ICD-10 has added another subtype: postschizophrenic depression, in which mood symptoms predominate, although it appears that anhedonia, inactivity, and amotivation are more predominant than any true depression. It is important to emphasize that there is no subtype "childhood schizophrenia" per se.

These classical subtypes are poorly studied (McGlashan and Fenton 1991), and only the paranoid one seems well established. The hebephrenic and undifferentiated subtypes are less well established. The catatonic, residual, and simple subtypes have no data at all. The catatonic subtype seems rare; the simple subtype (found only in ICD-10 [1992] and in older literature) is characterized only by progressive negative symptoms, and its validity is a matter of debate.

Phases

DSM-IV also describes three phases. The prodrome is characterized by a change in function and may have any or none of the psychotic symptoms, but not enough to make the diagnosis of schizophrenia. It may last hours to months or even over a year. The active phase requires the full panoply of psychotic symptoms, lasting at least 1 month. The residual phase, discussed above, is the one that is often the most persistent and produces the most long-lasting disability.

As noted, ICD-10 has a subcategory called "postschizophrenic depression," which is not available in DSM-IV. In my opinion, this is much more a phase of the disorder that occurs with regularity after the first few acute episodes than it is a true subtype. For some months after losing the psychotic symptomatology, the child or adolescent seems lethargic, lacking in zest, and just not the person that he or she was before the illness began. It has much in common with a convalescent period after a serious illness.

Symptomatology

Symptomatology has not been well studied in EOS, and usually any data come from informal methodology, although this is less true of studies in the last few years—especially those from UCLA (see Russell 1992) and in the area of cognition. Reviews (Beitchman 1985; Russell 1992; Werry 1992a, 1992b) have shown that most core symptoms can be found in children and adolescents and apparently are sufficient to enable the diagnosis to be made. However, there are both quantitative and developmental differences. It is not surprising that the greatest differences are in VEOS and in children under 10 years of age; these cases may require special techniques for diagnosis.

The core symptoms of passivity phenomena, so emphasized by Schneider and ICD-10, may be rare in children (Garralda 1985; Spencer et al. 1991), as may be poverty of thinking and incoherence (Caplan et al. 1989, 1990), systematized delusions, and delusions with adult (e.g., sexual) themes (Russell 1992; Russell et al. 1989). These differences are no doubt due to immature cognitive development and suggest a need for modification of diagnostic criteria in DSM and ICD insofar as these are made cardinal. The particular area of immaturity may be primarily one of egocentricity—that is, insensitivity to a listener's need to be able to follow thoughts that are without idiosyncratic references and breaks in logic. This area thus involves both language and communication skills (Caplan et al. 1989, 1990; Tompson et al. 1990).

Nonschizophrenic children or those with other disorders (such as conduct disorder) may show some of the core symptoms, such as disorganized thinking and hallucinations (Burke et al. 1985; Caplan et al 1989, 1990; Garralda 1984; Rothstein 1981; Werry 1992b), rather more frequently than adults. This reduces the specificity of these symptoms and calls for particular care in making the diagnosis of EOS. But there are also issues of false negatives, such as the boundary between EOS and schizotypal disorder (see below) and—the most controversial—whether EOS may be diagnosed in preverbal or nonverbal subjects. The latter has particular relevance in very young or language-impaired children and in the severely developmentally disabled (Cantor et al. 1982; Reid 1983; Russell et al. 1989). However, neither problem has been resolved.

There are also indubitably cultural effects on symptomatology that may add problems of culture clash as to what is abnormal (such as possession by dead relatives that may be quite acceptable in some ancestor-oriented cultures such as Polynesian culture). So far, however, there seems to be no study of how these affect children in particular. The obvious way to deal with such problems is to anticipate them and to rely on cultural validation of abnormality by the use of indigenous professionals or interpreters.

Reliability and Validity Issues

In adults, both the diagnosis and individual symptoms have been shown to be reliable (Bland and Kaloda 1988; Kay 1991), although mostly in research settings using complex structured interviews and scales. In EOS there are few data, especially formal calculations—although what there are suggest similarity to adults (Caplan et al. 1989; Russell et al. 1989; Volkmar et al. 1988; Werry et al. 1991ba). However, the situation in clinical practice is unknown, and the DSM field trials and other studies of child psychiatric disorders in general yield very few cases of EOS and variable levels of reliability (Quay 1986; Werry et al. 1983).

Test-retest reliability or stability of diagnosis is not as good, with frequent changes away from schizophrenia to bipolar disorder, schizo-affective disorder, and even personality disorder several years on (Eggers 1989; McClellan and Werry 1991; Werry et al. 1991a). There is also a slippage away from bipolar disorder to schizophrenia (McClellan and Werry 1991), although this is less marked than vice versa (Carlson 1990; Werry 1992b). All this suggests that there may be much more serious problems of reliability than are revealed by the usual interrater reliability studies.

Validity of diagnosis is dependent on demonstration of specific correlates, outcomes, or treatment response that will be described in detail below. In adults there is ample evidence to support considerable, though imperfect, validity of schizophrenia as a diagnostic category in all these areas. In EOS, although the data are thin, the indications are that it is similarly valid (McClellan and Werry 1991; Tompson et al. 1990; Werry, in press; Werry et al. 1991a, 1991b).

One of the most difficult validity areas in diagnosis is distinctiveness from schizotypal personality disorder. This seems to be very much an issue of severity rather than qualitative differences, to the extent that the UCLA group no longer separate them in children but speak of schizophrenia spectrum disorder (e.g., Caplan et al. 1989, 1990; Tompson et al. 1990). The other problem is schizoaffective disorder (Eggers 1989; Werry et al. 1991a). However, both these problems bedevil schizophrenia in adults and are discussed under "Differential Diagnosis."

Although reliability and validity of the diagnosis may be reasonably satisfactory, there are problems with phases, most particularly the prodrome (American Psychiatric Association 1991), the beginning of which is not always easy to date, especially in EOS where lifelong premorbid abnormality is usual (Werry 1992a). Likewise, the beginning of the residual phase may be difficult to pinpoint and/or to differentiate from exaggeration of preexisting personality disorder.

Least reliable and valid are the subcategories (Angst 1988; McGlashan and Fenton 1991). There is conflict among studies of EOS (Werry 1992a, 1992b) as to which subcategories predominate, which suggests that reliability is equally low in children and adolescents.

Prevalence and Epidemiology

Schizophrenia has a whole life prevalence of less than 1% and an incidence of about one-tenth of that per year. There is considerable variation in rates across cultures and regions (Torrey 1987; Torrey and Bowler 1990) and, probably most profoundly, according to definitional criteria (Bland and Kaloda 1988). There is some evidence that the incidence is declining in affluent societies (Torrey 1987). There is a "pole to equator" gradient and the disorder is said to be more benign in developing countries, although this could be a matter of problems in applying Western criteria to other cultures. It is more common in lower social classes, although this is true only in urban areas and is not explicable solely by urban drift, because certain regions such as the Pacific Northwest have remained stable for a century despite urbanization (Torrey and Bowler 1990). Schizophrenia is, however, common in the homeless, including homeless adolescents (Mundy et al. 1990). It is also more common in immigrants, although different groups have different risk rates (e.g., Afro-Caribbeans and Asians in the United Kingdom [Harrison 1990]).

Variations in prevalence in regions, races, cultures, and immigrants have attracted a variety of explanations: psychosocial stress, social drift, genetic selection, environmental hazards (toxins, viruses), and differences in maternal and child health care, but so far no single explanation is proven. It seems more likely that a melange of factors is involved.

The epidemiology of EOS is unstudied except that it is clear that VEOS is rare. The only substantial numbers of cases come from megalopolises like New York or Los Angeles or from samples built up over very many years (e.g., Eggers 1989). Thus, conclusions about demographic and other correlates cannot be derived except to say that male gender is much more common in VEOS (Werry 1992a). This, however, is not peculiar to EOS, because first admission in males is, on average, some 10 years earlier than females. Age of maximum incidence is 15–25 in males and 25–35 in females (Zigler and Levine 1981). Lifetime prevalence is equal in both sexes, but since the disease is milder in females, it is possible that admission might be more delayed after first onset.

For child and adolescent psychiatry, however, the implications of these figures are that, certainly in males, schizophrenia is a major disorder of adolescence and the question must be asked as to why it has been so little studied.

Clinical Features

Variability

It should be unnecessary to point out that although every "case" of schizophrenia resembles every other, no child or adolescent with schizophrenia is quite like any other. This is because the illness occurs in a unique human being living in a unique family and small social system. It is these unique features that often cause difficulty and that cause skeptics to deride the value of diagnosis. The most characteristic things about schizophrenia then, clinically, are its predictability and its unpredictability. Although one can state a usual course, the time frames, symptomatology, and phases show infinite individual variations and combinations (J. R. Asarnow et al. 1991; Eggers 1978), although within broad confines of the definition of the disorder.

Associated Features

Apart from core symptomatology, a wide range of other symptoms has been reported. In children and adolescents, mood symptoms appear especially common (J. R. Asarnow et al. 1991; Werry et al. 1991a) and this is not simply due to the problem of separating early-onset psychotic mood disorder from EOS (Werry et al. 1991b). Disruptive symptoms are also common (e.g., Russell 1992; Werry 1992a), especially in prodromal stages. However, the most characteristic associated feature must be the decline in all areas of function, especially personal-social and academic.

Age at Onset

The youngest age reported so far is 3 (Russell et al. 1989), although cases below ages 6–7 are rare indeed. Cases before age 11 continue to be unusual, but after that the frequency rises steadily into maximum incidence (about .1% per year) of late adolescence to early adulthood (Werry 1992a, 1992b). Some claim that schizophrenia can begin at birth or soon after and that only the fact that the definition emphasizes language-derived symptoms prevents the diagnosis from being made (Cantor et al. 1982); however, this is still a matter of speculation because earliest reported cases have still not reached the time of onset of language.

Premorbid Personality and Function

The literature here is clear: the earlier the onset of schizophrenia, the more likely there will be long-standing (usually lifelong) abnormality of personality and other function (R. F. Asarnow et al. 1989; Walker and Lewine 1990; Werry 1992a). The types of abnormality extend beyond personal-social function to include a wide range of other developmental areas (see below). The type of personality abnormality is usually within the rubric of DSM-III's "odd eccentric" cluster, but the "anxious/fearful" cluster is also common. The UCLA group found a 40% frequency of the third cluster, "antisocial/histrionic/narcissistic" (Werry 1992a), which is consistent with the pioneering follow-up study by Lee Robins of children seen in St. Louis child guidance clinics before World War II (Robins 1979). Put another way, premorbid abnormality is common but may be of any type.

However, especially in adolescent schizophrenia, up to 50% may have no previous abnormality, and in this group this always serious disorder takes the form of a sudden family catastrophe.

Family Correlates

The most consistent finding here is a raised frequency of the disorder in relatives that obeys the laws of consanguinity, being highest in homozygous twins and children of two schizophrenic parents and being consistent with a genetic basis (Gottesman et al. 1987; Werry 1992a). There is some suggestion that the frequency of disorder in relatives decreases, with age at onset being highest in VEOS (Hanson and Gottesman 1976; Pulver et al. 1990; Werry 1992a, 1992b). Objective indicators of family function suggest some association with family adversity and family dysfunction (Goldstein 1987).

Most of the research on parent/family interaction and dynamics is of poor quality (Goldstein 1987), although myths such as the "schizophrenogenic mother" still abound. The most striking thing about families and parents of schizophrenic patients is their diversity and heterogeneity (Goldstein 1987). However, two abnormal findings seem to be reasonably robust. The first is that near relatives have an increased frequency of schizotypal personalities, abnormal cognitive styles (especially in span of attention), deviant communication patterns (R. F. Asarnow et al. 1989; J. R. Asarnow et al. 1991; Goldstein 1987; Tompson et al. 1990), or all three. Some good studies of families of children and adolescents with EOS have found communication deviation more commonly in parents of children with schizophrenia and schizotypal disorder than in parents of depressed children (J. R. Asarnow et al. 1991; Tompson et al. 1990), suggesting that the findings from adults can probably be extrapolated to EOS.

However, the second and most robust finding about families is that there is no pattern that characterizes the disorder, but rather one that seems to make the disorder worse once it has begun and seems to make relapse more likely. This is expressed as a (negative) emotion to the patient (see Goldstein 1987). Studies in children are only just beginning and so far have shown only some of what would be expected from research in adults: that high expressed emotion is not specific to families of children with EOS but is found in other disorders as well (see Werry 1992b).

Impairment

Most studies of VEOS report severe impairment (Werry 1992a), but it is difficult to disentangle the impact of the illness from the premorbid abnormalities. However, in EOS, in general, the onset of the active (psychotic) phase brings a discernible, significant impairment that usually lasts for several months even after the active phase passes (Werry 1992a). Subsequent episodes increase the level of impairment in a stepwise fashion, but there is also generally a continuing slow increase in impairment for several years. Chronic severe disability is common. The kinds of impairment are protean and range from inability to attend to activities of daily living, disruption of social contacts and interests, general disorganization of behavior, and loss of academic ability, to the child or adolescent putting himself or herself at serious risk, including sexually and through drug abuse.

Complications

Morbidity and mortality in schizophrenia are increased, although the reasons for this are unclear. Factors posited are self-neglect, poor nutrition, overactivity, stress, impairment of the immune system, drug abuse, and even toxicity of psychotropic drugs (Levinson and Simpson 1987). Suicide occurs in about 10% of persons with schizophrenia. Most cases occur within 10 years of onset of the disorder and are twice as high in males as in females. Other risk factors for suicide, while of great theoretical interest, have too low a level of prediction to be useful clinically (Caldwell and Gottesman 1990). Only two studies of EOS have been in progress long enough to assess the frequency of suicide. One study (Eggers 1978) reported only suicide attempts. The other (Werry et al. 1991a) noted that four patients (15% of the schizophrenic group) had committed suicide, although in some instances death may have resulted from accidents motivated by psychotic activity—for example, jumping out a window in response to a hallucination or a delusion.

Especially if gruesome or against persons of eminence, crimes by psychiatric patients are sensationalized by the media, and the public may be misled into believing that most patients are dangerous. However, there is almost certainly a small increase (possibly a doubling) of crimes of violence by persons with a history of psychiatric illness. Some of these are delusionally motivated and others exaggerations of premorbid patterns of behavior (Shore et al. 1989). Each year, White House police deal with a surprising number and array of threatening psychotic persons (Shore et al. 1989). However, the great complication is one of downward social mobility or deterioration accruing from impaired personal, social, and academic function that may end in homelessness (Lamb 1990; Mundy et al. 1990), vagrancy, dependency, social nuisance, or, formerly, in custodial "back" ward care.

Neurological and Developmental Features

These are grouped together because they are interrelated. A wide variety of "minor" neurological and neurodevelopmental abnormalities, especially impaired language and motor skills, has been reported in EOS mostly by the UCLA group (R. F. Asarnow et al. 1989; Russell 1992; Russell et al. 1989). This finding gains strength when the definition of EOS is extended to include younger adults (Foerster et al. 1991; Walker and Lewine 1990). However, there is reason to believe that schizophrenia comes in two clinical phenotypes, one of which is associated with a life-long history of neurosocial and personal-social developmental abnormalities and in which the psychosis is a rather late stage, and one that seems to begin with psychosis in previously unaffected persons (Crowe 1985; Foerster et al. 1991; Murray and Lewis 1987). Whereas the first phenotype is negatively correlated with age and is thus very common in VEOS, about 20% of cases of VEOS may be unaffected before the onset of the psychosis (see Werry 1992a).

The picture in EOS is contradictory, but in schizophrenia as a whole there is some association between prenatal and perinatal brain damage and the disorder (O'Callaghan et al. 1991; Pogue-Geile 1991), although in many individuals there may be no observable neurological sequelae. Negative studies may reflect the well-known errors of reminiscence, selective history taking, and examination. Werry et al. (1991a) have argued that if lowered IQ is admitted as evidence of brain damage, the case in EOS becomes somewhat more convincing.

Studies using brain imaging techniques have shown a wide variety of abnormalities in adults, but these are abnormalities of degree only, not specific to schizophrenia, and it is not clear how much is primary and secondary to the disorder and/or its treatment and how much is coincidental (Hendren et al. 1991; Meltzer 1987; Pogue-Geile 1991). So far, there has been little attempt to use these methods in EOS (Hendren et al. 1991).

Neuropsychological and Cognitive Studies

It is generally agreed that schizophrenia can occur at a high IQ level but that there is some association between lowered IQ and schizophrenia. Although this is consistent with the posited role of brain damage in etiology, depression of intellectual function is most evident during the acute phase (Aylward et al. 1984). The picture is unclear in EOS, although the percentage of those with a premorbid IQ less than 80 is probably increased slightly (Werry 1992a).

A stronger finding is that of selectively impaired cognitive function, most particularly span of apprehension (R. F. Asarnow et al. 1989; J. R. Asarnow et al. 1991; Goldstein 1987). In children, an additional finding is language defects in addition to core symptoms of illogicality and thought disorder—notably sensitivity to the listener and communication deviance (Caplan et al. 1989, 1990) and defects of executive function (inability to change set [Butler et al. 1991]).

Most of these cognitive findings are also increased in schizotypal personality disorder in children and in relatives, and in other disorders (except thought disorder), but they are less severe than in EOS (J. R. Asarnow et al. 1991; Caplan et al. 1989, 1990; Tompson et al. 1990). This suggests that the onset of the disorder greatly augments any prior defects.

From a clinical point of view, these defects in basic cognition must have a serious impact in a rapidly developing organism where such emphasis is placed on formal learning. They must impair social learning as well.

Neuropsychological tests have been used in localization studies in adults, and, although less than consistent, these tests suggest some pathology in the frontal areas, temporal/limbic areas, or both (Gur et al. 1990).

Psychophysiological, Biochemical, and Other Laboratory Tests

As with most areas of schizophrenia, psychophysiological studies in adults suggest that a substantial group of patients with schizophrenia have quantitative but nonspecific deviations from nonschizophrenic individuals, especially in measures of selective attention (Holzman 1987). Saccadic eye movements may also be found in schizophrenia and familially and may serve as a genetic marker (Holzman 1987).

In biochemistry, the same pattern as in most other tests is to be found in adults; that is, quantitative departures are common, but these are not peculiar to schizophrenia. Most interest centers on the catecholamine and serotonin systems because of their link to antipsychotic drugs. Understandably, little work has been done in children.

Schizophrenia is a serious disorder with profound impact on cognitive and social function. In children and adolescents it is found more often in boys and is often preceded by marked premorbid personality and developmental abnormality. Frequency in relatives is probably higher than in nonrelated adults, and symptomatology shows expected developmental differences most marked in VEOS. There is no particular family dynamic pattern associated with the disorder, although, after it is established, the course may be influenced by psychosocial factors such as expressed negative emotion. Laboratory or neuropsychological differences are only quantitatively different, found in some patients but not all, and are not specific to schizophrenia.

There has been little study of these features in children and adolescents, but what data there are suggest that most are likely to be similar to adults with developmental and quantitative (probably mostly more extreme) differences. Most findings are of little use in diagnosis but may be helpful in assessing disability of individual patients and advising their families. Variability is a feature of the disorder both across individuals and their families and time.

Course and Prognosis

Onset is dramatic and acute in VEOS in 25% or less; in EOS, in 90%. A prodrome is probably much more common in EOS than VEOS (Werry

1992a). The acute psychotic episode in VEOS lasts about a year or so (J. R. Asarnow et al. 1991; Spencer et al. 1991) and in EOS about 4 months (McClellan and Werry 1991; Werry et al. 1991a, 1991b), but some do not ever lose psychotic symptoms. As noted above, in those who do there is usually a period of several months of convalescence resembling a postschizophrenia depression. What this means is that considerable patience in and steadiness of treatment is required.

Course is profoundly influenced by diagnostic criteria. DSM-IV criteria are among the most conservative, because of the 6-month requirement and first-ranked symptomatology (Andreasen 1987; Angst 1988; Westermeyer and Harrow 1988). Although ICD-10 uses much the same symptomatology as DSM, the fact that there is more flexibility, more left to clinical judgment, and a shorter (2-week) criterion almost certainly means that less severe cases would be included in the diagnosis and that therefore the prognosis should be somewhat better.

In their comprehensive review of outcome, Westermeyer and Harrow (1988) concluded that schizophrenia, narrowly defined, has a poor outcome in the vast majority of cases (about 70%). Put another way, modern definitions of the disorder have more in common with Kraepelin's concept of dementia praecox than with Bleuler's schizophrenia.

There have been only two long-term studies of outcome of any size in EOS: one in Germany (Eggers 1978) and one in New Zealand (Werry et al. 1991a, 1991b), and the results are in conflict (50% versus 80% poor outcome). Some of the difference may have been due to Eggers' less stringent diagnostic criteria and the inclusion of a number of cases subsequently rediagnosed as schizoaffective (Eggers 1989), although this did not seem to influence outcome much. The New Zealand findings are more in line with what is suggested by shorter-term outcome (see Werry 1992a) and one small longer-term study in the United States (McClellan and Werry 1991). Also, Eggers found that none of the individuals he studied with onset under the age of 11 recovered.

Both the adult and the much more limited child and adolescent literature show that the lifelong course is highly variable, although several acute episodes against a backdrop of slowly deteriorating function appear to be the usual prognosis. The disease is said to burn itself out after 10 years and there is even evidence to suggest that there may be some modest improvement after that (see Werry 1992b). Although there may be a few cases involving individuals who do well, with EOS one is usually a witness to a family tragedy.

Etiology and Pathogenesis

The pendulum has swung away from psychogenic views, begun by Bleuler and carried to extreme limits by the psychoanalytic and radical psychiatric movements (e.g., Bettelheim or R. D. Laing), back to Kraepelin's genetic-biogenic one. Even so, although there are some plausible and interesting hypotheses, the actual pathogenic base remains unknown (Meltzer 1987). However, Bleuler's view that the disorder was biogenic but symptomatology and outcome were shaped by psychosocial factors is probably the most parsimonious way of summarizing the research. It is a great pity—especially for families of that era, who often found themselves unwittingly accused of causing the disorder in their child (see Werry 1979)—that American psychiatry between 1950 and 1975 took only half of Bleuler's idea, caricatured it at first, and then embraced it to death.

Schizophrenia is unlikely to be a single disease. It is much more a phenotype in which symptomatology is rather too far downstream and too much influenced by homeostatic and adventitious factors to give more than very crude pointers to etiology. Also, modern concepts of disease—although not denying the place of major or sine qua non factors (such as bacteria in infection)—see the final disorder as a complex multivariate outcome, well illustrated in schizophrenia in the schematic model of Neuchertelein and Liberman (Goldstein 1987).

A very influential theory taking several different forms suggests that there are at least two broad groups of schizophrenia. Crowe (1985) has argued for a genetic versus a nongenetic (brain damage) dichotomy, while others suggest one based, at least in part, on male gender (Foerster et al. 1991; Pulver et al. 1990).

Biological Hypotheses

Genetic

This is not so much a true pathogenic hypothesis as one that indicates the mechanism for where and how to search for the "lesion." Although the field of molecular biology that is intimately tied to genetics is a glamour area of modern science, there are enormous difficulties in proceeding (Gottesman et al. 1987). The genetic base of at least some schizophrenia is the well-established risk with increasing consanguinity, being about 8% for siblings, 12% for children, 40% in homozygous twins, and 40% when both parents are affected. Risk rates for relatives of those with EOS are probably higher (Hanson and Gottesman 1976; Pulver et al. 1990; Werry 1992a). The mode of transmission is unlikely to be that of a single major gene (or several such) but polygenic with protective and vulnerability genes influencing outcome (Gottesman et al. 1987). This would explain variations in family history just as well as the etiologically phenotypic view.

Biochemical

Most of the theories in this class are derived from knowledge of cellular effects of drugs effective in schizophrenia, making it worse or mimicking it (e.g., amphetamines). Postsynaptic dopamine hypersensitivity is the current favorite, although noradrenaline, serotonin, and other amines also attract interest (Meltzer 1987). Clinicians need know little more than the above at this stage of knowledge.

Neuropathological

Brain damage—especially of the prenatal and perinatal types—has long been suspected, but has best been demonstrated in high-risk longitudinal studies and, less successfully, in separating out familial and nonfamilial types (Murray and Lewis 1987). Temporal lobe epilepsy, itself nearly always a sign of early brain damage, is another long-known risk factor (Crowe 1985) supportive of this hypothesis.

This view, which has a direct derivative in the developmental hypothesis (see below), holds that somehow the brain-damaging factor beginning early in life distorts the process of brain development in a cumulative fashion so that the disorder emerges only years later. Elegant views of how this might operate at a brain level are offered by Weinberger (1987), Crowe (1990), and Robins (1979), among others (see Buchsbaum 1990). The preferred sites or systems for any abnormality are in the temporal or frontal regions, although the basal ganglia and other sites are favored by some (Buchsbaum 1990). Temporal lobe dysfunction would best explain the language and thought disorders. Frontal lobe dysfunction would best explain the problems of executive function in schizophrenia, so perhaps both are involved. The developmental theory of Weinberger is of particular interest to child and adolescent psychiatrists. To explain the mainly adolescent and young adult onset of schizophrenia, he posits that puberty may be associated with maturation of some brain system; that system is then activated as a result of the developmental challenges of that period. This in turn puts stress on that part of the brain that is damaged, and schizophrenia results. Changes in dopaminergic systems in the limbic system fit this model very well and, further, by their slow decline after early adulthood, could explain why active symptoms are most prominent only in the first few years of the disorder.

Infective and Immunological

As noted above, the waxing and waning of the schizophrenia "epidemic" between 1800 and 1995 are consistent with a virus. The existence of a greater risk in recent immigrants and across different ethnic groups and countries is also consistent with a virus (Harrison 1990; Torrey 1987). This view is disputed and so far lacks the immunological evidence needed. Others have proposed an autoimmune response (see Meltzer 1987).

Developmental

This will appeal to those in child and adolescent psychiatry, since it proposes that, although the brain is injured in some way very early in life, the effect is slowly cumulative so that psychosis and deterioration is a kind of end stage that does not emerge until considerably later in life. It offers the possibility of some degree of reconciliation between the biogenic and psychogenic views, particularly as proposed by Weinberger (1987). It is also able to explain the lifelong premorbid abnormalities of personal and social adjustment and neurodevelopment and the gradual emergence of more severe psychological and neuropsychological pathology as life proceeds (see Goldstein 1987).

Such a view ordinarily is taken to assume two kinds of schizophrenia:

congenital or developmental schizophrenia, which is associated with life-long abnormalities, and acquired schizophrenia, in which the child is unaffected up to the time of psychosis. However, abnormal development does not necessarily imply that the critical disease process begins then, nor vice versa, because the developmental abnormalities reported in VEOS and EOS are seen in many other child and adolescent psychiatric disorders and in nonschizophrenic children, are not universal in schizophrenia, and could be coincidental or could merely expedite the later emergence of genetic factors (Pogue-Geile 1991). After all, there are a large number of genetic disorders, such as Huntington's disease and muscular dystrophy, which do not manifest themselves until adolescence or later.

Psychosocial Views

After the excesses of 1950–1975, psychosocial hypotheses have withered away partly because of theoretical vagueness and poor research (see Goldstein 1987) and partly because of credibility issues. What remains is rather different and much more robust. It has been repeatedly demonstrated in over 20 excellent studies and in several countries that after schizophrenia has developed, families or other small social systems in which the patient lives—through the medium of negative expressed emotion to the patient—influence the rate of relapse (Hirsch and Leff 1975) and may interact with the effects of antipsychotic medication (see Goldstein 1987; Kane 1987). Even more compelling is that treatment aimed specifically at changing this expressed emotion reduces the rate of relapse (Goldstein 1987; Leff et al. 1982). The old double-bind hypothesis also survives, if rather tenuously and in greatly modified, less doctrinaire form. This hypothesis views the family problem as a genetically determined language or cognitive disorder called communication deviance (R. F. Asarnow et al. 1989; Goldstein 1987).

Good research in EOS in these two facets of family pathogenesis is just beginning, and although these facets are found in families of children with schizophrenia, they are not specific and their impact on the disorder remains to be demonstrated (Hibbs et al. 1991; Sanchez-Lachay et al. 1991; Stubbe et al. 1991; Tompson et al. 1990).

Probably the most clinically practical demonstration of the importance of psychosocial factors in established schizophrenia comes from the repeatedly demonstrated (if little formally researched) fact that institutions cause regression of social skills in persons with schizophrenia (and other disorders) and that active rehabilitation programs can ameliorate disability significantly (Liberman 1988).

Assessment

Assessment has three main purposes: diagnosis, management of the child with the disorder, and monitoring progress. In most clinical situations, there seems little doubt that the usual method of diagnosis is informal, based on loosely organized history taking and examination half-remembered from residency training. As in all child and adolescent psychiatry, this would include parents, child, teachers, and significant others as informants. Dissatisfaction with the revealed inaccuracy of such methods (e.g., Gutterman et al. 1987; Prendergast et al. 1988), the need for reliable and valid research, and the profound thrust by DSM-III, with its operational diagnostic criteria and field trials, have led to less informal methods.

Structured Diagnostic Interviews

This is not the place to give a review of this topic, which transcends just one disorder such as schizophrenia and for which competent reviews can be found elsewhere (Gutterman et al. 1987). Epidemiological studies may, for economic reasons, prefer lay interview methods such as the Diagnostic Interview Schedule for Children (DISC) (Edelbrock and Costello 1988), which have to be rigidly structured to suit the lack of training in interviewers. But in clinical practice, any child or adolescent suspected of having a psychotic disorder requires a competent psychiatric interview, and the clinician should seek to check such a devastating diagnosis as EOS by formal methods, despite their tediousness. The three best-known (see Russell 1992) and most suitable are the Schedule for Affective Disorders and Schizophrenia for School-Age Children (K-SADS) (Ambrosini et al. 1989); the Diagnostic Interview for Children and Adolescents (DICA) (Herjanic and Reich 1982), which is also available in microcomputerized form (Reich 1990); and the Interview Schedule for Children (ISC) (Kovacs 1978). The UCLA group has developed a focused and expanded (to include pervasive developmental disorder [PDD] and schizotypal disorder) derivative of the K-SADS: the Interview for Childhood Disorders and Schizophrenia (ICDS) (Russell et al. 1989). Russell (1992) has reviewed the limited data on reliability for these instruments in EOS and concludes that the most satisfactory are the K-SADS for adolescents and the ICDS for children, although the others have not yet had any test of their diagnostic power in EOS. In older adolescents, adult methods may be just as, or even more, suitable (see Werry 1992b).

Symptomatology and Function

Although assessment of symptomatology is important for diagnosis, it is as important for management of the individual child as for monitoring progress. This is because, as in all of medicine, it is symptoms affecting individuals that cause distress and disability, not schizophrenia. Westermeyer and Harrow (1988), in their exhaustive review of outcome in schizophrenia, argue for a two-dimensional system of measures of symptoms and adaptive function typified in DSM-III-R's Axis V (Global Assessment of Functioning).

Symptomatology

The biggest revolution in symptomatology since Kraepelin, Bleuler, and Schneider is in the division into positive and negative symptoms (see Andreasen 1987; Kay 1990, 1991), although a recent study suggests there may be a third dimension of disorganization (Dollfus et al. 1991). Positive symptoms incorporate the classical Germanic first-ranked symptoms; the negative ones are largely ones of deficit such as flattened affect, avolition, asociality, and so on. There are two reliable and valid schedules for assessing these symptoms on a diagnostic and continuing basis: the Scale for the Assessment of Positive Symptoms and the Scale for the Assessment of Negative Symptoms (SAPS and SANS) (see Andreasen 1987); and the Positive and Negative Symptom Scale (PANSS) (Kay 1990, 1991). Though designed for positive and negative symptoms, both also can yield a disorganization score (Dollfus et al. 1991), which appears to have high face validity as a particular facet of the disability seen in EOS.

Recently there has been some excellent research in symptomatology in children, including pilot efforts to adapt the adult scales for children (Fields et al. 1991); the use of pictorial methods of elicitation (Ernst et al. 1991); and laboratory tests, such as the Kiddie Formal Thought Disorder Rating Scale (Caplan et al. 1989, 1990) and the Span of Attention Test (R. F. Asarnow et al. 1989). These studies show that children require special methods of elicitation and that some of the defining symptoms in adults, such as passivity phenomena (Garralda 1985; Spencer et al. 1991), disorganization, and poverty of thinking (Caplan et al. 1989, 1990) are strongly age-dependent and may not be seen at all in VEOS.

A great deal more research is needed in this area to develop methods for clinicians to assess and monitor progress of children and adolescents with schizophrenia.

Adaptive Function

No attempt will be made here to survey measures of function except to note that because of the profound disability caused by schizophrenia, methods that are known to any competent occupational therapist and that place emphasis on activities of daily living and on academic achievement, however limited, are particularly indicated.

Differential Diagnosis

Bipolar Mood Disorder

This is the most serious problem, since misdiagnosis leads to mistreatment. In the past the error has operated mostly against bipolar disorder (see Carlson 1990; Werry et al. 1991a) but a recent study suggests this may be changing (McClellan and Werry 1991). There is now strong evidence that floridly psychotic adolescents—and probably children, too, although proven bipolar disorder in that age group is exceedingly rare (Carlson 1990)—often cannot be definitively differentially diagnosed except by following the adolescents for several years (Carlson 1990; McClellan and Werry 1991; Werry et al. 1991a, 1991b). Werry et al. (1991b) showed that the reason for misdiagnosis is not necessarily due to overlooking fundamental symptoms at initial diagnosis as originally suggested (Carlson 1990).

According to the only substantial long-term follow-up study of both disorders in children and adolescents (Werry et al. 1991a, 1991b), indicators of schizophrenia are long-standing premorbid abnormality, especially oddness and neurodevelopmental abnormalities; psychosis lasting more than 3 months; a deteriorating course and a family history of schizophrenia; and for bipolar disorder, lack of premorbid abnormality and rapid onset, plus a family history of bipolar disorder. However, none of these is absolute, and they are based on one study only. The most important thing is to recognize that florid psychosis requires an open mind and punctilious follow-up. Child and adolescent psychiatrists may take comfort in the fact that the situation is no easier in young adults.

Schizoaffective Disorder

This disorder has an ambiguous status but is generally felt to represent overlapping extremes of the two parent disorders. One extreme, which is marked by prominent manic episodes, is closer to bipolar disorder; the other extreme, in which depressive symptoms (and schizophrenic course) predominate, is closer to schizophrenia. Family pedigrees sometimes support such thinking and sometimes do not, although increased frequencies of both disorders in families are rather more consistent, thus suggesting a truly mixed disorder (Samson et al. 1988). Studies suggest that the course lies midway between that of the two disorders and that both antimanic and antipsychotic treatment should be tried (Samson et al. 1988).

The disorder is defined somewhat differently in DSM-IV and ICD-10. The former system is more stringent and requires at least two characteristic symptoms during 1 month (less if treated), which must occur either in the absence of major mood disturbance or with a mood disturbance (if present) whose total duration is brief relative to the schizophrenic features. ICD-10 allows greater flexibility to the clinician, particularly with regard to the present of mood disturbance. The issue of whether the active psychotic phase can include mixed features remains controversial.

There are only two studies of early-onset schizoaffective disorder (Eggers 1989; Werry et al. 1991a, 1991b) and one has only six cases.

Eggers found little difference in outcome or other characteristics, but this was not true in the other study, where, if anything, schizoaffective disorder was more severe. In the New Zealand study, few of the misdiagnosed bipolar cases had schizoaffective disorder at outcome; therefore, use of this label in difficult early-onset cases at initial diagnosis should be subject to the same doubt and longitudinal surveillance as with the two parent disorders. Clearly, more study is needed.

Schizotypal Disorder

This disorder is characterized by insufficient "doses" of symptoms found in schizophrenia (see Raine 1991), an increased, although still low, risk of developing schizophrenia (Battaglia et al. 1991), and an absence of a clear onset. DSM defines symptomatology as occurring in nine areas (ideas of reference, social anxiety, odd beliefs and thinking, unusual perceptual experiences, eccentric behavior, no friends, odd speech, constricted affect, and suspiciousness). The similarity to schizophrenia is obvious. A promising seven-item questionnaire tied to DSM criteria (Raine 1991) can assist with diagnosis. This questionnaire, although probably suitable for adolescents, would require considerable adaptation for children.

The absence of clear onset presents a particular problem in VEOS and in EOS, in which premorbid function is often one of significant lifelong abnormality (Werry 1992a). In DSM-IV, VEOS and EOS are included in the personality disorders, but in ICD-10 (World Health Organization 1992) they are in the schizophrenia section. The latter approach fits well with the schizophrenia spectrum concept emphasized in children and adolescents by the UCLA and Yale groups (Russell 1992; Volkmar et al. 1988). These groups have pointed out the difficulty of differentiating between schizotypal disorder and insidious-onset schizophrenia in children with lifelong personality abnormality. They have also demonstrated the qualitative similarity between symptomatology and associated (especially family) characteristics. Wolff's (1991) long-term prospective study of schizotypal children found that very few developed schizophrenia but most remained discernibly eccentric, although enjoying variable and sometimes quite successful levels of social adaptation in adulthood. Wolff's review also suggests that Asperger's original group of children contained many schizotypal children with similar outcomes. There is also some unproven clinical lore that antipsychotic medications may be just as helpful in schizotypal disorder as they are in schizophrenia, although in lower dosages (McClellan and Werry 1991). Certainly, when in doubt, a trial of medication is indicated.

Most of what is known about schizotypal disorder is derived from studies on adults. It may be difficult with children to separate schizotypal disorder from atypical pervasive developmental disorder (Meijer and Treffers 1991), although the UCLA group seemed not to have this difficulty (Russell 1992).

Despite considerable debate, schizotypal disorder is listed in DSM-IV as a personality disorder under cluster A of the odd and eccentric disorders. This is at odds with the view of a schizophrenia spectrum and is a disadvantage in child psychiatry because it is often difficult to make a clear distinction between severe and very-early-onset schizotypal disorder and VEOS. The nine defining symptoms and the number required (five) are much the same. The illustrative examples and definitions have been pruned a little, but not as much as they have been in the case of schizophrenia.

There is now in DSM-IV specific reference to schizotypal disorder and its features in children and adolescents in the text not found in DSM-III-R, and a caveat about not confusing it with turmoil in adolescence. It should be noted, however, that there is a debate in child psychiatry as to how common and how inexorable such turmoil really is. This is important because there is reason to suspect that this disorder ordinarily is lifelong and should be detectable for adulthood (see Werry et al. 1991b; Wolff 1991).

The main difference between the DSM-IV and ICD-10 definitions is that in ICD-10, schizotypal disorder has no reference in its name to "personality" and is found in the same section as schizophrenia. As noted, this is much more appropriate for children. Both DSM-IV and ICD-10 list nine symptoms for schizotypal disorder. Although there are a couple of differences, these symptoms are much the same; however, no particular threshold is stated. This leaves the diagnostic decision to the clinician, which ought to lead to wide variations by individual and country. As in schizophrenia, there is no mention of children.

Schizoid Disorder

This presents less of a problem because cognition is normal; the outstanding characteristic is a self-centeredness and a lack of interest in human relationships. Schizoid disorder may have more in common with autism and Asperger's disorder than with schizophrenia.

It should be noted, too, that in the past this term was used in error for schizotypal disorder. Indeed, the best longitudinal study of "schizoid" children, by Wolff (1991) in Edinburgh, was mostly a study of schizotypal children—an error that Wolff corrected only when the children were grown up (see Russell 1992).

The differences in diagnostic criteria between DSM-III-R and DSM-IV are minimal and only matters of wording. The disorder remains within cluster A of the personality disorders. The biggest change is in the text, which specifies that schizoid disorder may be found in children and adolescents and also mentions the difficulty of differentiating schizoid disorder from autism and Asperger's disorder (see Werry et al. 1991b; Wolff 1991). The differential diagnosis refers to the distinguishing features of more seriously impaired social relationships, language impairments, and stereotyped behavior. However, it should be noted that language may be quite normal in Asperger's disorder and that there are those who argue that schizoid disorder is sometimes merely the adult outcome (see Werry, in press; Wolff 1991).

Schizoid personality disorder is much the same in ICD-10 as in DSM-IV, and at least three of the "traits" (symptoms) are required. There is no specific mention of children. However, the text notes that personality disorders usually begin in late childhood or adolescence but, for reasons not stated, suggests that the diagnosis of personality disorder should not be made before late adolescence.

A major difference is that ICD refers to "schizoid disorder of childhood" in the exclusions. Although this is not a separate category, it turns out to be a synonym for Asperger's disorder, which may reflect the origins of some cases of adult schizoid disorders but might also cause some confusion.

Organic Psychoses

Organic psychoses should cause little difficulty, because in delirium, disorientation, and fluctuating consciousness, as well as in dementia, memory impairment is found, whereas careful study (including particularly neuropsychological testing) in schizophrenia shows an intact sensorium.

Substance use disorders are the most common comorbid disorders. They may present problems of differential diagnosis in the acute phase, but only within the first few hours, because most substances last less than 24 hours at most. Drug screening is an essential part of differential diagnosis of any acute psychotic state anyway. There is some evidence to suggest that illicit drugs, especially cannabis, may precipitate the onset of schizophrenia and cause relapses, but the evidence is controversial. There is also some evidence to support the idea that cannabis may actually be useful as an anxiolytic in schizophrenia (Dixon et al. 1991).

Autism, Asperger's Disorder, and Other Pervasive Developmental Disorders

These are discussed by Volkmar and coauthors (Chapter 6), Szatmari (Chapter 7), and Volkmar (Chapter 8).

Treatment

Management may be subdivided into that of the disorder and that of the patient, the family, the school, and the community. Although only those areas relating to the disorder will be discussed here, I hope that it is unnecessary to emphasize in a monograph about children and adolescents the importance of the other areas, or how to go about examining them.

The lack of knowledge about EOS and the need to extrapolate from adult studies have been lamented repeatedly throughout this chapter. Nowhere is this more true than in treatment, where there are almost no studies at all (Werry 1992a).

Pharmacotherapy and Electroconvulsive Therapy

This area has recently been reviewed in detail in adults (Baldasserini 1991; Kane 1987) and in EOS (Campbell et al. 1993; McClellan and Werry 1991). In adult psychiatry it is well established that antipsychotic drugs (neuroleptics)

- are the mainstay of specific treatment
- reduce active symptoms both acutely and during subsequent phases of the disorder but have less (but some) effect on negative symptoms
- take between 4 and 6 weeks to produce maximal effect on psychosis and up to 1 year in untreated chronic cases
- reduce the frequency of relapses
- reduce the duration of relapses if they occur
- are all equally effective and differ only in side-effect profile (mainly atropinic/autonomic or mainly extrapyramidal plus or minus idiosyncratic effects)—with the possible exception of clozapine, which may have a special role in treatment-resistant schizophrenia (Birmaher et al. 1992)
- are effective in the acute phases in doses of about 400–600 mg/70 kg in chlorpromazine equivalents, and in lower doses in maintenance/prophylaxis
- are generally given in doses that are much too high, thereby increasing patient discomfort, side effects, and the risk of tardive dyskinesia and dystonia, which are dose related
- are only partially or poorly effective in about one-third of patients, a lack of response that is usually not helped by raising the dose above usual levels
- seem to have no specific effect on the underlying disorder so that they must be given for many years until the disorder burns itself out, although they are able to improve symptomatology and function
- have one of the highest therapeutic ratios in medicine and produce, in the main, only minor or treatable annoyances, such as sedative, atropinic, autonomic, or extrapyramidal effects (Baldasserini 1991)—yet occasionally have more serious effects, such as blood dyscrasias, seizures, neuroleptic malignant syndrome, neurological sequelae, endocrine dysfunctions, dermatitides, hepatotoxicity, retinal pigmentation, and (only possibly) cardiotoxicity and sudden death (Levinson and Simpson 1987)
- present a serious problem of compliance and challenge to clinicians to get patients and families informed and on board with the treatment program

- may be combined with other drugs (notably the benzodiazepines) in the first few days of hospitalization in the acute phase in very excited or disturbed patients; this would be done to reduce the amount of medication needed, although it increases the risks of serious interactions. Neuroleptics may also be combined with antidepressant medication for postschizophrenic depression but not for mere residual states (Plasky 1991)
- are the subject of a huge clinical mythology: that is, that some drugs are better than others in general or for negative rather than for positive symptoms, or that raising the dose to high levels increases the size of the effect (only clozapine and possibly resperidone offer advantages over other neuroleptics)
- are poorly understood and unjustly vilified as "tranquilizers" or "chemical straitjacketing" by a largely scientifically illiterate, prejudiced, and/or hostile media industry and public

In VEOS, it is assumed that pharmacotherapy is largely ineffective, yet the only systematic study points otherwise (Spencer et al. 1992). In EOS some data also suggest that pharmacotherapy is effective (see Birmaher et al. 1992; McClellan and Werry 1991). It is worth noting that young persons seem more prone to acute dystonic reactions than older persons (Dollfus and Petit 1988); these reactions can be both terrifying and a disincentive to treatment and need to be anticipated. They almost always occur within the first 72 hours of starting treatment or increasing dosage.

In summary, then, extrapolation from adult studies, the limited child and adolescent data, and the devastation produced by the disorder make it negligence not to try antipsychotic drugs at some point in treatment.

Before leaving the topic of medication, it is important to identify the common errors implicit in the list above. These are 1) overdosage, 2) failure to appreciate the slow time frame of antipsychotic action, leading to premature cessation of medication or, more commonly, a frenetic switching among different antipsychotics, 3) polypharmacy, 4) failure to monitor progress and side effects in a systemic way as outlined above, and 5) total reliance on medication instead of on multidisciplinary, multimodal treatment (McLellan and Werry 1991).

Electroshock treatment is mentioned only to dismiss it, because its role in schizophrenia in any except the rare malignant catatonia with fluid and electrolyte imbalance is at best unproven (Abrams 1992) and at worst highly controversial.

Psychosocial

There are only two forms of individual or family treatment of proven value as specific treatments in schizophrenia (Goldstein 1987), and these are both behavioral. One is family treatment aimed at reducing (negative) expressed emotion (Leff et al. 1982), and the other is the Camarillo rehabilitation package (Liberman 1988). Neither has yet been tried in EOS, but both should be. Psychoanalytic and other insight-oriented psychotherapies are contraindicated not only because they are largely ineffective, but also because where there is some impact, it seems mostly negative (Goldstein 1987).

However, the exercise of common sense, as well as general supportive, educational, activity, and occupational measures for families and children, on a strictly pragmatic basis, is to be encouraged. This should not be extended to unproven, expensive, ideologically driven treatments such as family therapy, multivitamins, or quasi-neurological interventions.

Summary and Directions for Research

Schizophrenia is rare in children, but its frequency rises steeply in adolescence. It is usually a devastating disorder with a poor prognosis. As such, it requires all the skills of child and adolescent psychiatry and of rehabilitation medicine. Although most of the useful knowledge about schizophrenia comes from adult studies, there are important developmental differences and needs revealed by what little research there is in EOS. Further, the similarity between adult and early-onset forms of the disorder is no argument for ceding children and adolescents to the care of adult psychiatrists or facilities as happens to most adolescents at present. This is a violation of their basic needs and rights under the WHO charter. This situation is primarily caused by a lack of interest and advocacy on the part of child and adolescent mental health professionals, reflected in the grossly underdeveloped state of research in EOS.

Case Report

Kyle was the youngest of three children born to a working-class family. His mother had immigrated as a child; his father was employed as a laborer. The pregnancy, labor, and delivery had been uncomplicated. Kyle was born at term. His early development was within normal limits, although he was slow to talk. He attended preschool and began primary school without academic difficulty; he was, however, noted by his teachers to be overly reserved, shy, and rather clumsy.

Shortly before his 10th birthday, Kyle seemed to become more withdrawn. His parents and teacher felt that he was overly preoccupied with fantasy figures. Over the next several months his schoolwork, previously at an average level, began to deteriorate. His parents noted that he had started to talk to himself at times. He was seen by the school psychologist who found problems of disorganized thinking, attention, and reality testing. Before the completion of the evaluation, Kyle's speech and behavior became markedly disorganized and testing had to be discontinued.

Child psychiatric examination revealed that Kyle was having auditory hallucinations in which voices commented about him and his behavior. He appeared anxious and fearful and worried that a radio had been planted in his head. He had ideas of reference, believing that the television was talking to him. His speech was disorganized and he exhibited tangential thinking and loose associations. There was no history of exposure to drugs. His mother reported that her brother had been hospitalized for a similar problem when he was an adolescent.

Because of the need for a full diagnostic workup and the family's distress, Kyle was hospitalized. Thioridazine, a neuroleptic, in doses of 5 mg/kg, led to a marked reduction in the hallucinations and delusions over a 6-week period, although some affective flattening and anergia remained. Kyle was subsequently discharged to the care of his parents. The dose of thioridazine was reduced to 3 mg/kg and supportive counseling was provided. Medications were discontinued after a period of over 1 year, but another psychotic episode occurred after 9 months, and medications were therefore reinstituted. At the time of follow-up, when Kyle was 15, he continued to have some difficulties with unusual experiences and idiosyncratic speech, but the bigger problems were his negative symptoms: anergia and poverty of thinking. He was managing to stay in school, although his academic performance was poor. A trial of clozapine was carried out with significant

improvement, but he remains socially and academically disabled and
has put on 10 kg excess weight.

References

Abrams R: Electroconvulsive Therapy, 2nd Edition. New York, Oxford University Press, 1992, p 18

Ambrosini PJ, Metz C, Prabucki K, et al: Video tape reliability of the third revised edition of the K-SADS. J Am Acad Child Adolesc Psychiatry 28:723–728, 1989

American Psychiatric Association: Diagnostic and Statistical Manual of Mental Disorders, 2nd Edition. Washington, DC, American Psychiatric Association, 1968

American Psychiatric Association: Diagnostic and Statistical Manual of Mental Disorders, 3rd Edition. Washington, DC, American Psychiatric Association, 1980

American Psychiatric Association: Diagnostic and Statistical Manual of Mental Disorders, 3rd Edition, Revised. Washington, DC, American Psychiatric Association, 1987

American Psychiatric Association: DSM-IV Options Book: Work in Progress. Washington, DC, American Psychiatric Association, 1991, pp F1–26

American Psychiatric Association: Diagnostic and Statistical Manual, 4th Edition. Washington, DC, American Psychiatric Association, 1994

Andreasen NC: The diagnosis of schizophrenia. Schizophr Bull 13:25–34, 1987

Angst J: European long-term follow-up studies of schizophrenia. Schizophr Bull 14:501–513, 1988

Asarnow RF, Asarnow JR (eds): Childhood Onset Schizophrenia. Schizophr Bull 20:591–746, 1994

Asarnow RF, Asarnow JR, Strandburg R: Schizophrenia: a developmental perspective, in Rochester Symposium on Developmental Psychology. Edited by Cicchetti D. New York, Cambridge University Press, 1989, pp 189–220

Asarnow JR, Bates S, Tompson M, et al: Depressive and schizophrenia spectrum disorders in childhood. A follow-up study. Paper presented at the annual meeting of the American Academy of Child and Adolescent Psychiatry, San Francisco, October 1991

Aylward E, Walker E, Bettes B: Intelligence in schizophrenia: meta-analysis of the research. Schizophr Bull 10:430–459, 1984

Baldasserini RJ: Drugs and the treatment of psychiatric disorders, in Goodman and Gilman's Pharmacological Basis of Therapeutics, 8th Edition. Edited by Goodman-Gilman A, Rall TW, Nies AS, et al. New York, Pergamon, 1991, pp 383–435

Battaglia M, Gasperini M, Sciuto G, et al: Psychiatric disorders in the families of schizotypal subjects. Schizophr Bull 17:659–668, 1991

Beitchman JH: Childhood schizophrenia: a review and comparison with adult-onset schizophrenia. Psychiatr Clin North Am 8:793–814, 1985

Birmaher B, Baker R, Kapur S, et al: Clozapine for the treatment of adolescents with schizophrenia. J Am Acad Child Adolesc Psychiatry 31:160–164, 1992

Bland RC, Kaloda J: Nosology, epidemiology and genetics, in Handbook of Schizophrenia, Vol 3. Edited by Tsuang ML, Simpson JS. Amsterdam, Elsevier, 1988, pp 1–25

Buchsbaum MS: Frontal lobes, basal ganglia, temporal lobes: three sites for schizophrenia? Schizophr Bull 16:377–546, 1990

Burke P, Del Becarro M, McCauley E, et al: Hallucinations in children. J Am Acad Child Adolesc Psychiatry 24:71–75, 1985

Butler P, Whitaker A, Setterberg S, et al: Executive function deficits in early onset schizophrenia. Paper presented at the annual meeting of the American Academy of Child and Adolescent Psychiatry, San Francisco, October 1991

Caldwell CB, Gottesman II: Schizophrenics kill themselves too: a review of risk factors for suicide. Schizophr Bull 16:571–589, 1990

Campbell M, Gonzalez NM, Ernst M, et al: Antipsychotics (neuroleptics), in A Practitioner's Guide to Psychoactive Drugs for Children and Adolescents. Edited by Werry JS, Aman MG. New York, Plenum, 1993, pp 269–296

Cantor S, Evans J, Pearce J, et al: Childhood schizophrenia: present but not accounted for. Am J Psychiatry 139:758–762, 1982

Caplan R, Guthrie D, Fish B, et al: The kiddie formal thought disorder rating scales: clinical assessment, reliability and validity. J Am Acad Child Adolesc Psychiatry 28:408–416, 1989

Caplan R, Perdue S, Tanguay PE, et al: Formal thought disorder in childhood onset schizophrenia and schizotypal personality disorder. J Child Psychol Psychiatry 31:1103–1114, 1990

Carlson GA: Child and adolescent mania: diagnostic considerations. J Child Psychol Psychiatry 31:331–342, 1990

Crowe TJ: The two syndrome concept: origins and current status. Schizophr Bull 11:471–486, 1985

Crowe TJ: Temporal lobe asymmetries as the key to the etiology of schizophrenia. Schizophr Bull 16:433–444, 1990

Dixon L, Haas G, Weiden PJ, et al: Drug abuse in schizophrenic patients: clinical correlates and reason for use. Am J Psychiatry 148:224–230, 1991

Dollfus S, Petit M: Efficacité et tolérance des psychotropes chez l'enfant. Paris, Expansion Scientific Francaise, 1988

Dollfus S, Petit M, Lesieur P, et al: Principal components analysis of PANSS and SANS-SAPS: global ratings in schizophrenic patients. European Journal of Psychiatry 6:251–259, 1991

Edelbrock C, Costello AJ: Structured psychiatric interviews for children, in Assessment and Diagnosis in Child Psychopathology. Edited by Rutter M, Tuma AH, Lam I. London, David Fulton Publishers, 1988, pp 87–112

Eggers C: Course and prognosis in childhood schizophrenia. Journal of Autism and Childhood Schizophrenia 8:21–36, 1978

Eggers C: Schizoaffective disorders in childhood: a follow-up study. J Autism Dev Disord 19:327–342, 1989

Eisenberg L: The course of childhood schizophrenia. Archives of Neurology and Psychiatry 78:69–83, 1957

Ernst M, Pouget E, Silva RR, et al: Pictorial instrument for children: psychosis and conduct disorder subscales. Paper presented at the annual meeting of the American Academy of Child and Adolescent Psychiatry, San Francisco, October 1991

Fields J, Kay S, Grochowski S, et al: Assessing positive and negative symptoms in children and adolescents. Paper presented at the annual meeting of the American Academy of Child and Adolescent Psychiatry, San Francisco, October 1991

Foerster A, Lewis S, Owen M, et al: Premorbid adjustment and personality in psychosis: effects of sex and diagnosis. Br J Psychiatry 158:171–176, 1991

Garralda ME: Hallucinations in children with conduct and emotional disorders: the clinical phenomena. Psychol Med 14:589–596, 1984

Garralda ME: Characteristics of the psychoses of late onset in children and adolescence (a comparative study of hallucinating children). Journal of Adolescence 8:195–207, 1985

Goldberg D: Cost effectiveness studies in the treatment of schizophrenia. Schizophr Bull 17:453–460, 1991

Goldstein MJ: Psychosocial issues. Schizophr Bull 13:157–171, 1987

Gottesman II, McGuffin P, Farmer AE: Clinical genetics as clues to the "real" genetics of schizophrenia: a decade of modest gains while playing for time. Schizophr Bull 13:39–64, 1987

Gur RE, Gur RC, Saykin AJ: Neurobehavioral studies in schizophrenia: implications for regional brain dysfunction. Schizophr Bull 16:445–451, 1990

Gutterman EM, O'Brien JD, Young JG: Structured diagnostic interviews for children and adolescents: current status and future directions. J Am Acad Child Adolesc Psychiatry 26:621–630, 1987

Hanson DR, Gottesman II: The genetics, if any, of infantile autism and childhood schizophrenia. Journal of Autism and Childhood Schizophrenia 6:209–234, 1976

Harrison G: Searching for the causes of schizophrenia: the role of migrant studies. Schizophr Bull 16:663–671, 1990

Hendren RL, Hodde-Vargas JE, Vargas LA, et al: Magnetic resonance imaging of severely disturbed children. J Am Acad Child Adolesc Psychiatry 30:466–470, 1991

Herjanic B, Reich W: Development of a structured psychiatric interview for children: agreement between child and parent of individual symptoms. J Abnorm Child Psychol 10:307–324, 1982

Hibbs EE, Hamburger SD, Lenane M, et al: Determinants of expressed emotion in families of disturbed and normal children. J Child Psychol Psychiatry 32:757–770, 1991

Hirsch SR, Leff JP: Abnormalities in parents of schizophrenics. London, Oxford University Press, 1975

Holzman PS: Recent studies of psychophysiology in schizophrenia. Schizophr Bull 13:49–75, 1987

Kane JM: Treatment of schizophrenia. Schizophr Bull 13:171–186, 1987

Kay SR: Significance of the positive/negative distinction in schizophrenia. Schizophr Bull 16:635–652, 1990

Kay SR: Positive and Negative Syndromes in Schizophrenia: Assessment and Research. New York, Brunner/Mazel, 1991

Kolvin I: Studies in the childhood psychoses. Br J Psychiatry 118:381–419, 1971

Kovacs M: The Interview Schedule for Children (ISC), Form C. Pittsburgh, PA, Western Psychiatric Institute, 1978

Kydd RR, Werry JS: Schizophrenia in children under 16 years. J Autism Dev Disord 12:343–357, 1981

Lamb HR: Will we save the homeless mentally ill? Am J Psychiatry 147:649–657, 1990

Leff J, Kuipers L, Berkowitz R, et al: A controlled trial of social intervention in the families of schizophrenic patients. Br J Psychiatry 141:121–134, 1982

Levinson DF, Simpson GM: Serious nonextrapyramidal adverse effects of neuroleptics: sudden death, agranulocytosis, and hepatotoxicity, in Psychopharmacology: The Third Generation of Progress. Edited by Meltzer H. New York, Raven Press, 1987, pp 1433–1436

Liberman RP: Psychiatric Rehabilitation of Chronic Mental Patients. Washington, DC, American Psychiatric Press, 1988

Makita K: The age of onset of childhood schizophrenia. Folia Psychiatrica Neurologica Japonica 20:111–121, 1966

McClellan JM, Werry JS: Schizophrenia. Psychiatr Clin North Am 15:131–148, 1991

McGlashan TH: A selective review of recent North American long-term follow-up studies of schizophrenia. Schizophr Bull 14:515–542, 1988

McGlashan TH, Fenton WS: Classical subtypes for schizophrenia: literature review for DSM-IV. Schizophr Bull 17:609–632, 1991

McGuire TG: Measuring the economic costs of schizophrenia. Schizophr Bull 17:375–388, 1990

Meijer M, Treffers PDA: Borderline and schizotypal disorders in children and adolescents. Br J Psychiatry 158:205–212, 1991

Meltzer HY: Biological studies in schizophrenia. Schizophr Bull 13:93–128, 1987

Mundy P, Robertson M, Robertson J, et al: The prevalence of psychotic symptoms in homeless adolescents. J Am Acad Child Adolesc Psychiatry 29:724–731, 1990

Murray RM, Lewis SW: Is schizophrenia a neurodevelopmental disorder? BMJ 295:681–682, 1987

O'Callaghan E, Sham P, Takei N, et al: Schizophrenia after prenatal exposure to 1957 A2 influenza epidemic. Lancet 337:1248–1250, 1991

Plasky P: Antidepressant usage in schizophrenia. Schizophr Bull 17:649–658, 1991

Pogue-Geile MF: The development of liability to schizophrenia, in Schizophrenia: A Life Course Developmental Perspective. Edited by Walker EF. New York, Academic Press, 1991, pp 277–298

Prendergast M, Taylor E, Rapoport JL, et al: The diagnosis of hyperactivity: a US-UK cross national study of DSM-III and ICD-9. J Child Psychol Psychiatry 16:289–301, 1988

Pulver AE, Brown CH, Wolyntec P, et al: Schizophrenia: age at onset, gender and familial risk. Acta Psychiatr Scand 82:344–351, 1990

Quay HC: Classification, in Psychopathological Disorders of Childhood, 3rd Edition. Edited by Quay HC, Werry JS. New York, Wiley, 1986, pp 1–34

Raine A: The SPQ: a scale for the assessment of schizotypal personality based on DSM-III-R criteria. Schizophr Bull 17:555–564, 1991

Reich W: The Diagnostic Interview for Children (DICA). Toronto, Multihealth Systems, 1990

Reid AH: Psychiatry of mental handicap. Journal of the Royal Society of Medicine 76:587–592, 1983

Robins L: Follow-up studies, in Psychopathological Disorders of Childhood, 2nd Edition. Edited by Quay HC, Werry JS. New York, Wiley, 1979, pp 481–513

Rothstein A: Hallucinatory phenomena in children. J Am Acad Child Psychiatry 20:623–635, 1981

Russell AT: Schizophrenia, in Assessment and Diagnosis of Child and Adolescent Psychiatric Disorders: Current Issues and Procedures. Edited by Hooper SR, Hynd GW, Mattison RE. Hillsdale, NJ, Lawrence Erlbaum, 1992, pp 23–63

Russell AT, Bott L, Sammons C: The phenomenology of schizophrenia occurring in childhood. J Am Acad Child Adolesc Psychiatry 28:399–407, 1989

Rutter M: Childhood schizophrenia reconsidered. Journal of Autism and Childhood Schizophrenia 2:315–337, 1972

Samson JA, Simpson JC, Tsuang MT: Outcome studies of schizoaffective disorder. Schizophr Bull 14:543–549, 1988

Sanchez-Lachay A, Trautaman PD, Lewin N: Expressed emotion and cognitive family therapy of suicide attempters. Paper presented at the annual meeting of the American Academy of Child and Adolescent Psychiatry, San Francisco, October 1991

Shore D, Filson CR, Johnson WE, et al: Murder and assault arrests of White House cases: clinical and demographic correlates of violence subsequent to civil commitment. Am J Psychiatry 146:645–651, 1989

Spencer EK, Meeker W, Kafantaris V, et al: Symptom duration in schizophrenic children: DSM-III-R compared with ICD-10 criteria. Paper presented at the annual meeting of the American Academy of Child and Adolescent Psychiatry, San Francisco, October 1991

Spencer EK, Kafantaris V, Padron-Gayol M, et al: Haloperidol in schizophrenic children. Psychopharmacol Bull 28:183–186, 1992

Stubbe D, Zahner GR, Goldstein MJ, et al: Diagnostic specificity of a brief measure of expressed emotion. Paper presented at the annual meeting of the American Academy of Child and Adolescent Psychiatry, San Francisco, October 1991

Tompson MC, Asarnow JR, Goldstein MJ, et al: Thought disorder and communication problems in children with schizophrenia spectrum and depressive disorders and their parents. Journal of Clinical Child Psychology 19:159–168, 1990

Torrey EF: Prevalence studies in schizophrenia. Br J Psychiatry 150:598–608, 1987

Torrey EF, Bowler A: Geographical distribution of insanity in America. Schizophr Bull 16:592–604, 1990

Volkmar FR, Cohen DJ, Hoshino Y, et al: Phenomenology and classification of the childhood psychoses. Psychol Med 18:191–201, 1988

Walker E, Lewine RJ: Prediction of adult-onset schizophrenia from childhood home movies of the patient. Am J Psychiatry 147:1052–1056, 1990

Weinberger DR: Implications of normal brain development for the pathogenesis of schizophrenia. Arch Gen Psychiatry 44:660–669, 1987

Werry JS: The childhood psychoses, in Psychopathological Disorders of Childhood, 2nd Edition. Edited by Quay HC, Werry JS. New York, Wiley, 1979, pp 43–89

Werry JS: Child and early adolescent schizophrenia: a review in the light of DSM-III-R. J Autism Dev Disord 22:610–614, 1992a

Werry JS: Child psychiatric disorders: are they classifiable? Br J Psychiatry 161:472–480, 1992b

Werry JS: Long-term outcome of pervasive developmental, psychotic and allied disorders, in Do They Grow Out of It? Long-Term Outcome of Childhood Disorders. Edited by Hechtman L. Washington, DC, American Psychiatric Press (in press)

Werry JS, Methven RJ, Fitzpatrick J, et al: The interrater reliability of DSM-III in children. J Abnorm Child Psychol 11:341–354, 1983

Werry JS, McClellan JM, Chard L: Childhood and adolescent schizophrenia, bipolar and schizoaffective disorders: a clinical and outcome study. J Am Acad Child Adolesc Psychiatry 30:457–465, 1991a

Werry JS, Andrews LK, McClellan JM: Do mood symptoms differentiate misdiagnosed early onset bipolar disorder from schizophrenia? Paper presented at the NIMH Workshop on Early Onset Schizophrenia, Bethesda, MD, September 1991b

Westermeyer JF, Harrow M: Course and outcome in schizophrenia, in Handbook of Schizophrenia, Vol 3: Nosology, Epidemiology and Genetics. Edited by Tsuang MT, Simpson JS. Amsterdam, Elsevier, 1988, pp 205–244

Wing JK: The functions of asylum. Br J Psychiatry 157:822–827, 1990

Wolff S: Schizoid personality in childhood and adult life, I: the vagaries of diagnostic labelling. Br J Psychiatry 159:615–620, 1991

World Health Organization: International Classification of Diseases, 9th Revision. Geneva, World Health Organization, 1978

World Health Organization: International Classification of Diseases, 10th Revision. Geneva, World Health Organization, 1992, pp 84–95

Zigler E, Levine J: Age on first hospitalization of schizophrenia. J Abnorm Psychol 90:458–467, 1981

Chapter 2

Affective Psychoses, I: Major Depression With Psychosis

Rameshwari V. Tumuluru, M.D., Shahnour Yaylayan, M.D.,
Elizabeth B. Weller, M.D., and Ronald A. Weller, M.D.

Introduction

The occurrence of depression in children and adolescents has been reported since the seventeenth century. However, in the mid-twentieth century the prevalent theory was that children could not develop depression because they had immature superegos. Thus, depression in children was largely ignored for many years. However, a meeting of the fourth Congress of the Union of European Paedopsychiatrists in Stockholm in 1970 concluded that depression could occur in children and adolescents. This resulted in increased recognition of depression in childhood and adolescence and an awareness that additional information regarding its diagnosis and treatment was needed (Akiskal and Weller 1989).

Although depression in children has now become a well-established entity, interest in psychotic symptoms associated with depression did not begin to develop until studies published by Chambers et al. (1982) and Freeman et al. (1985) described their occurrence. However, the clinical significance of psychotic symptoms with depression in children and adolescents has not been well studied and remains poorly understood.

Definition: Criteria in DSM-III, DSM-III-R, DSM-IV, and ICD-10

In 1977, researchers of mood disorders in children proposed that criteria used to diagnose depression in adults could also be used to diagnose depression in children, with minor modifications to make these criteria appropriate.

DSM-III, DSM-III-R, and DSM-IV

More recently, DSM-III (American Psychiatric Association 1980), DSM-III-R (American Psychiatric Association 1987), and now DSM-IV (American Psychiatric Association 1994) indicated that mood disorders in children and adolescents are similar to mood disorders in adults. Though the DSM-III-R has been commonly used in the United States and Canada, the International Classification of Diseases (ICD) criteria are used more in other parts of the world in both age groups (World Health Organization 1992).

In DSM-III-R and in DSM-IV, a major depressive episode is diagnosed when five or more of the following signs and symptoms are present for at least two weeks: 1) depressed mood; 2) loss of interest or pleasure; 3) significant weight loss or weight gain; 4) insomnia or hypersomnia; 5) psychomotor retardation or agitation; 6) fatigue or loss of energy; 7) feelings of worthlessness or excessive guilt; 8) diminished ability to think or concentrate and/or indecisiveness; 9) recurrent thoughts of death, suicidal ideation, suicide plan, or suicide attempt. According to DSM-III-R, a major depression was, by definition, not caused by "organic" factors or recent bereavement; rather, similar criteria are included in DSM-IV, which also explicitly requires significant distress, impairment, or both (see Table 2–1). Criteria for adults and children are generally the same with a few modifications as they apply to children. For example, in children and adolescents the predominant mood may be one of irritability, and failure to gain expected weight, rather than weight loss, may be observed.

Table 2–1.   DSM-IV criteria for major depressive episode

A.   Five (or more) of the following symptoms have been present during the same 2-week period and represent a change from previous functioning; at least one of the symptoms is either (1) depressed mood or (2) loss of interest or pleasure.

Note: Do not include symptoms that are clearly due to a general medical condition, or mood-incongruent delusions or hallucinations.

   (1)   depressed mood most of the day, nearly every day, as indicated by either subjective report (e.g., feels sad or empty) or observation made by others (e.g., appears tearful).   **Note:** In children and adolescents, can be irritable mood.
   (2)   markedly diminished interest or pleasure in all, or almost all, activities most of the day, nearly every day (as indicated by either subjective account or observation made by others)
   (3)   significant weight loss when not dieting or weight gain (e.g., a change of more than 5% of body weight in a month), or decrease or increase in appetite nearly every day.   **Note:** In children, consider failure to make expected weight gains.
   (4)   insomnia or hypersomnia nearly every day
   (5)   psychomotor agitation or retardation nearly every day (observable by others, not merely subjective feelings of restlessness or being slowed down)
   (6)   fatigue or loss of energy nearly every day
   (7)   feelings of worthlessness or excessive or inappropriate guilt (which may be delusional) nearly every day (not merely self-reproach or guilt about being sick)
   (8)   diminished ability to think or concentrate, or indecisiveness, nearly every day (either by subjective account or as observed by others)
   (9)   recurrent thoughts of death (not just fear of dying), recurrent suicidal ideation without a specific plan, or a suicide attempt or a specific plan for committing suicide

B.   The symptoms do not meet criteria for a mixed episode (see p. 335).

C.   The symptoms cause clinically significant distress or impairment in social, occupational, or other important areas of functioning.

D.   The symptoms are not due to the direct physiological effects of a substance (e.g., a drug of abuse, a medication) or a general medical condition (e.g., hypothyroidism).

E.   The symptoms are not better accounted for by bereavement (i.e., after the loss of a loved one, the symptoms persist for longer than 2 months or are characterized by marked functional impairment, morbid preoccupation with worthlessness, suicidal ideation, psychotic symptoms, or psychomotor retardation).

Source.   American Psychiatric Association: Diagnostic and Statistical Manual of Mental Disorders, 4th Edition. Washington, DC, American Psychiatric Association, 1994, p. 327. Used with permission.

Once diagnosed, depression in the DSM-IV system can be further classified on the basis of severity (mild, moderate, or severe but without psychotic features) and by the presence of psychotic features such as hallucinations and delusions, which can be either mood-congruent or mood-incongruent. Mood-congruent hallucinations or delusions are consistent with typical depressive themes such as guilt, death, disease, nihilism, inadequacy, or deserved punishment. Mood-incongruent delusions or hallucinations do not involve such typically depressive themes. Examples of mood-incongruent psychotic features include persecutory delusions and delusions of thought insertion, thought withdrawal, and thought broadcasting. It is possible for a major depressive disorder either to occur as a single episode or to be recurrent. The combination of major depression with schizophrenia, schizophreniform disorder, and so forth, which was excluded in DSM-III-R, was included in DSM-IV. In this chapter we focus on individuals who meet the DSM-IV criteria for major depressive episode with psychotic features.

Although DSM-IV indicates that the essential features of a major depressive episode are similar across different age groups, there may be age-specific features that differentiate depression in children and adolescents from depression in adults. For example, somatic complaints, psychomotor agitation, and mood-congruent hallucinations may be particularly frequent in depressed prepubertal children. Likewise, depressed adolescents may show increased antisocial behavior, drug and alcohol abuse, conduct disorder, aggression, or school difficulties compared with other age groups. At times, these problems may be significant enough to justify making another diagnosis in addition to depression. Thus, age may affect the overall clinical picture of depression in children and adolescents (Poznanski et al. 1985b).

ICD-10 Criteria

Though the ICD criteria are used worldwide, the description of criteria for depression with psychotic features is not as well defined as in DSM-IV. Depressive episode in ICD-10 is characterized by 1) a lowering of mood, 2) decreased activity, 3) reduction of energy, 4) impaired concentration, interest, and enjoyment, 5) sleep and appetite disturbance, 6) low self-esteem (feelings of guilt or worthlessness in the milder form),

7) suicidal thoughts and acts, and 8) diurnal variations of mood.

Depression is usually diagnosed if the index episode is so severe it causes distress and interference with ordinary activities for at least 2 weeks. The mood change must be accompanied by symptoms described above.

There may be individual variation in presentation, and atypical presentations are common in adolescence. For example, anxiety, distress, and agitation may be more prominent than depression. Mood changes may be measured by irritability, excessive alcohol use, histrionic behaviors, exacerbation of preexisting phobic or obsessional symptoms, or hypochondriacal preoccupations.

Feelings of worthlessness, guilt and sinfulness, fear of imminent disasters, and mood-congruent hallucinations may be present along with symptoms of severe depression.

Prevalence and Epidemiology

Studies of the epidemiology of depression in children and adolescents are limited. Although available studies have included children from all age groups who were drawn from different sources—the community, psychiatrically ill inpatients, and outpatients—the number of subjects in each study has been low. Furthermore, there are only one or two studies in each age category. Thus, these studies should be interpreted with caution.

At the time this book was published, there was only one epidemiological study of preschool depression. In a sample of 100 preschool children (ages 1–6 years) referred to an outpatient child development unit, Kashani et al. (1984) reported that 4% of children received a diagnosis of possible or definite depression by DSM-III criteria.

Two studies have been reported on the incidence of depression in prepubertal children. A study of 100 children admitted to an inpatient community mental health center (Kashani et al. 1982) found a 13% prevalence of major depression. Another study (Kashani and Simonds 1979) examined a community-based sample of children ages 7–12 years. The incidence of depression was 1.9% by DSM-III criteria.

In a sample that included both children and adolescents, Carlson and Cantwell (1979a, 1979b) studied 1,000 patients ages 7–17 years who had been screened in the inpatient and outpatient department at the University of California at Los Angeles. Symptoms of depression were noted in 210 of these patients. Of those, 102 children were interviewed and diagnosed by DSM-III criteria; 60% had depressive symptoms and 28% met criteria for an affective disorder.

In adolescents there have been two epidemiological studies of depression with community samples. Kandel and Davies (1982) administered a six-item self-report inventory to adolescents (ages 13–19 years) and their parents. In this study, female adolescents reported more depressive symptoms than did male adolescents. Increased delinquency was noted more often among boys than girls. Adolescents also reported more symptoms than did their parents. Kashani et al. (1987) interviewed 150 adolescents from the community sample, using the Diagnostic Interview for Children and Adolescents (DICA). They found a 4% prevalence of major depression and a 3% prevalence of dysthymia. Among the adolescents who met criteria for depression and dysthymia, anxiety was the most frequent comorbid diagnosis.

Unfortunately, none of these epidemiological studies mentioned the prevalence of psychotic symptoms in depression.

Clinical Features

Although the criteria for diagnosis of depression are similar to those for adults, the clinical presentation can vary across age groups. Differences in presentation may be related to differences in cognitive and developmental abilities, especially with regard to verbal and nonverbal communication. Compared with adults, more attention needs to be paid to nonverbal signs of depression in children. A study by Poznanski et al. (1985a) demonstrated that the nonverbal rating was strongly associated with a diagnosis of depression and was the best predictor of the severity of depression.

Affective expression of depression can vary across developmental stages. Preschoolers who are relatively nonverbal may appear withdrawn and anxious, with little spontaneous smiling. Prepubertal children and adolescents have less trouble expressing their sadness in words.

Depressed children and adolescents are usually bored, unhappy, or apathetic and enjoy few pleasurable activities, such as playing sports or games. Some very depressed children engage in solitary activities, such as staring at the television or sitting in a park without playing.

Morbid preoccupation is not uncommon. A child may think about the death of others. Sometimes the child will focus on the death of a pet. Self-esteem is lowered. However, children developmentally younger than 6 years have little abstract concept of self-image, and their expression of self-concept is focused on their appearance and whether or not friends like them. Children above the age of 6 can express their ideas of self-esteem better. They are particularly sensitive to nicknames and name-calling. Children and teenagers can express guilt either verbally or by actions. Social withdrawal, poor peer relationships, rejection by peers, and poor social skills are common. Lack of acceptance by peers is particularly difficult for teenagers.

A sudden decline in school performance is significant. This may be due to lack of interest or poor concentration. Psychomotor retardation, also called hypoactivity, may be present. Somatic complaints and fatigue are quite common. Parents and teachers often describe irritability in depressed children, along with frequent, excessive weeping, poor sleep habits, and decreased appetite (Poznanski 1982a). Input from school is important in diagnosing depression because teachers can be more objective than parents, who often are afflicted with depression themselves.

The severity and frequency of depressive symptoms were studied in children being treated in an outpatient clinic (Ryan et al. 1987). Ninety-five children and 92 adolescents, ages 6–18 years, who met research diagnostic criteria (RDC) for major depressive episode in the K-SADS, were studied. Prepubertal children had more somatic complaints, depressed appearance, psychomotor agitation, separation anxiety, phobias, and hallucinations. By contrast, adolescents had greater anhedonia, hopelessness, hypersomnia, weight change, alcohol and illicit drug use, and lethal suicide attempts (but no increase in severity of suicidal ideation or intent). Anxiety as a symptom of depression was common among children and adolescents. In addition, they had negative cognitions, appetite changes, weight changes, and conduct symptoms.

Carlson and Kashani (1988) compared the frequency of depressive symptoms between several developmental stages. There were no differences in the occurrence of depressed mood, poor concentration, insomnia, and suicidal ideation among different age groups. However, there was an increased frequency of anhedonia, diurnal variation, hopelessness, psychomotor retardation, and delusions with increasing age. Occurrence of depressed appearance, low self-esteem, and somatic complaints decreased with increasing age.

Course and Prognosis

It is generally believed that the earlier the age at onset, the poorer is the prognosis. The outcome for children and adolescents who have mood disorders appears to be poor. For example, an earlier age at onset of depression in children predicted a longer duration and multiple episodes of illness (Kovacs et al. 1984b). Also, children who had dysthymia had increased risk for recurrence (Kovacs et al. 1984a). Comorbid anxiety disorders and conduct disorders also have a negative impact on outcome.

Sixty adolescents, ages 13–16 years, hospitalized for major depression were followed prospectively for 3–4 years by Strober and Carlson (1982). Twenty percent of these had a bipolar outcome. The factors that predicted a bipolar outcome included the presence of mood-congruent psychotic features, rapid onset of depression, psychomotor retardation, a family history "loaded with affective illness" and pharmacologically induced mania or hypomania. Kovacs et al. (1984b) reported that 30% of dysthymic children developed bipolar illness. Although the presence of psychotic features during depression may predict future bipolarity in adolescents, further studies are needed to determine the long-term outcome for depressed children with psychotic features.

Etiology and Pathogenesis

Currently, the etiology of depression in children and adolescents must be considered unknown. However, several etiologies have been theorized as having a role in the pathogenesis of depression. These include genetic theories (Gershon 1982; Weissman et al. 1984), neuroendocrine theories (Poznanski et al. 1982; Puig-Antich et al. 1979, 1989), psychodynamic theories (Kashani and Sherman 1988), cognitive theories (Kashani and

Sherman 1988), and problems in parent-child relationships. The bio-psychosocial approach to the etiology of depression assumes that each of these mechanisms or theories contributes to the pathogenesis of major depression in children and adolescents. However, none of these theories specifically addresses the issue of how psychotic symptoms develop in depressed children and adolescents. Furthermore, the diagnostic significance and prognostic value of psychotic symptoms require further study in this age group.

Assessment

The assessment of depression in children and adolescents is more time consuming than it is in adults because information from parents, teachers, and children should be obtained. Developmental and cognitive factors must be considered. In addition to the standard clinical interview, the assessment of children and adolescents may include structured or semistructured diagnostic interviews, self-report inventories, and biological markers.

Standard Clinical Interview

Symptoms of depression in children, adolescents, and adults can vary by developmental stage (see the section "Clinical Features"in this chapter). Herzog and Rathbun (1982) proposed developmentally specific criteria to diagnose depression from ages 36 months to 18 years. At approximately the same time, Poznanski (1982b) devised developmentally appropriate questions for evaluating symptoms of depression. In addition, Poznanski stressed the importance of assessing nonverbal communication in this age group.

In addition to the standard clinical interview of the child and adolescent as the primary source of information, diagnostic information must be corroborated by others, usually parents and teachers (Weller and Weller 1986).

Diagnostic Interviews

The standard clinical interview can also can be supplemented by structured or semistructured interviews. Carlson and Cantwell (1979a) reported that a systematic interview coupled with the Children's Depression Inventory (CDI) was able to unmask depression more than the standard evaluation procedure alone. In their study, the standard evaluation missed the current diagnosis in 60% of the cases. Structured and semistructured interviews have the added advantage of allowing for data collection for research purposes.

Several instruments are commonly used to assess childhood depression. The Diagnostic Interview for Children and Adolescents—Revised (DICA-R) (Reich and Welner 1992) is a widely used structured interview. The Schedule for Affective Disorders and Schizophrenia for School-Age Children (K-SADS) devised by Chambers et al. (1985) is a semistructured interview for children ages 6–12 years and is based on the adult version of the instrument (SADS). The Children's Depression Rating Scale (CDRS-R) is based on the Hamilton Rating Scale for Depression (Hamilton 1960). It rates the severity of depression on the basis of information obtained from child, parent, teacher, and clinician (Poznanski et al. 1979, 1984).

Self-Report Inventories

The Children's Depression Inventory (CDI) (Kovacs 1981) is probably the most widely used self-report questionnaire. It is based on the Beck Depression Inventory (Beck and Beamesderfer 1974). The drawback of the CDI is its lack of face validity; children can easily identify appropriate and inappropriate responses.

Biological Markers

Although there are no laboratory tests to diagnose depression in children, biological markers may be used to supplement the clinician's diagnostic impression. Biological markers have been better studied in depressed adults. Such markers include the dexamethasone suppression test (DST), polysomnography, and growth hormone secretion. Although these tests have been studied in children and adolescents (see the section "Etiology and Pathogenesis" in this chapter), this work should be considered preliminary. The DST is the only test that has been widely studied in children and adolescents. It is considered a state marker and may prove useful in predicting treatment response. The results are abnormal when the child is in a depressed state (Weller and Weller 1986). However, further studies of biological markers are needed to identify more accurately their role in assessing depression in children and, more specifically, their relationship to psychotic symptoms in depression.

Assessment of Psychosis in Children

In evaluating young children, it may be difficult to determine whether a child is fantasizing or experiencing true hallucinations or delusions. Thus, there has been some controversy as to how old a child must be before psychotic symptoms such as hallucinations and delusions can be accurately diagnosed. Over the years, there have been repeated efforts to establish the age at which children can distinguish between fantasy and reality. Despert (1948) suggested that a normal child can distinguish between fantasy and reality around the age of 3 years. However, Piaget (1962) reported that children start to believe that dreams are not real and their dreams begin to have an internal quality at approximately 6 years of age. If the ability to distinguish between fantasy/dream and reality is related to the ability to distinguish hallucinations from fantasy, then a child could be diagnosed as psychotic only after 3 years, according to Despert (1948), or after 6 years, according to Piaget (1962).

Pilowsky (1986) reviewed the problem of assessing hallucinations in children. He recommended direct observation of children to assess their involvement with internal stimuli. He also felt it was extremely helpful to interview the child and the parents separately for information about psychotic symptoms. Spontaneous reports by the child were often more reliable than information obtained by direct questioning of the child. Pilowsky suggested that a child is more likely to be actually hallucinating if

- the hallucinations are vivid (if voices are heard like the voice of a real person or if visual images look like real-life pictures)
- there is credence to the hallucinations (if the child is certain that whatever she or he is perceiving is actually present, and hence acts on the hallucinations)
- the source of hallucinations is ego-alien (if the origin of these hallucinations is outside the child's internal world)

■ the hallucinations have no volitional quality (if the child cannot
  make the voices or the images come and go at will)

Pilowsky (1986) also distinguished between parahallucinations and
hallucinations. Parahallucinations, a frequent occurrence in normal
children, include the following:

■ Eidetic imagery: this occurs when a child looks carefully at an object
  and then later perceives the object as present when it is no longer
  there. The child is aware that it is not real but just an image.
■ Imaginary companions: imaginary play companions and objects
  should be considered normal phenomena, according to Bender and
  Fogel (1941).
■ Hypnagogic and hypnopompic hallucinations: these occur while
  the child is falling asleep (hypnagogic) or is waking up (hypnopompic) and are normal phenomena (Weiner 1961).

Although it is always a difficult task to assess hallucinations in children, following the above guidelines should help distinguish real hallucinations from parahallucinations. It is also important to take a careful
history from the child and other informants such as parents, teachers,
friends, and siblings. With attention to such details, it becomes easier to
assess the presence or absence of hallucinations.

Several authors have examined the frequency, characteristics, and
phenomenology of psychotic symptoms in depressed children and adolescents. A selected review of such studies follows.

Chambers et al. (1982) studied 58 prepubertal children, ages 6–12
years, who met RDC for major depressive disorder. The sample was
equally divided between endogenous ($n = 29$) and nonendogenous
($n = 29$) subjects. All forms of hallucinations were more common in the
endogenous than the nonendogenous children. For example, 21 of the
58 children (36%) reported auditory hallucinations. Of these, 14 were
endogenously depressed and 7 were nonendogenously depressed. This
difference in the occurrence of psychotic symptoms in endogenously
depressed and nonendogenously depressed children (48% versus 24%)
represented a trend that approached statistical significance ($\chi^2 = 2.69$,
$P = .12$). More than half the patients for whom data were recorded (16

of 25) reported auditory hallucinations that came from outside their heads. Nine of 25 (36%) experienced auditory hallucinations that came from inside their heads. Other hallucinations reported by the cohort of 25 children included visual hallucinations ($n = 7$) and tactile hallucinations ($n = 4$). None had olfactory hallucinations. Eighty-six percent of these hallucinations were mood-congruent; only 14% were mood-incongruent. Hallucinatory phenomena such as illusions, imaginary companions, hypnagogic or hypnopompic hallucinations were reported by 9 children (16%). No child reported eidetic imagery.

Delusions in the Chambers et al. (1982) group were far less common than hallucinations. Only 4 children (7%) had delusions. These included ideas of control, feelings of persecution, delusions of guilt or sin, somatic preoccupation, and nihilism or delusions of catastrophe. In all cases, the onset of hallucinations and delusions was reported as occurring simultaneously with or subsequent to the onset of the major depressive episode. The authors found that only a third of the parents were aware of the psychotic symptoms their children reported. In the majority of patients, the diagnosis of psychotic subtype was based solely on information from the child.

Psychotic symptoms reported by these depressed children were then compared to those reported by adults with depression. Psychotic symptoms in both children and adults were found to be similar in form, content, and temporal characteristics. The authors made several conclusions: 1) About one-third of prepubertal depressed children reported psychotic symptoms, usually hallucinations, 2) these psychotic symptoms were similar in form, content, and temporal characteristics to those reported by adults with depression, although their frequency differed, and 3) the clinical and theoretical implications of the occurrence of psychotic symptoms in children with major depression remain uncertain because of the immature cognition of prepubertal children.

Freeman et al. (1985) found that 6 of 33 children (18%) diagnosed with major depressive disorder at a youth affective disorders clinic had hallucinations or delusions. These 6 children met RDC and DSM-III criteria for major depression. They could be further classified as having the endogenous subtype of major depression. These 6 psychotically depressed children were more severely depressed than the 27 nonpsychotically depressed children, as measured by the CDRS-R. In 5 children

(83%), psychotic features were mood-incongruent, and in 1 (17%), psychotic features were mood-congruent.

The most common psychiatric diagnoses in the parents of these children were mood disorders, alcohol abuse, and substance abuse, alone or in combination. The most frequent psychiatric diagnoses of the children's second-degree adult relatives were mood disorders and alcohol abuse. Four out of five (80%) of these psychotically depressed children had a DST that was positive. The authors concluded that psychotic features are frequent in depressed prepubertal children and that further investigation and longitudinal follow-up are needed to determine how to classify depressed children accurately.

Ryan et al. (1987) compared symptom frequency and severity in 95 children and 92 adolescents, ages 6–18 years, who fulfilled RDC for major depressive disorder. Exclusion criteria were physical illnesses, obesity, seizures, IQ less than 70, anorexia nervosa, bulimia, autism, schizophrenia, and/or alcohol/substance use. The mean age was 9.6 years for prepubertal children and 14.7 years for adolescents. In prepubertal children, depressive hallucinations were present in 37%, compared with 21% of depressed adolescents. Of the 92 adolescents, 17 had psychotic symptoms (18%). The psychotically depressed adolescents had more depressed mood ($P < .02$), less diurnal variation with mood worse in the morning ($P < .04$), more diurnal variation with mood worse in the evening ($P < .04$), more guilt ($P < .03$), and more use of alcohol ($P < .005$) and illicit drugs ($P < .05$) than the nonpsychotically depressed adolescents. Of the 95 prepubertal children with major depression, 30 had psychotic features (32%). The psychotic prepubertal children had more depressed mood ($P < .01$) and less diurnal variation (evenings worse) ($P < .04$) than the nonpsychotically depressed prepubertal children.

Carlson and Kashani (1988) compared the phenomenology of depression in children, adolescents, and adults with data from three different studies: 1) 100 adults with major depression (Baker et al. 1971), 2) 95 depressed prepubertal children and 92 adolescents (Ryan et al., 1987), and 3) 9 depressed preschoolers (Kashani et al. 1984). On the basis of their review of these studies, Carlson and Kashani (1988) reported that delusions (as part of psychotic depression) were most common in depressed adults (16%) compared with depressed adolescents (4%) and prepubertal children (4%). None of the depressed preschoolers had delusions. However, hallucinations were more common in depressed prepubertal children (22%) than in depressed adolescents (14%) and depressed adults (9%). None of the preschoolers had hallucinations. The authors concluded that age modified symptom frequency but did not alter the basic phenomenology of major depression. They also suggested that hallucinations in children may not have the same diagnostic specificity that they have in adults.

Differential Diagnosis

In major depression with psychosis, as in any diagnosis, an attempt should be made to look for other symptoms and to rule out other diagnoses. In the child and adolescent population, alternative diagnoses over each of the developmental stages must be considered.

Although the incidence of psychosis in depression in preschoolers has not been documented, diagnoses to consider when there is a depressed mood in preschoolers include separation anxiety disorder, physical or sexual abuse, failure to thrive, and adjustment disorder with depressed mood (Weller and Weller 1991).

In prepubertal children who are diagnosed with psychotic features, a diagnosis of schizoaffective disorder may also be considered (Freeman et al. 1985). In addition, children at risk for affective disorder may have a comorbid diagnosis of attention-deficit/hyperactivity disorder (ADHD) (Weller and Weller 1991), conduct disorder, or separation anxiety disorder (Mitchell et al. 1988).

In adolescents, anxiety disorder and conduct disorder need to be ruled out (Kovacs et al. 1984c). Ryan et al. (1987) found a high incidence of substance abuse associated with depression. Thus, a primary diagnosis of substance abuse must be ruled out. Finally, in the past, adolescents with psychotic symptoms have been misdiagnosed as schizophrenic (Carlson and Strober 1978), and therefore depression and schizophrenia should be carefully evaluated in an adolescent with psychotic symptoms.

Treatment

In general, the biopsychosocial approach should be used to treat all mood disorders in children and adolescents. However, the efficacy of psychopharmacological agents is of particular interest in treating psychotic depression. Antidepressants have been used in depressed children and adolescents. However, studies have not determined the efficacy of pharmacotherapy in psychotically depressed children and adolescents.

In a study of six children who were psychotically depressed, Freeman et al. (1985) reported that two children responded to a combination of desipramine and psychotherapy. One improved with a combination of desipramine, haloperidol, and psychotherapy. One responded to psychotherapy alone. Two received no treatment.

Geller et al. (1985) compared the plasma levels of nortriptyline in eight nondelusional depressed adolescents and six delusional depressed adolescents treated with nortriptyline and chlorpromazine. The delusional depressed group required less nortriptyline.

Asarnow and Carlson (1988) reported on a 5-year follow-up of a 10-year-old girl diagnosed as having major depression with psychotic features. She responded initially to a combination of imipramine and cognitive-behavior therapy. At the 5-year follow-up, she was responding to cognitive-behavior therapy alone.

Clearly, additional studies are needed to determine the role of pharmacotherapy in the treatment of depression with psychotic features in children and adolescents.

Summary and Directions for Research

Although there are a number of studies of depression in children and adolescents, the short- and long-term outcome for depressed children and adolescents with psychotic features has not been well studied. In addition to the phenomenology and outcome, treatment studies need to be undertaken. Given that early onset has a poorer prognosis, identification and treatment of children at risk may prevent a misdiagnosis (e.g., of schizophrenia) and facilitate early intervention.

Mood disorders are being increasingly recognized and diagnosed in childhood. Several studies have reported a higher frequency of psychotic features in depressed children than in depressed adults. The psychotic symptoms reported by children are similar in form, content, and temporal characteristics to those reported in samples of adults with depression. However, the pattern and frequency of symptoms may differ. The theoretical and clinical implications of psychotic symptoms in children and adolescents with major depression are currently uncertain. Further investigation, including longitudinal follow-up studies, is needed to clarify the significance of psychotic features in depressed children and adolescents.

Case Report

Donald is a 10-year-old white male who was initially evaluated as an outpatient for ongoing problems at home and school. Donald was described as a shy and introverted boy who became more withdrawn after starting kindergarten. In the first grade, he was unable to concentrate and understand his schoolwork, but no testing was done. In the second grade, he continued to have difficulty and it was necessary for him to repeat the grade. When he was 9 years old, his parents separated. While in third grade, Donald became progressively more depressed and withdrawn. He also had poor self-esteem and performed poorly in school.

Prior to his outpatient evaluation, he was described as angry and sad. He was isolated and was noted to be pounding objects and injuring himself (he hit himself on the head with a hammer and had to have stitches). Donald also suffered from decreased energy, poor concentration, insomnia (initial and middle), and "gory dreams" when he did sleep. The content of these dreams, which occurred nightly, included skeletons being hung by nooses, with bloody daggers going through them. A coffin with a basketball player with no skin or muscle, whose internal organs could be seen, was described in the background.

Donald also had irritability, poor concentration, suicidal thoughts, and feelings of tearfulness. He described vivid visual and auditory hallucinations. His visual hallucinations included monsters in his closet, a skeleton hanging through a noose, and a "weird-looking man with a blown-off arm and with a machete coming out of his head." His auditory hallucinations consisted of "people talking to me like in a weird movie," and a voice sounding like someone being stabbed calling his name over and over again. He also described feeling things crawling on him (e.g., a tarantula on his neck), things touching and stabbing him, and smelling gas when no one else could smell it.

Donald also reported frequent headaches and feeling anxious about his mother when he was away from her. At the time of the evaluation, he had a blunted affect, sad mood, and mild articulation problems. He also had a CDRS score of 84, which is in the severely depressed range.

His mother had been prescribed diuretics during pregnancy to lower her blood pressure. Otherwise, the pregnancy and delivery had been uneventful. Donald's developmental milestones were normal. At the age of 2 years, however, he developed serious otitis media and now has poor hearing in one ear.

Family history was significant for parents' divorce when Donald was 9 years old. His mother had a single depressive episode with suicidal ideation following the divorce. She was treated with oxazepam (Serax). Donald's maternal aunt has a history of depression and generalized anxiety disorder. A paternal aunt had alcohol and drug abuse.

Following his evaluation, Donald was diagnosed as having major depression with psychotic features. He was treated successfully with a combination of individual therapy and imipramine 75 mg hs. One year later he remained symptom free.

References

Akiskal HS, Weller EB: Mood disorders in children and adolescents, in Comprehensive Textbook of Psychiatry, 5th Edition. Baltimore, MD, Williams & Wilkins, 1989

American Psychiatric Association: Diagnostic and Statistical Manual of Mental Disorders, 3rd Edition. Washington, DC, American Psychiatric Association, 1980

American Psychiatric Association: Diagnostic and Statistical Manual of Mental Disorders, 4th Edition. Washington, DC, American Psychiatric Association, 1994

Asarnow JR, Carlson GA: Childhood depression: five year outcome following combined cognitive behavior therapy and pharmacotherapy. Am J Psychother 42:456–464, 1988

Baker M, Dorzob J, Winokur G, et al: Depressive disease: classification and clinical characteristics. Compr Psychiatry 12:354–365, 1971

Beck AT, Beamesderfer A: Assessment of depression: The Depression Inventory. In Psychological Measurements in Psychopharmacology, Vol 7, Modern Problems in Pharmacopsychiatry. Edited by Pinchot P. Basel, Switzerland: Karger, 1974

Bender L, Fogel FB: Imaginary companions of children. Am J Orthopsychiatry 11:56–65, 1941

Carlson GA, Cantwell DP: A survey of depressive symptoms in a child and adolescent psychiatric population: interview data. J Am Acad Child Psychiatry 18:587–599, 1979a

Carlson GA, Cantwell DP: A survey of depressive symptoms, syndromes and disorders in a child and adolescent psychiatric population. J Child Psychol Psychiatry 21:19–25, 1979b

Carlson GA, Kashani JH: Phenomenology of major depression from childhood through adulthood: analysis of three studies. Am J Psychiatry 145:1222–1225, 1988

Carlson G, Strober M: Manic depressive illness in early adolescence: a study of clinical and diagnostic characteristics in six cases. J Am Acad Child Psychiatry 17:138–153, 1978

Chambers WJ, Puig-Antich J, Tabrizi MA, et al: Psychotic symptoms in prepubertal major depressive disorder. Arch Gen Psychiatry 39:921–927, 1982

Chambers WJ, Puig-Antich J, Hirsch M, et al: The assessment of affective disorder in children and adolescents by semistructured interview: test-retest reliability of the Schedule for Affective Disorders and Schizophrenia for School-aged Children, Present Episode Version. Arch Gen Psychiatry 39:921–927, 1985

Despert J: Delusional and hallucinatory experiences in children. Am J Psychiatry 104:528–537, 1948

Freeman LN, Poznanski EO, Grossman JA, et al: Psychotic and depressed children: a new entity. J Am Acad Child Psychiatry 1:95–102, 1985

Geller B, Cooper TB, Farooki ZQ, et al: Dose and plasma levels of nortriptyline and chlorpromazine in delusionally depressed adolescents and of nortriptyline in nondelusionally depressed adolescents. Am J Psychiatry 142:336–338, 1985

Gershon ES: Genetic studies of affective disorder and schizophrenia, in Human Genetics, A: The unfolding genome. New York, Alan R. Liss, 1982, pp 417–432

Hamilton M: A rating scale for depression. J Neurol Neurosurg Psychiatry 23:56–62, 1960

Herzog DB, Rathbun JM: Childhood depression: developmental considerations. Am J Dis Child 136:115–120, 1982

Kandel DB, Davies M: Epidemiology of depressive mood in adolescents: an empirical study. Arch Gen Psychiatry 39:1205–1212, 1982

Kashani JH, Sherman DD: Childhood depression: epidemiology, etiological models, and treatment implications. Integrative Psychiatry 6:12–21, 1988

Kashani JH, Simonds JF: The incidence of depression in children. Am J Psychiatry 136:1203–1205, 1979

Kashani JH, Cantwell DP, Shekim WO, et al: Major depressive disorder in children admitted to an inpatient community mental health center. Am J Psychiatry 139:671–672, 1982

Kashani JH, Ray JS, Carlson GA: Depression and depressive-like states in pre-school-age children in a child development unit. Am J Psychiatry 141:1397–1402, 1984

Kashani JH, Carlson G, Beck NC, et al: Depression, depressive symptoms and depressed mood among a community sample of adolescents. Am J Psychiatry 144:931–934, 1987

Kovacs M: Rating scale to assess depression in school aged children. Acta Paedopsychiatr 46:305–315, 1981

Kovacs M, Feinberg TL, Crouse-Novak MA: Depressive disorders in childhood, I: a longitudinal prospective study of characteristics and recovery. Arch Gen Psychiatry 41:229–237, 1984a

Kovacs M, Feinberg TL, Crouse-Novak MA, et al: Depressive disorders in childhood, II: a longitudinal study of the risks for a subsequent major depression. Arch Gen Psychiatry 41:643–649, 1984b

Kovacs M, Gatsonis C, Paulauskas S, et al: Depressive disorders in childhood, IV: a longitudinal study of comorbidity with and risk for anxiety disorders. Arch Gen Psychiatry 46:776–782, 1984c

Mitchell J, McCauley E, Burke PM, et al: Phenomenology of depression in children and adolescents. J Am Acad Child Adolesc Psychiatry 27:12–20, 1988

Piaget J: Play Dreams and Imitation in Children. New York, WW Norton, 1962

Pilowsky D: Problems in determining the presence of hallucination in children, in Hallucinations in Children. Edited by Pilowsky D, Chambers W. Washington, DC, American Psychiatric Press, 1986

Poznanski EO: The clinical characteristics of childhood depression, in Basic Handbook of Child and Adolescent Psychiatry, 3: Psychiatry. Edited by Noshpitz JD. New York, Basic Books, 1982a, pp 296–307

Poznanski EO: The clinical phenomenology of childhood depression. Am J Orthopsychiatry 52:308–313, 1982b

Poznanski EO, Cook SC, Carroll BJ: A depression rating scale for children. Pediatrics 64:442–450, 1979

Poznanski EO, Carroll BJ, Banegas MA, et al: Dexamethasone suppression test in prepubertal depressed children. Am J Psychiatry 139:321–324, 1982

Poznanski EO, Grossman JA, Buchsbaum Y, et al: Preliminary studies of the reliability and validity of the Children's Depression Rating Scale. J Am Acad Child Psychiatry 23:191–197, 1984

Poznanski EO, Freeman LN, Moklos HB: Children's depression rating scales, revised (September 1984). Psychopharmacol Bull 21:979–989, 1985a

Poznanski EO, Mokros HB, Grossman J, et al: Diagnostic criteria in childhood depression. Am J Psychiatry 147:1168–1173, 1985b

Puig-Antich J, Chambers W, Halpern F, et al: Cortisol hypersecretion in prepubertal depressive illness: a preliminary report. Psychoneuroendocrinology 4:191–197, 1979

Puig-Antich J, Dahl R, Ryan N, et al: Cortisol secretion in prepubertal children with major depressive disorder: episode and recovery. Arch Gen Psychiatry 46:801–809, 1989

Reich W, Welner Z: The Diagnostic Interview for Children and Adolescents— Revised. Unpublished manuscript, Washington University, St. Louis, MO, June 1992

Ryan ND, Puig-Antich J, Ambrosini P, et al: The clinical picture of major depression in children and adolescents. Arch Gen Psychiatry 44:854–861, 1987

Strober M, Carlson G: Bipolar illness in adolescents with major depression. Arch Gen Psychiatry 39:549–555, 1982

Weiner MF: Hallucinations in children. Arch Gen Psychiatry 5:544–553, 1961

Weissman MM, Gershon ES, Kidd KK, et al: Psychiatric disorder in the relatives of probands with affective disorder: the Yale NIMH Collaborative Family Study. Arch Gen Psychiatry 4:13–21, 1984

Weller EB, Weller RA: Assessing depression in prepubertal children. Hillside Journal of Clinical Psychiatry 8:193–201, 1986

Weller EB, Weller RA: Mood disorders, in Comprehensive Text of Child and Adolescent Psychiatry. Edited by Lewis M. Baltimore, MD, Williams & Wilkins, 1991, pp 646–664

World Health Organization: International Classification of Diseases, 10th Revision. Geneva, World Health Organization, 1992, pp 57–67

Chapter 3

Affective Psychoses, II: Bipolar Disorder With Psychosis

Shahnour Yaylayan, M.D., Rameshwari V. Tumuluru, M.D., Elizabeth B. Weller, M.D., and Ronald A. Weller, M.D.

Introduction

Bipolar disorders have been recognized in childhood since Kraepelin (1921) reported that, in a sample of 900, 0.4% of first attacks of manic-depressive illness (bipolar disorder) occurred before age 10. Lately, there has been increasing interest in examining subtypes of mood disorders, especially those associated with psychotic symptoms.

Psychotic symptoms occurring with childhood mania were reported by Graves (1884) more than a century ago. Behr (1930) believed that mania was the distinctive insanity of early childhood, with hallucinations appearing first and delusions later. Subsequently, several authors have reported that psychotic symptoms were associated with childhood mania (Anthony and Scott 1960; Ballenger et al. 1982; J. D. Campbell 1952;

71

72 *Psychoses and PDDs in Childhood and Adolescence*

Carlson and Strober 1978; McGlashan 1988; Varanka et al. 1988). Over the years, many children and adolescents who have mania with psychotic features may have been diagnosed as schizophrenic (J. D. Campbell 1952; Carlson and Strober 1978; Esman et al. 1983; Varanka et al. 1988; Weller et al. 1986).

Definition: Criteria in DSM-IV and ICD-10

Historically, the criteria for diagnosing mania in children and adolescents were developed by Anthony and Scott (1960). Their criteria were modified by Weinberg and Brumback (1976) on the basis of DSM-II (American Psychiatric Association 1968) criteria. DSM criteria underwent several revisions from the development of DSM-I (American Psychiatric Association 1952) to the criteria used in DSM-III-R (American Psychiatric Association 1987). DSM-IV (American Psychiatric Association 1994) represents a further revision of this system. Though the use of DSM nomenclature is common in the United States and Canada, the ICD-10 (World Health Organization 1992) criteria are in more worldwide use.

In DSM-IV, the essential feature of a manic episode is a distinct period (at least 1 week, but less if hospitalization is required) during which the predominant mood is either elevated, expansive, or irritable. The DSM-IV criteria also require that at least three of the following symptoms be present during the mood disturbance (four symptoms are required if the mood is only irritable): 1) inflated self-esteem or grandiosity, 2) decreased need for sleep, 3) more talkative than usual or pressured speech, 4) flight of ideas or racing thoughts, 5) distractibility, 6) psychomotor agitation or increase in goal-directed activity, and 7) excessive involvement in pleasurable activities with high potential for painful consequences. To diagnose mania, the mood disturbance must be severe enough to cause marked impairment in occupational or social activities or relationships with others or to necessitate hospitalization. The manic episode cannot be due to the direct effects of a substance or a general medical condition. These conditions would also preclude a diagnosis of depression, as discussed in detail in the chapter "Affective Psychoses, I: Major Depression With Psychosis."

As with a major depressive episode, a manic episode may be classified according to severity (mild, moderate, severe without psychotic features, or severe with psychotic features). If psychotic features are present, they can be either mood-congruent or mood-incongruent. In mood-congruent psychotic features, the content of hallucinations or delusions is consistent with typical manic themes such as inflated worth, power, knowledge, identity, or a special relationship with a deity or famous person. In mood-incongruent psychotic features, the content of the hallucinations or delusions does not involve typical manic themes as described above, but it may include persecutory delusions not related to grandiose themes or ideas, delusions of being controlled, and thought insertion. Also, catatonic symptoms such as stupor, mutism, and posturing would be considered a mood-incongruent psychotic feature (American Psychiatric Association 1994). Table 3–1 presents the DSM-IV criteria for a manic episode. Criteria for a hypomanic episode are similar, except that the episode is not severe enough either to cause marked impairment in social or occupational functioning or to require hospitalization, and, by definition, no psychotic features are present.

In DSM-IV it is possible to diagnose bipolar I disorder or bipolar II disorder if there has been more than one episode and if the clinical picture is one of mixed mania/hypomania and depression. It is also possible to diagnose cyclothymic disorder in children or adolescents if there have been numerous periods of hypomanic symptoms and numerous periods of depressed mood or loss of interest or pleasure (not meeting criteria for a major depressive episode) over the course of a year. This diagnosis is excluded if the child or adolescent has met criteria for a major depressive episode or if the symptoms are better accounted for by schizoaffective disorder and are not superimposed on schizophrenia, schizophreniform disorder, delusional disorder, and so forth. A diagnosis of bipolar disorder not otherwise specified can also be made if the disorder has bipolar features that do not meet criteria for other disorders within the diagnostic class.

According to ICD-10 (World Health Organization 1992), a typical manic episode is characterized by 1) elevated or irritable mood, 2) elation, 3) increased energy, 4) overactivity, 5) decreased need for sleep, 6) loss of social inhibitions, 7) inflated self-esteem, 8) grandiose delusions, 9) extravagant spending, 10) aggressiveness, 11) sexual preoccu-

---

Table 3–1. DSM-IV criteria for manic episode

A. A distinct period of abnormally and persistently elevated, expansive, or irritable mood, lasting at least 1 week (or any duration if hospitalization is necessary).

B. During the period of mood disturbance, three (or more) of the following symptoms have persisted (four if the mood is only irritable) and have been present to a significant degree:

    (1) inflated self-esteem or grandiosity
    (2) decreased need for sleep (e.g., feels rested after only 3 hours of sleep)
    (3) more talkative than usual or pressure to keep talking
    (4) flight of ideas or subjective experience that thoughts are racing
    (5) distractibility (i.e., attention too easily drawn to unimportant or irrelevant external stimuli)
    (6) increase in goal-directed activity (either socially, at work or school, or sexually) or psychomotor agitation
    (7) excessive involvement in pleasurable activities that have a high potential for painful consequences (e.g., engaging in unrestrained buying sprees, sexual indiscretions, or foolish business investments)

C. The symptoms do not meet criteria for a mixed episode (see p. 335).

D. The mood disturbance is sufficiently severe to cause marked impairment in occupational functioning or in usual social activities or relationships with others, or to necessitate hospitalization to prevent harm to self or others, or there are psychotic features.

E. The symptoms are not due to the direct physiological effects of a substance (e.g., a drug of abuse, a medication, or other treatment) or a general medical condition (e.g., hyperthyroidism).

    Note: Manic-like episodes that are clearly caused by somatic antidepressant treatment (e.g., medication, electroconvulsive therapy, light therapy) should not count toward a diagnosis of bipolar I disorder.

Source. American Psychiatric Association: Diagnostic and Statistical Manual of Mental Disorders, 4th Edition. Washington, DC, American Psychiatric Association, 1994, p. 332. Used with permission.

---

pation, and, in some episodes, 12) delusions of persecution.

If the symptoms are mild, the subject may appear to be "boorish, garrulous and conceited" (World Health Organization 1990). At the height of the illness, delusions, incomprehensible speech, or violent excitement may result in an erroneous diagnosis of schizophrenia. The first attack most commonly occurs between ages 15 and 30, but it may occur at any age from late childhood to the seventh or eighth decade.

The episode should last at least 1 week. The term *manic episode* is used for a single episode. If there is a history of mania or a subsequent episode of mania, the illness is termed a bipolar affective disorder and is characterized by at least two episodes, in which the subject's mood and activity are profoundly disturbed, and by periods of mania and depression.

Prevalence and Epidemiology

Bipolar disorder occurs in 1% of adults and affects males and females equally (Regier and Burke 1989). A nonreferred community sample of 150 adolescents, 14–16 years old, from Columbia, Missouri, was studied by Carlson and Kashani (1988), using the Diagnostic Interview for Children and Adolescents (DICA). When severity and duration were taken into account, only 0.6% of the adolescents met diagnostic criteria for mania. The occurrence of psychotic symptoms with mania has been documented, but there are no published prospective epidemiological studies, and there are no published epidemiological studies of mania in prepubertal children.

The increasing prevalence of bipolar, schizoaffective, and unipolar disorder has been explained by a phenomenon called the cohort effect. This effect was observed by Gershon et al. (1987) and Klerman et al. (1985). These authors found that the age at onset of these disorders was getting younger and that the lifetime prevalence of mood disorder was higher in people born after 1940. The cohort effect has been explained as being caused, not by genetics alone, but possibly by an interaction between cultural, environmental, and biological phenomena. This observation implied an increasing incidence of mood disorders in children and adolescents in future generations and hence warrants further study.

Clinical Features and Phenomenology

Carlson (1983) reported that some symptoms of mania vary with age. Children under the age of 9 presented with more irritability, aggressiveness, and emotional lability, whereas children over the age of 9 were more grandiose, euphoric, paranoid, and had flight of ideas. Both age groups had hyperactivity, push of speech, and distractibility. Also, discrete episodes were difficult to delineate in children (Carlson 1983).

Extremes of mood are reported more frequently after puberty. Adolescents with mania often have clinical presentations similar to those of adults. However, psychotic features are more common in adolescents than adults (Ballenger et al. 1982). As a result, the tendency has been to make a diagnosis of schizophrenia.

Strober and Carlson (1982) examined treatment outcome in 60 adolescents ages 3–16 who were hospitalized for major depressive disorder. Twenty percent had developed a bipolar disorder 3–4 years later. Bipolarity was predicted by rapid symptom onset, psychomotor retardation, mood-congruent psychotic features, a "loaded" family history of affective illness in three successive generations, and pharmacologically induced hypomania.

Before lithium was introduced, mania was underdiagnosed in the United States. About 50% of adults with mania had been previously diagnosed as having schizophrenia (Horgan 1981; Mendelwicz et al. 1972). To determine whether mania had been similarly underdiagnosed in prepubertal children, Weller et al. (1986) conducted a retrospective review of all English-language case descriptions of children ages 6–12 who were diagnosed as having manic depression, psychosis, schizophrenia, or atypical manic depression or as being "severely disturbed." It was felt that children with mania would most probably be found in these diagnostic classifications. Of the 157 children ages 6–12 whose cases were reviewed, there were 42 girls and 115 boys. A total of 33 children were diagnosed as having, probably having, or possibly having mania. Of these, 17 (52%) had previously been diagnosed as having mania, but 16 (48%) had been diagnosed as having some other disorder. Thus, about one-half of the children diagnosed with mania by DSM-III criteria had originally received another diagnosis. The most common prior diagnosis was schizophrenia. The authors concluded that mania should be in the differential diagnosis of children who present with psychotic symptoms, particularly if affective symptoms are also present.

To determine the phenomenology and course of illness in adolescents with mania who had been previously diagnosed as having schizophrenia, Carlson and Strober (1978) did a retrospective chart review. Subjects were all adolescent patients since 1971 who were diagnosed as having schizophrenia when first admitted to the University of California at Los Angeles (UCLA) Neuropsychiatric Institute, but were diagnosed as having manic-depressive disorder on a subsequent admission. This had occurred in 6 adolescents. All underwent a follow-up evaluation when they were relatively asymptomatic. Mean age at the follow-up was 19 years. There were 3 males and 3 females. Mean age at onset of first episode was 14 years and 9 months. These 6 subjects had a total of 23 episodes of illness during the 54-month follow-up period. Seventeen of the episodes were manic and 6 were depressive. Psychotic symptoms were present in 10 of the 23 episodes (6 manic and 4 depressive). All subjects had experienced psychotic symptoms at some point during their illness. The hallucinations and delusions had all occurred during affective episodes. One adolescent had experienced command hallucinations. Grandiose, nihilistic, paranoid, and religious delusions were present during manic episodes. Incoherent speech, loose associations, regressive behavior, and cognitive disorganization were also reported. All 6 subjects had sexual preoccupation during manic episodes. Prior to being diagnosed as having an affective illness, all 6 had been treated with phenothiazines with minimal change in their symptoms. Eventually, they were placed on lithium carbonate at therapeutic serum levels; 50% responded with a reduction in manic symptoms. The response of the remaining 3 subjects to lithium was less dramatic.

To ascertain whether psychotic symptoms occur more frequently in patients with early-onset bipolar disorder than in those with late-onset bipolar illness, Ballenger et al. (1982) reviewed the histories of all patients admitted to the National Institute of Mental Health (NIMH) from 1971–1978 with a diagnosis of manic-depressive illness. There were 9 adolescents with episodes of mania observed and treated before age 21. Their manic symptoms were compared with those of 12 adults whose manic episodes were first observed after they reached the age of 30. Adolescent patients had significantly more delusions and more ideas of reference and more than 3 schizophrenic symptoms. They also had considerably more confusion (55% versus 25%), thought disorder (44% versus 17%), and bizarre behavior (33% versus 8%). Diagnosis was also supported by a positive response to lithium in 19 adolescent patients. The authors emphasized the diagnostic importance of recognizing affective symptoms in psychotic adolescents with mixed manic and schizophrenic symptoms. They suggested that the correct diagnosis of bipolar disorder would be made if primary importance was given to manic symptoms rather than schizophrenic symptoms.

Similar findings were reported by McGlashan (1988), who studied 66 psychiatric patients discharged from a long-term residential treatment facility between 1950 and 1975. These patients were reevaluated by telephone interviews 15 years after discharge. Of the 66 patients, 35 had an adolescent-onset mania (occurrence of the first symptom was at age 19 or below) and 31 had adult onset (occurrence of the first symptom was at age 20 or older). Of these, 28 with adolescent onset and 31 with adult onset were located. Adolescent-onset patients displayed more delusions, hallucinations, or both than adult-onset patients. The majority of adolescent-onset patients had enough psychotic symptoms to have a diagnosis of schizoaffective disorder rather than bipolar disorder. Eighty-three percent of the adolescent-onset subjects had a diagnosis of schizoaffective disorder, and 17% had a diagnosis of bipolar disorder. Corresponding rates for adult-onset subjects were 45% and 55%. This difference was significant ($P < .003$). Adolescent-onset patients also had significantly more trouble with the law than adult-onset subjects (30% versus 7%) and more psychotic assaultiveness (70% versus 36%). Thus, subjects with adolescent-onset mania manifested with more psychotic symptoms than did subjects with adult-onset mania. This study also found that patients with adolescent-onset mania were more severely ill at their index admission.

Rosen et al. (1983) reported more psychotic symptoms in bipolar patients with earlier ages of onset. The study included 71 bipolar subjects who attended the Lithium Clinic at the New York State Psychiatric Institute between 1977 and 1978. Of the 71 patients, 53 had been psychotic at some time during the course of their illness. Of these 53 psychiatric patients, 25 met research diagnostic criteria (RDC) for schizoaffective disorder. The authors found a negative correlation between age at onset and psychotic symptoms for the entire group of patients ($r = -.4$, $P < .001$) and for the 25 schizoaffective patients ($r = -.48$, $P < .01$). Bipolar subjects with an age at onset prior to 20 years of age had more psychotic symptoms (≥ 5) than bipolar patients with an age at onset over 40 years (38% versus 0%). The authors suggested that bipolar subjects with an earlier age at onset have more psychosis than do those with a later age at onset.

Course and Prognosis

McGlashan's (1988) study revealed that patients who had mania with symptom onset in adolescence had significantly more trouble with the law and were more assaultive than those with a later onset. However, their social functioning and work history were significantly superior following treatment. Strober et al. (1990) found a threefold increase in relapse rates in a prospective study of bipolar adolescents who discontinued lithium prophylaxis after discharge. Early relapse in patients treated with lithium was associated with a greater risk of subsequent relapses. Unfortunately, there are no published long-term prospective follow-up studies of bipolar children.

Etiology and Pathogenesis

Numerous etiologies have been proposed for the development of mania. The following are some of the major theories put forth.

Biological Theories

To explain the etiology of mood disorders, various biological theories have been proposed. Though these theories have been extensively studied in adults, such studies are limited in children and adolescents.

Bipolar children and adolescents have an increased incidence of affective illness in their family members (Dwyer and DeLong 1987; Strober et al. 1988; Varanka et al. 1988). In one study, affective illness in first-degree relatives of probands who had mania with prepubertal onset was three times greater than in those with an adolescent onset (29.4% versus 8.6%). Furthermore, prepubertal-onset probands had a poorer response to lithium than did adolescent-onset probands (33.3% versus 65.7%) (Strober et al. 1988).

Klein et al. (1985) reported higher rates of affective disorder (especially cyclothymia) among adolescent offspring of parents with bipolar affective disorder compared to control subjects.

Another study (Dwyer and DeLong 1987) reported that 62.5% of parents of affectively ill children had a major affective disorder.

Psychosocial Theories

Psychoanalytic theories describe mania as a defense against depression (Regier and Burke 1989). Anthony and Scott (1960) believed that stressful life events could trigger manic episodes. Carlson and Strober (1978) noted an association between repeated object loss and onset of manic episodes in adolescents.

It is well known that offspring of affectively ill parents are at increased risk of developing affective illness. Pelligrini et al. (1986) compared the psychosocial characteristics of offspring of bipolar type I patients with offspring of psychiatrically healthy control subjects. This study was directed toward identifying characteristics of children who maintain psychiatric well-being despite a family history of affective illness. In their study, 23 children of parents with bipolar type I disorder were compared to 33 children of psychiatrically healthy control parents. Their study revealed that of the 23 resilient children, their personal resources and support from family members, peers, and a best friend contributed to their well-being. The affected children, on the other hand, had poor resources, little family support (and thus depended on nonfamily adult support), and no best friend. This study has important ramifications because it contributes to the understanding of vulnerable yet resilient children who have a family/genetic predisposition to a mood disorder.

Cytryn et al. (1984) reported that affect regulation and social interactions are impaired in the young children of bipolar parents.

Assessment

There are no laboratory studies to diagnose bipolar disorder in children and adolescents. However, diagnostic instruments are helpful in establishing the diagnosis. Structured interviews include the Diagnostic Interview Schedule for Children (DISC) (Gioia 1988) and the Diagnostic Interview for Children and Adolescents—Revised (DICA-R) (Reich and Welner 1992). These instruments are most useful when augmented with a clinical interview. Semistructured interviews that can be used to assess mania include the Schedule for Affective Disorders and Schizophrenia for School-aged Children (K-SADS) (Chambers et al. 1982) and the Interview Schedule for Children (ISC) (Kovacs 1978).

Differential Diagnosis

Attention-deficit/hyperactivity disorder (ADHD) may at times resemble mania, but careful evaluation will help differentiate the two disorders. Dvoredsky and Stewart (1981) reported two cases of "childhood hyperactivity," which were followed by manic depression at ages 17 and 27. The authors concluded from these two case reports that there may be a subgroup of patients who show an initial clinical picture of behavior problems and develop an affective disorder later.

Bipolar disorder can also be confused with adjustment reaction, behavior disorder, narcissistic disorder (Carlson 1983), or schizophrenia (Carlson 1983; Carlson and Strober 1978).

Treatment

The use of antimanic agents like lithium carbonate, carbamazepine, and valproate is well established in adults. However, there are no large systematic treatment studies of these agents for bipolar disorder in children and adolescents. Several investigators have studied the use of lithium in bipolar disorder in this age group. In 1977, the Academy of Child Psychiatry (M. Campbell et al. 1978) issued a position paper stating the following:

> The areas where lithium should be explored because of its potential therapeutic value and its possible advantage over other currently available standard psychoactive drugs, include: manic depressive illness, emotionally unstable character disorder, aggressiveness and high risk offspring of lithium responders. (p. 718)

Youngerman and Canino (1978) reviewed the charts of 190 children and adolescents treated with lithium. The researchers used DSM-III criteria to divide the children into the following diagnostic groups: major affective disorder, behavior disorder of childhood and adolescence, and schizophrenia—childhood type. Forty-six cases were described in detail; of these, 30 responded positively to lithium, and they all had affective symptomatology.

The first use of lithium in an adolescent was described by Van Krevelen and Van Voorst (cited in Lena 1979) in a 14-year-old boy who suffered from periodic psychosis with manic phases that were longer than the depressive phases. Lena (1979) emphasized the need for checking renal and thyroid function prior to starting lithium.

Carlson and Strober (1978) reported the use of lithium carbonate in six adolescents previously diagnosed as having schizophrenia who were retrospectively rediagnosed as manic-depressive. Following the rediagnosis, three of the six patients had complete remission on lithium. Improvement in the other three children was not as dramatic, and they had recurrences on lithium maintenance.

DeLong (1978) reported dramatic improvement in hostility, aggressiveness, and distractibility in 12 children on lithium. Six to 33 months later, 9 of these children also had cyclic mood swings.

Varanka et al. (1988) studied 10 prepubertal manic children admitted to a children's inpatient unit between 1981 and 1985. There were nine boys and one girl. Ages ranged from 6 years 9 months to 12 years 7 months. None had received previous inpatient psychiatric treatment. All had either elevated (50%) or irritable (50%) mood, all had increased motor activity, and 60% had increased sexual interest and racing thoughts. Ninety percent reported decreased need for sleep. Almost all had been previously diagnosed as hyperactive, and all 10 showed mood-congruent psychotic features. Seven children (70%) had visual hallucinations such as "seeing the devil," "seeing people with purple eyes," and "seeing the bogeyman." Five children (50%) had auditory hallucinations: "The devil and angel talk to me." Seven children (70%) reported persecutory delusions such as "the wolfman is after me" or "people are watching me." Two (20%) had grandiose delusions such as being the President of the United States. None of these psychotic symptoms had been present before the manic episode.

All 10 children had a positive family history for psychiatric disorder: 20% had a family history of manic episodes, 50% had a family history of depression, and 60% had alcoholism in their families. All were treated with lithium carbonate only. A mean dose of 1,270 mg (40 mg/kg/day) was used, and lithium levels were in the therapeutic range (0.6–1.4 meq/L). No neuroleptics were given except to one subject, who received two doses of haloperidol 0.5 mg for aggressive behavior. Significant improvement occurred in all 10 patients.

DeLong and Aldershof (1987) studied the long-term efficacy of lithium treatment of childhood behavior disorders in 190 children followed for 10 years. Lithium was effective for childhood bipolar disorder. Of the 59 children diagnosed, 66% were treated successfully.

Although lithium has been used successfully in treating mania, double-blind, placebo-controlled studies have not been performed in children. Even less is known about the treatment of bipolar disorder with psychotic features in this age group.

Summary and Directions for Research

Psychotic symptoms have been reported in childhood and adolescent mania. Although the extent of psychotic symptoms in mania in this age group is not currently known, their occurrence may be more common than previously believed. When the onset of bipolar illness occurs in adolescence or prepuberty, there may be significant psychotic symptoms, which might lead to a diagnosis of schizoaffective disorder or even schizophrenia. To avoid such potential misdiagnosis, mania should be carefully considered in the differential diagnosis of psychosis with affective features in children and adolescents.

Several reports suggest that early onset of depression with psychotic features, psychomotor retardation, or both puts such children and adolescents at high risk for developing bipolar illness (Akiskal et al. 1985; Strober and Carlson 1982). Also, Kovacs et al. (1984), in a study of depressed and dysthymic children, reported that 30% of dysthymic children who were followed longitudinally developed bipolar disorder. Hence, children with a history of depression with psychotic features, a history of dysthymia, or a history of bipolar illness in their parents may all be at high risk to develop bipolar disorder. Such high-risk children could be systematically followed to study the prodrome, onset, and phenomenology of the first episode of mania. Such information would lead to a better understanding of bipolar disorder in children and adolescents and would result in improved diagnosis and treatment in children and adolescents with this disorder.

Case Report

Janet, a 7-year-old white female, was initially evaluated as an outpatient for ongoing problems with volatile mood and physical aggression. Janet was described by her parents as having been difficult and uncontrollable since birth. She was a colicky baby who only slept for half an hour a night during the first year of her life. Though she walked and had a vocabulary of 100 words by 12 months, she had been difficult to manage. At the age of 18 months, she was uncontrollable. She would pull off her clothes and scream constantly. Treatment with an antispasmodic and anticholinergic and with a barbiturate for short periods was ineffective. At the age of $3\frac{1}{2}$ years, she was talking nonstop, was always on the go, and was aggressive with her peers and infant sibling. Inappropriate behavior included smearing feces and urinating on her clothes. Because of episodic problems with aggressiveness and other behavior, she was treated at age $4\frac{1}{2}$ years with methylphenidate 2.5 mg q am, which resulted in dysphoric mood and increased irritability. As a result of an initial diagnosis of ADHD, other stimulant medications were tried, with similar side effects. A trial on imipramine slowed her down but caused hallucinations. At the time of the initial evaluation, she was being treated with thioridazine 10 mg tid, which had been discontinued a few days before the evaluation. In addition to the symptoms of unpredictability, mood swings, and alternately irritable or dysphoric mood, she had continued to be aggressive to her brother, age $3\frac{1}{2}$ years, and had attempted to choke her father with a cord. She had also reported hearing voices, buzzing noises, and bells at the age of 5. Though there was no history of fire setting or suicide attempts, she had been mean to the family cat; at the age of $3\frac{1}{2}$ years, she had tied a helium balloon to the cat, to see if it would float.

Significant family history included a history of depression in the mother, a history of undifferentiated psychosis in the maternal grandmother, and alcoholism in the maternal grandfather. The father's paternal grandfather was diagnosed as having paranoid schizophrenia, and the father's brother was diagnosed as having bipolar affective disorder.

Nine months after the initial outpatient evaluation and continued treatment with thioridazine, she was hospitalized as a result of symptoms of increasing aggressiveness and mood swings. She was discharged after a successful trial of lithium carbonate at a dose of 150 mg bid and 300 mg po q hs.

Four months after discharge from the hospital, Janet became dysphoric, had sleep difficulties and low self-esteem, and was quite irritable despite an increase of lithium carbonate to 300 mg bid and 450 mg q hs.

Imipramine was started and increased up to 75 mg/day. Despite initial improvement of mood, it was noted that Janet progressively worsened 4 months later and became moody, silly, and dysphoric, with low self-esteem. Therefore, to target what was seen to be rapid cycling, imipramine was tapered to 25 mg hs and carbamazepine was started. The current dosage of medications of lithium carbonate 1,050 mg/day, imipramine 25 mg hs, and carbamazepine 200 mg bid have yielded good results.

References

Akiskal HS, Downs J, Jordan P, et al: Affective disorders in referred children and younger siblings of manic depressives. Arch Gen Psychiatry 42:996–1004, 1985

American Psychiatric Association: Diagnostic and Statistical Manual: Mental Disorders. Washington, DC, American Psychiatric Association, 1952

American Psychiatric Association: Diagnostic and Statistical Manual of Mental Disorders, 2nd Edition. Washington, DC, American Psychiatric Association, 1968

American Psychiatric Association: Diagnostic and Statistical Manual of Mental Disorders, 3rd Edition, Revised. Washington, DC, American Psychiatric Association, 1987

American Psychiatric Association: Diagnostic and Statistical Manual of Mental Disorders, 4th Edition. Washington, DC, American Psychiatric Association, 1994

Anthony J, Scott P: Manic depressive psychosis in childhood. J Child Psychol Psychiatry 1:53–72, 1960

Ballenger JC, Reus VI, Post RM: The "atypical" clinical picture of adolescent mania. Am J Psychiatry 139:602–606, 1982

Behr MA: Psychiatric problems in children. Journal of the Indiana Medical Association 23:7–11, 1930

Campbell JD: Manic depressive psychosis in children: report of 18 cases. J Nerv Ment Dis 116:424–439, 1952

Campbell M, Schulman D, Rapoport J: The current status of lithium therapy in child and adolescent psychiatry. J Am Acad Child Adolesc Psychiatry 17:717–720, 1978

Carlson GA: Bipolar affective disorders in childhood and adolescence, in Affective Disorders in Childhood and Adolescence: An Update. Edited by Cantwell DP, Carlson GA. New York, NY, Spectrum Publications, 1983

Carlson GA, Kashani JH: Manic symptoms in a nonreferred adolescent population. J Affect Disord 15:219–226, 1988

Carlson GA, Strober M: Manic-depressive illness in early adolescence: a study of clinical and diagnostic characteristics in six cases. J Am Acad Child Psychiatry 17:138–153, 1978

Chambers NJ, Puig-Antich J, Hirsch M, et al: The assessment of affective disorders in children and adolescents by semistructured interview. Arch Gen Psychiatry 42:698–702, 1982

Cytryn L, McKnew DH, Zahn-Waxler C, et al: A developmental view of affective disturbances in the children of affectively ill parents. Am J Psychiatry 141:219–222, 1984

DeLong GR: Lithium carbonate treatment of select behavior disorders in children suggesting manic depressive illness. J Pediatr 93:689–694, 1978

DeLong GR, Aldershof AL: Long-term experience with lithium treatment in childhood: correlations with clinical diagnosis. J Am Acad Child Adolesc Psychiatry 26:389–394, 1987

Dvoredsky AE, Stewart MA: Hyperactivity followed by manic depressive disorder: two case reports. J Clin Psychiatry 42:212–214, 1981

Dwyer JT, DeLong GR: A family history study of twenty probands with childhood manic depressive illness. J Am Acad Child Adolesc Psychiatry 26:176–180, 1987

Esman AH, Hertzig M, Aarons S: Juvenile manic depressive illness: a longitudinal perspective. J Am Acad Child Adolesc Psychiatry 22:302–304, 1983

Gershon ES, Hamovit JH, Guroff JJ, et al: Birth cohort changes in manic and depressive disorders in relatives of bipolar and schizoaffective patients. Arch Gen Psychiatry 44:314–319,1987

Gioia P: A revised version of the Diagnostic Interview Schedule for Children (DISC-R): results of a field trial and proposals for a new instrument (DISC-2). Bethesda, MD, Epidemiology and Psychopathology Research Branch, Division of Clinical Research, National Institute of Mental Health, 1988

Graves HE: Acute mania in a child of five years: recovery and remarks. Lancet:824–826, 1884

Horgan D: Change of diagnosis to manic-depressive illness. Psychol Med 11:517–523, 1981

Klein DN, Depue RA, Slater JF: Cyclothymia in the adolescent offspring of parents with Bipolar Affective Disorder. J Abnorm Psychol 94:115–127, 1985

Klerman GL, Lavori PW, Rice J, et al: Birth-cohort trends in rates of major depressive disorder among relatives of patients with affective disorder. Arch Gen Psychiatry 42:689–693, 1985

Kovacs M: The Interview Schedule for Children (ISC). Psychopharmacol Bull 21:991–994, 1978

Kovacs M, Feinberg TL, Crouse-Novak M, et al: Depressive disorders in childhood. Arch Gen Psychiatry 41:643–649, 1984

Kraepelin E: Manic Depressive Insanity and Paranoia. Edinburgh: E & S Livingstone Ltd., 1921

Lena B: Lithium in child and adolescent psychiatry. Arch Gen Psychiatry 36:854–855, 1979

McGlashan TH: Adolescent versus adult onset mania. Am J Psychiatry 145:221–223, 1988

Mendelwicz J, Fieve RR, Rainer JD, et al: Manic depressive illness: a comparative study of patients with and without a family history. Br J Psychiatry 120:523–530, 1972

Pelligrini D, Kosisky S, Nackman D, et al: Personal and social resources in children of patients with bipolar affective disorder and children of normal control subjects. Am J Psychiatry 143:856–861, 1986

Reich W, Welner Z: The Diagnostic Interview for Children and Adolescents—Revised. Unpublished manuscript, Washington University, St. Louis, MO, June 1992

Regier DA, Burke JD: Quantitative and experimental methods in psychiatry, in Comprehensive Textbook of Psychiatry, 5th Edition, Vol. 1. Edited by Kaplan HI, Sadock BI. Baltimore, MD, Williams & Wilkins, 1989, p 324

Rosen LN, Rosenthal NE, VanDusen PH, et al: Age at onset and number of psychotic symptoms in bipolar I and schizoaffective disorder. Am J Psychiatry 140:1523–1524, 1983

Strober M, Carlson GA: Bipolar illness in adolescents with major depression: clinical, genetic and psychopharmacologic predictors in a 3–4 year prospective follow-up investigation. Arch Gen Psychiatry 39:549–555, 1982

Strober M, Morrell W, Burroughs J, et al: Family study of bipolar I disorder in adolescence: early onset of symptoms linked to increased familial loading and lithium resistance. J Affect Disord 15:255–268, 1988

Strober M, Morrell W, Lampert C, et al: Relapse following discontinuation of lithium maintenance therapy in adolescents with bipolar I illness: a naturalistic study. Am J Psychiatry 147:457–461, 1990

Varanka TM, Weller RA, Weller EB, et al: Lithium treatment of manic episodes with psychotic features in prepubertal children. Am J Psychiatry 145:1557–1559, 1988

Weinberg WA, Brumback RA: Mania in childhood, case studies and literature review. Am J Dis Child 130:380–385, 1976

Weller RA, Weller EB, Tucker SG, et al: Mania in prepubertal children: has it been underdiagnosed? J Affect Disord 11:151–154, 1986

World Health Organization: International Classification of Diseases, 10th Edition, Criteria for Research [draft]. Geneva, World Health Organization, 1990, pp 57–67

World Health Organization: The ICD-10 Classification of Mental and Behavioural Disorders: Clinical Descriptions and Diagnostic Guidelines. Geneva, World Health Organization, 1992

Youngerman J, Canino IA: Lithium carbonate use in children and adolescents. Arch Gen Psychiatry 35:216–224, 1978

Chapter 4

Borderline Features in Childhood Disorders

Melvin Lewis, M.B.B.S., F.R.C.Psych., D.C.H.

Introduction

The term *borderline* in relation to children is elusive and idiosyncratic, in part because of the dearth of rigorous scientific validation studies. Further, findings from scientific research on borderline conditions in adults simply cannot be extrapolated backward to childhood, if only for developmental reasons. Nor can the adult borderline condition be equated with all the multiple conditions that have been called borderline in children. In the early child psychiatry literature the definitions were largely drawn from inferences based on psychoanalytic theory and psychodynamic descriptions (e.g., Bemporad et al. 1982; Ekstein and Wallerstein 1956; Frijling-Schreuder 1969; Kernberg 1975; Pine 1983; Robson 1983). Petti and Vela (1990), in their review of the extensive child literature, including more recent contributions, noted that "the amount

---

This chapter is modified from an earlier version, Lewis (1994).

of space required to present a topic area is inversely proportional to the degree of scientific certainty associated with it" (p. 334) and concluded that "there appear to be a number of borderline disorders with different etiologies, phenomenology, associated features, and required treatments" (p. 335). However useful the diagnosis of borderline might be in clinical practice, it has to be said that the validity of the concept has simply not been scientifically established.

Definition

Minimally, a personality trait may be defined as an enduring pattern of perceiving, relating to, and thinking about one's environment and oneself (Lewis and Volkmar 1990). This is a dimensional concept, which in its extreme form may be recognized as pathological, although possibly not fulfilling the criteria for a disorder. A personality trait becomes a personality disorder (i.e., a disease) when the trait is not only severe, but becomes inflexible and maladaptive and causes either distress or impairment in social or occupational functions. How might one proceed from these definitions to a classification of borderline disorders?

DSM-IV (American Psychiatric Association 1994) codes adult personality disorders on Axis II. Clinically, personality disorders appear to be divided among three broad clusters (see Table 4–1). In contrast to DSM-III-R (American Psychiatric Association 1987), a category for passive-aggressive personality disorder (previously in cluster C) is no longer included. Several conditions listed in DSM-III-R were not accorded formal diagnostic status as categories that were in need of further study (e.g., sadistic and self-defeating disorders).

ICD-10 (World Health Organization 1988) classifies abnormalities

Table 4–1. DSM-IV clusters of adult personality disorders

Cluster A	Cluster B	Cluster C
Paranoid	Antisocial	Avoidant
Schizoid	Borderline	Dependent
Schizotypal	Histrionic	Obsessive-compulsive
	Narcissistic	Not otherwise specified

of personality in adults into personality disorders, personality trait accentuation, and enduring personality change, and it also has a separate category for organic personality disorder, but it does not include schizotypal, borderline, or narcissistic personality disorder under personality disorders.

Under the heading "Disorders of Adult Personality," ICD-10 (1992) somewhat reluctantly included a description of borderline personality disorder (F60.31) as a subcategory of emotionally unstable personality disorder. Among the particular additional characteristics noted are the presence of a disturbance of self-image, aims, and internal preferences (including sexual) and chronic feelings of emptiness. "Intense and unstable relationships may cause repeated emotional crises and may be associated with excessive efforts to avoid abandonment and a series of suicidal threats or acts of self harm" (p. 205). There is no specific description of borderline disorders in children or adolescents.

Children and adolescents under 18 years of age who seem persistently, and over a long time, to have the essential characteristic features (perhaps modified by developmental factors) of any of the personality disorders described for adults may be diagnosed in the same way as adults. However, in only one instance (in DSM-IV) is the child given a separate diagnostic label thought to be appropriate for the child's level of development. Thus, conduct disorder is diagnosed in children, whereas in adults the term *antisocial personality disorder* is used if appropriate. This represents a change from DSM-III-R, where the term *avoidant disorder of childhood* was presumed to have some continuity with avoidant personality disorder in adulthood (the former diagnostic category has been eliminated in DSM-IV).

The implications of the DSM-IV approach to personality disorders in children are twofold: first, that personality disorders are most appropriately diagnosed in adulthood (when the constellation of traits subsumed under the term *personality* are presumably more stable) and, second, that with the exception of conduct disorder there is not a presumed correspondence of childhood disorders to adult personality disorders. The evidence regarding borderline personality disorder in childhood is clearly not satisfactory at present; that is, there is not a substantial body of evidence that what we call borderline personality disorder in children is the same as, or goes on to be, borderline personality disorder as described in adulthood. On the contrary, a wide variety of outcomes, including depression and schizophrenia, have been observed. The DSM-IV definition of borderline personality disorder is presented in Table 4–2. This definition differs from that employed in DSM-III-R in terms of its greater emphasis on transient (stress related) paranoid ideation, dissociative symptoms, or both.

Prevalence

Given the uncertain validity of the concepts and poorly established diagnostic criteria, true prevalence figures are not available.

Clinical Features

In general, there are seven common clinical features (see Table 4–3). There may be rapid, unpredictable (so-called "predictably unpre-

---

Table 4–2.   DSM-IV diagnostic criteria for borderline personality disorder

A pervasive pattern of instability of interpersonal relationships, self-image, and affects, and marked impulsivity beginning by early adulthood and present in a variety of contexts, as indicated by five (or more) of the following:

(1) frantic efforts to avoid real or imagined abandonment. **Note:** Do not include suicidal or self-mutilating behavior covered in Criterion 5.
(2) a pattern of unstable and intense interpersonal relationships characterized by alternating between extremes of idealization and devaluation
(3) identity disturbance: markedly and persistently unstable self-image or sense of self
(4) impulsivity in at least two areas that are potentially self-damaging (e.g., spending, sex, substance abuse, reckless driving, binge eating). **Note:** Do not include suicidal or self-mutilating behavior covered in Criterion 5.
(5) recurrent suicidal behavior, gestures, or threats, or self-mutilating behavior
(6) affective instability due to a marked reactivity of mood (e.g., intense episodic dysphoria, irritability, or anxiety usually lasting a few hours and only rarely more than a few days)
(7) chronic feelings of emptiness
(8) inappropriate, intense anger or difficulty controlling anger (e.g., frequent displays of temper, constant anger, recurrent physical fights)
(9) transient, stress-related paranoid ideation or severe dissociative symptoms

---

Source.   American Psychiatric Association: Diagnostic and Statistical Manual of Mental Disorders, 4th Edition. Washington, DC, American Psychiatric Association, 1994, p. 654. Used with permission.

Table 4–3.   Borderline conditions in children: common presenting features

1. Rapid regression in thinking, reality testing, and affective control
2. Extreme vulnerability to stress, with psychotic decompensation
3. Chronic regressed state
4. Severe separation anxiety and regression
5. Generalized restricted development (e.g., in relationships, affect, cognition, and language)
6. Schizoid retreat into preoccupation with fantasy life and withdrawal from relationships
7. Overwhelming rage and violent fantasies with extreme anxiety and loss of control

Source. Lewis 1994. Used with permission.

dictable") regression in thinking, reality testing, and affective control. Extreme vulnerability to external stress may lead to sudden suicidal or homicidal behavior, or psychotic manifestations, including hallucinations. Such children may reintegrate quickly once the stress stops—for example, when they are placed in a safe, structured, stress-free environment, such as a hospital. The child may be chronically regressed. Severe regression on separation from the parent, who often also has a borderline condition, and reintegration when reunited with the parent may occur, as though the child can function only within the symbiotic relationship with the parent. In other words, in theoretical terms, there seems to be a failure of individuation and object constancy. A generalized restriction of development in relationships, in affective range, in cognitive functions, and in language may occur. Retreat into a preoccupation with fantasy and emotional withdrawal from relationships may occur, leading to a schizoid clinical picture. The child may be overwhelmed with rage and violent fantasies that flood the child, threaten the child's self-control, and produce extreme anxiety.

Symptoms such as rage, temper outbursts, violent fantasies, regression, and impulsivity may all occur, sometimes mimicking certain cases of attention-deficit/hyperactivity disorder (ADHD) or anxiety disorders with depression (see Table 4–4).

Associated symptom clusters may be conceptualized as "comorbidity." Alternately, this total clinical picture may actually constitute borderline personality disorder in children, comparable perhaps to the way

---

Table 4–4.   Comorbid disorders (symptom clusters) in borderline
conditions in childhood

Attention-deficit/hyperactivity disorder
Anxiety disorders
Major depressive disorder

---

in which the term *conduct disorder* is used as an all-inclusive term that
covers a wide range of behaviors (and possibly conditions).

As it happens, few conditions in child and adolescent psychiatry are
mutually exclusive (in the sense that, say, autism and Down's syndrome
rarely, if ever, coexist in the same child). More often a child has more
than one diagnosis (e.g., major depressive disorder and conduct disorder). Indeed, as Puig-Antich (1982) demonstrated, treatment of the one
disorder (depression) may lead to improvement in symptoms of the
other disorder (behavior). In the case of children with a borderline disorder, several other diagnoses can co-occur, including ADHD, anxiety
disorder, major depressive disorder, and posttraumatic stress disorder.

Hypotheses to account for these coexistent diagnoses include the
following:

1. The child with a borderline disorder may be particularly vulnerable
   to the other listed diagnoses.
2. The borderline condition may itself be an atypical variant of one or
   more of these other disorders.
3. A more fundamental disorder may be the basic factor common to
   all the co-occurring diagnoses.
4. True comorbidity, that is, the co-occurrence of one or more of the
   conditions by chance alone, may account for the multiple diagnoses.
5. The appearance of comorbidity or coexistence may be an artifact
   of our classification systems (DSM-IV and ICD-10), which are currently based largely on symptom lists and, except in rare instances
   such as conversion disorder, are not based on mechanisms, etiology, or natural history of the alleged disorder.
6. The reported apparent coexistence in some instances may result
   from flawed research design and may not be significant.

Whatever the explanation, clinicians report that they are not surprised to find that a child with a borderline condition has several other diagnoses over the course of the illness.

In general, the behavior of a child or adolescent with a so-called borderline disorder is characterized by unpredictable moods and a pervasive, fluctuating, and unstable level of organization in multiple functions in such major areas as impulse control, affect modulation, attention, cognition, and relationships. Relationships are immature, often at a need-fulfilling stage, with a great deal of ambivalence and dependency and a minimal capacity for empathy. The child may have paranoid rages and may regress to the point of uncontrolled temper tantrums and loss of reality testing. A fluctuating thought disorder is often present, accompanied by a disorder of mood (especially depression), of behavior (which may be disorganized, aggressive, withdrawn, or bizarre), or of perception (with delusions and hallucinations). The anxiety level in these children is often quite high, and is poorly defended against, resulting in an interference with relationships and thinking. Compensatory omnipotent fantasies are often quite prominent. Unfortunately, the striking lack of empathy in the child may lead to a repetitious reinforcement of failure and rejection in almost every social interaction in which the child is involved, and a consequent increase in the child's depression, despair, and anxiety.

Course and Prognosis

Regrettably, most outcome studies use variable definitions and are poorly controlled. In essence there are no systematic studies on the course of children diagnosed as having a borderline condition (Petti and Vela 1990). Several clinically interesting treatment and follow-up case studies have been reported (Kestenbaum 1983; Petti and Unis 1981).

Etiology and Pathogenesis

The very difficulty of defining a case is in itself a research question. One possibility is that not only does the child have multiple comorbidities (however defined), but the comorbidities themselves may also have multiple causes. Such causal pathways may include those shown in Table 4–5.

Thus a working model for understanding the pathogenesis of this disorder (or perhaps cluster of disorders) might be a complex interactive model involving polygenic, organic, cognitive, intrapsychic and interpersonal, and socioenvironmental factors.

Genetic Factors

Personality styles (or temperament) in general are derived in part from genetic factors (Torgesen and Kringlen 1978). In addition, several disorders embedded in or comorbid with borderline personality disorder have been shown to have some genetic components. These associated disorders include antisocial personality disorder (Schulsinger 1972) and ADHD (Cantwell 1976; Zametkin and Rapoport 1987). The heritability of certain aspects of personality and of certain major psychopathological disorders may be in the range of 30% (Plomin 1990).

Organic Factors

There is no established pathognomonic organic finding in children who have a borderline condition. However, several reports support the presence of some form of organicity (Aarkrog 1981; Bemporad 1982), and one report suggests a disturbance of the enzyme dopamine-beta-hydroxylase (Rogeness et al. 1984, 1986). More research is required to confirm these reports.

Psychodynamic Factors

The psychoanalytic theories of Kernberg (1975) and Kohut's (1971) theories on borderline disorder are essentially "sleeper" theories. They

---

Table 4–5.   Borderline conditions in children: causal pathways

1. Genetic loading (Andrulonis 1990)
2. Organic factors (Bemporad et al. 1982)
3. Disturbances in the development of relationships (Pine 1982)
4. Serious disturbances in family functions and systems (Combrinck-Graham 1988)
5. Major parental psychopathology and major external stresses, especially abuse (Pine 1986)

---

imply a delayed effect of early psychological trauma during the separation-individuation phase, because the effects are not readily apparent at the time of the trauma but appear later—as a result, it is hypothesized, of an induced or heightened vulnerability to subsequent stresses. Curiously, children who do experience and manifest difficulties during the separation-individuation phase—because of, say, disordered parenting at that time—may develop symptoms of so-called borderline personality disorder during childhood, but they do not necessarily go on to have the syndrome of borderline personality disorder as adults. One would have to say that scientifically reliable documentation of the validity of these psychoanalytic etiological theories is not available.

Differential Diagnosis

The hypothesis of multiple comorbidities mentioned above often translates clinically into a difficult differential diagnosis (see Table 4–6).

Many of the children labeled borderline may have symptoms of ADHD, major depressive disorder, conduct disorder, somatoform disorder, dissociative disorder, posttraumatic stress disorder, cyclothymic disorder, schizophrenia, and partial complex seizure-type disorders.

In some instances, a child who presents with the clinical picture labeled borderline personality disorder (an Axis II diagnosis) may be suffering from a peculiar form of dissociative disorder, specifically disociative identity disorder (an Axis I diagnosis, rarely diagnosed in children). In both disorders there appears to be a similar etiology, including severe sexual abuse during childhood. In addition, the symptoms of the two conditions are often similar, including some form of thought dis-

Table 4–6. Borderline conditions in children: differential diagnosis

Attention-deficit/hyperactivity disorder
Major depressive disorder
Conduct disorder
Somatization disorder
Schizophrenia
Partial complex seizures
Posttraumatic stress disorder

order, and the course is often chronic and difficult, with suicide attempts a not infrequent occurrence.

The diagnostic distinction (between borderline personality disorder and dissociative identity disorder) is important because the treatments are different. In particular, in the treatment of children with dissociative phenomena (including dissociative identity disorder) an effort must be made to make the child conscious of dissociative defenses, such as splitting and regression, which appear to take place as a way of dealing with the terror of the sexual abuse, and the consequent seemingly inexplicable episodes of rage and violence that sometimes occur and which the child does not appear to remember.

The unrefined diagnosis of borderline personality disorder in childhood is often a dubious diagnosis because the symptoms are so all-inclusive and there are virtually no exclusion criteria. Further, such a global diagnosis may carry two other burdens: first, once the label is given, no further diagnostic studies may be done, and second, the treatment may be halfhearted because the prognosis is thought to be guarded, at best.

Because eventual adult outcomes are unclear (Rutter 1988), the term *borderline* in children may eventually turn out to represent an intermediate cluster of behaviors in the development of a child in whom multiple causes and possible multiple comorbidities (if that is what they are) are present. For this reason it is probably unwise to be easily satisfied with the diagnosis of borderline personality disorder in children.

Treatment and Outcome

The recognition of symptom clusters of other treatable conditions—including bipolar illness, ADHD, or complex partial seizure disorder—is very important because specific targeted treatment for these better-defined conditions may then be offered. Unfortunately, well-controlled treatment response studies for the basic borderline condition are not available at present. In one study (Bentivegna et al. 1985) only half the treated children improved, and in those who did improve, residential treatment was often requested and the treatment was long term. In any event, the fluctuating range of etiological factors and clinical features, along with the paucity of well-designed natural history and treatment outcome studies, leads to the present need to use multimodal treatment approaches (see Table 4–7).

Such treatments may include family therapy, individual therapy, parent therapy, pharmacotherapy, hospital and milieu therapy (residential treatment, day treatment, or both), and behavioral therapy. At present there are insufficient data to rely solely on any one of these approaches; all may be necessary when clinically indicated. Controlled follow-up studies are not presently available.

A major consideration in the intensive psychotherapy of borderline children, especially in the context of residential treatment, is the development of reality testing. Reality testing helps the child recognize and understand his or her reactions to various events within current life experiences, such as disappointments when parents fail to show up, provocations from peers, and imposition of controls by staff. Precipitating events, fantasies, and warded-off affects are defined for the child. In this way the child's regressive behavior is made more understandable not only to the child, but to the therapist, the staff, and the parents. Reality testing often requires the close day-to-day contact of residential treatment to understand the meaning of the child's behavior.

Reality testing clarifies not only what is real and what is fantasy, but which thoughts, fantasies, and ideas belong to the child and which belong to the therapist, parent, or child care staff member. Further, when the child demonstrates an essentially correct perception of his or her parents, this should be confirmed for the child.

Because of the instability of object representation, especially when the other person is not present, psychoanalytic interpretation of preconscious or unconscious affects, fears, or wishes is often limited in its effectiveness, at least during the early phases of treatment. In some instances, it seems as though the child can barely hold on to the concepts

Table 4–7. Borderline conditions in children: multimodal treatment

Family therapy	Individual therapy
Parent therapy	Pharmacotherapy
Hospital treatment	Milieu therapy
Behavior therapy	Residential/day hospital treatment

being conveyed in the verbal interpretation and only for the time it takes to say them; once the verbal interpretation is completed, the child seems to lose touch with the words and is at the mercy of other demands, usually primitive inner demands. Since interpretation is sometimes limited in its effectiveness in this way, working through is also difficult in these children.

This phenomenon of delayed object constancy may provide a key to an important therapeutic agent, perhaps even a key agent: the need for the reliable presence of a stable person in the child's life. Thus the single most important component of the treatment of these children may be the availability of a consistent, stable relationship.

This reflects in part a metapsychological view of the development of these children, in which early instinctual needs are still experienced, unstable early defenses (such as projection and identification) and impaired reality testing prevail, and primary process is clinically evident. The child manages to make the therapist feel a regressive pull toward similar chaotic and archaic levels of functioning. Whether the child does this intentionally as part of the child's desire to project his or her own feelings of impotence onto the therapist, leaving the child to feel temporarily more omnipotent and the therapist to feel acute discomfort, or whether the effect on the therapist is simply a product of being in the presence of such a child, is of less importance than the fact that the reaction occurs at all. That is to say, the therapist can use the reaction evoked to gain some understanding of what the child might be experiencing.

Essentially, the therapist conveys to the child, mostly through the metaphor of play, his or her understanding of what the child appears to be experiencing, consciously or preconsciously, in the here and now. Boundaries are defined: what is fantasy, what is actuality? The therapist then offers an explanation to the child that is simple and convincing—again, most often through the metaphor of play. The purpose of using the metaphor of play is to enable the child to maintain the buffer of distance and not be overwhelmed by anxiety.

At the same time, the therapist also begins to suggest other, more effective and realistic ways of obtaining gratification and dealing with staff or parents. This, too, is frequently done through play, but eventually it can be done in a straightforward, almost didactic way.

The therapist as well as the staff must maintain controls during the treatment in order to limit regressive, sexualized, and aggressive behavior to manageable levels and to avoid the excessive guilt and anxiety that is so quickly mobilized in the child who feels controls are slipping.

Similarly, when the child begins to act out aggressive impulses toward the therapist, this, too, must first be controlled before it is explored and interpreted. The acting out may begin as "accidentally" throwing some of the therapist's desk belongings on the floor, then kicking them. This may escalate to breaking the various objects, or throwing them out of the window. It is essential to prevent this kind of escalation by imposing controls early. Because children who are regressed or regressing feel acutely uncomfortable, limits must be set and regression halted to prevent any further increase in anxiety. Separations, for example, may precipitate intense feelings of abandonment, accompanied by characteristic regressive behaviors, which in turn need supportive but firm controls.

The high level of anxiety is not the only complication in the treatment of these children. Depression is often present, too. The sense of despair, hopelessness, and helplessness—as well as, at times, the frightening anger—need to be acknowledged, clarified, and understood. Usually this comes at a later stage in the treatment, when the child feels more secure in his or her relationship with the therapist, has a better defined sense of self, and is not in dread of being overwhelmed by inner feelings. Often a child who is ready to look at his or her depression is also ready to hear and comprehend a reconstruction that will help the child make some sense and give some order and meaning to his or her state of feelings and turmoil.

In any case, it is almost always useful, whether or not in the context of exploring depression, to provide the child with a meaningful history of his or her life—a history that will help the child understand why he or she had, or has, to feel and behave in certain ways. In some cases, it may be helpful to depict this pictorially, in a concrete way, with pictures and drawings, with the child participating in the drawing and labeling process.

Concomitant work with the parents is essential. Sometimes the parent is idealized by the child, even the parent who repeatedly fails the child. Sometimes the parent has an ambivalent, or unrealistic, expectation of the child. In some instances the parent must be helped to enable the child to live in another setting when that is in the best interests of the child.

The child may present to the staff a distorted picture of the parent as part of the child's unconscious attempts to ward off anxiety through splitting and projection. Sometimes the child will use the therapist and other staff members as convenient scapegoats in expressing rage at a parent.

The regressive pull and the reactions evoked in the therapist who treats a borderline child are almost pathognomonic. Anxiety and defensiveness in the presence of a child who is almost incomprehensible or threatening to lose control is a common experience. Rescue fantasies, unrealistic goals, and despair may also occur. The therapist often needs emotional support during this work with the child.

Summary and Directions for Research

The problem of the lack of definitive scientifically valid research must be addressed. In some ways, attempts at closure on the diagnosis of "borderline" are premature. Before closure, careful longitudinal studies of the developmental pathways ("chain of operations") and individual symptoms or clusters of symptoms, family studies, and both short-term and long-term treatment outcome studies are needed. There are indications that current studies are moving in these directions.

Finally, the term "borderline" in a diagnosis for children nowadays is a misleading adjective or label for a variable collection of symptoms that together may suggest the existence of multiple, pervasive, and unstable affective, behavioral, and cognitive regulatory dysfunctions, none of which has been fully validated. The clinical pictures described in this chapter might perhaps be categorized in the DSM-IV as pervasive developmental disorder not otherwise specified (PDD NOS). The clinical picture is qualified by specific dimensional descriptions of the prominent clinical features in a given child; these features can then be used as a basis for formulating and monitoring an idiosyncratic, multimodal treatment plan for that child.

Case Reports

Case 1

Timmy, a 9-year-old child, generally did fairly well in the on-grounds school. One week he became obsessed with fantasies about airplane crashes, boats being torpedoed, and people getting burned or drowned. At the same time, he began to smash toy cars and trucks, and developed a sleep disorder. The treatment team finally discovered that a few days earlier he had overheard his parents discussing a vacation trip they were going to take, and he was very resentful that they were not taking him. He was almost panicked at the thought that his hostility toward them for that, and for other things, might somehow endanger them. The "unpacking" of these fantasies and the terror that they evoked was made possible by a process of meticulous interstaff collaboration, whereby little bits of information were gathered from the school and child care staff and pieced together at a combined staff conference.

Case 2

Evelyn, a 10-year-old girl, would pull up her skirt and would tell her male therapist that he wanted to "fuck" her. She would stand on a chair, engaging in sexually provocative postures. The therapist at first attempted to reflect the child's wish for closeness, which was perceived by the child as a seduction, leading to more regressive behavior. Finally, when the child began to try to unzip the therapist's pants, the therapist recognized that it was necessary to control this behavior firmly and immediately before exploring with her why she was behaving in this way. (Early sexual abuse was suspected.)

References

Aarkrog T: The borderline concept in childhood, adolescence and adulthood. Acta Psychiatr Scand (Suppl) 293:1–300, 1981

American Psychiatric Association: Diagnostic and Statistical Manual of Mental Disorders, 3rd Edition, Revised. Washington, DC, American Psychiatric Association, 1987

American Psychiatric Association: Diagnostic and Statistical Manual of Mental Disorders, 4th Edition. Washington, DC, American Psychiatric Association, 1994

Andrulonis PA: Borderline personality subcategories in children. Paper presented at the annual meeting of the American Psychiatric Association, New York, May 1990

Bemporad JR, Smith HF, Hanson G, et al: Borderline syndromes in childhood: criteria for diagnosis. Am J Psychiatry 139:596–602, 1982

Bentivegna SW, Ward LB, Bentivegna NP: Study of a diagnostic profile of the borderline syndrome in childhood and trends in treatment outcome. Child Psychiatry Hum Dev 15:198–205, 1985

Cantwell DP: Genetic factors in the hyperkinetic syndrome. J Am Acad Child Psychiatry 15:214–233, 1976

Combrinck-Graham L: The borderline syndrome in childhood: a family systems approach. Journal of Psychotherapy 5:31–54, 1988

Ekstein R, Wallerstein J: Observations on the psychotherapy of borderline and psychotic children. Psychoanal Study Child 11:303–311, 1956

Frijling-Schreuder E: Borderline states in children. Psychoanal Study Child 24:307–327, 1969

Kernberg O: Borderline Conditions and Pathological Narcissism. New York, Aronson, 1975

Kestenbaum CJ: The borderline child at risk for major psychiatric disorder in adult life, in The Borderline Child. Edited by Robson KS. New York, McGraw-Hill, 1983, pp 49–81

Kohut HH: The Analysis of the Self. New York, International Universities Press, 1971

Lewis M: Borderline disorders in children. Child and Adolescent Psychiatry Clinics of North America 3:31–42, 1994

Lewis M, Volkmar FR: Clinical Aspects of Child and Adolescent Development, 3rd Edition. Malvern, PA, Lea & Febiger, 1990

Petti TA, Unis A: Imipramine treatment of borderline children: case reports with a controlled study. Am J Psychiatry 138:515–518, 1981

Petti TA, Vela RM: Borderline disorders of childhood: an overview. J Am Acad Child Adolesc Psychiatry 29:327–337, 1990

Pine F: A working nosology of borderline syndromes in children, in The Borderline Child. Edited by Robson KS. New York, McGraw-Hill, 1983, pp 83–99

Pine F: On the development of the "borderline" child. Am J Orthopsychiatry 56:450–457

Plomin R: The role of inheritance in behavior. Science 248:183–188, 1990

Puig-Antich J: Major depression and conduct disorder in prepuberty. J Am Acad Child Psychiatry 21:118–128, 1982

Robson KS (ed): The Borderline Child. New York, McGraw-Hill, 1983

Rogeness GA, Hernandez JM, Macedo CA, et al: Clinical characteristics of emotionally disturbed boys with very low activities of dopamine-B-hydroxylase. J Am Acad Child Psychiatry 23:203–208, 1984

Rogeness GA, Hernandez JM, Macedo CA, et al: Near-zero plasma dopamine-B-hydroxylase and conduct disorder in emotionally disturbed boys. J Am Acad Child Psychiatry 25:521–527, 1986

Rutter M: Epidemiological approaches to developmental psychopathology. Arch Gen Psychiatry 45:486–491, 1988

Schulsinger F: Psychopathology, heredity and environment. International Journal of Mental Health 1:190–206, 1972

Torgesen AM, Kringlen E: Genetic aspects of temperamental differences in infants: a study of same-sexed twins. J Am Acad Child Psychiatry 17:433–444, 1978

World Health Organization: Mental, behavioral and development disorders, clinical descriptions and diagnostic guidelines, in International Classification of Diseases, 10th Edition (draft). Geneva, World Health Organization, 1988

World Health Organization: International Classification of Diseases, 10th revision. Geneva, World Health Organization, 1992, pp 17, 198, 205

Zametkin AJ, Rapoport JL: Neurobiology of attention deficit disorder with hyperactivity: where have we come in 50 years? J Am Acad Child Adolesc Psychiatry 26:676–686, 1987

Chapter 5

Dissociative Hallucinosis and Allied Conditions

Barry Nurcombe, M.D., William Mitchell, M.D.,
Robert Begtrup, M.D., Michael Tramontana, Ph.D.,
Joseph LaBarbera, Ph.D., and John Pruitt, M.D.

Introduction

Pinel, Briquet, Charcot, Moebius, and other nineteenth-century psychiatrists linked mental disorder to life events, but Janet (1911) was the first to relate trauma to dissociation (désagrégation psychologique). In Janet's conceptual scheme, frightening experiences involving "vehement emotions" become separated or dissociated from conscious awareness as "subconscious fixed ideas." These dissociated ideas are not integrated into memory but remain latent and prone to return to consciousness as "psychological automatisms." The tendency to dissociate, Janet thought, is affected by constitutional defect (insuffisance psychologique), prior traumatic experience, the unfamiliarity and emotional impact of the decisive event, and the individual's physiological state at that time (van der Kolk and van der Hart 1989).

In *Studien in Hysterie [Studies on Hysteria]*, Breuer and Freud (1893–1895/1955) deferred extensively to Janet. Breuer and Freud described hysterical patients as suffering from inadmissible ideational "complexes," complexes that result in a "splitting" of the mind and the emergence of abnormal forms of consciousness ("hypnoid states"). Furthermore, pathological associations formed during hypnoid states fail to decay like ordinary memories, but reemerge to disrupt somatic processes in the form of hysterical sensorimotor symptoms or disturbances of consciousness. In the classic case of Anna O., for example, Breuer described a patient who suffered from hysterical paraphasia, paralyses, and episodes of trance ("somnambulism") associated with visual hallucinosis. Breuer and Freud disputed Janet's concept that dissociation is a passive process reflecting psychological weakness. Instead, they introduced the notion of an active defensive process that energetically deflects consciousness from distressing ideas. Out of this theory emerged the later concepts of repression and ego-defense.

Following World War I, Freud (1920/1955) described the "traumatic state," a condition of arousal and potential ego disintegration that occurs when stimulation overwhelms the stimulus barrier (reizschutz) and floods the ego. Those whose capacity to "bind" excitement is fully taken up by the maintenance of earlier repressions are more vulnerable to trauma. Unmastered excitement creates tension, with a debilitation of ego functions, spells of anxiety or rage, sleeplessness, repetitive traumatic dreams, mental repetitions during the day, and the secondary psychoneurotic complication known as "traumatic neurosis" (Fenichel 1946).

Interest in traumatic neurosis subsided until World War II, when massive dissociation was noted following combat stress (Grinker and Spiegel 1945; Kardiner 1941; Sargent and Slater 1940). Kardiner's studies of combat neurosis generated the concept of "physioneurosis," a persistent state of physiological hyperreactivity following a traumatic event. After the Vietnam War, Kardiner's original description of traumatic neurosis was incorporated into the definition of posttraumatic stress disorder (PTSD), a syndrome characterized by the following features: 1) intrusive traumatic thoughts and dreams, 2) traumatic reenactments, 3) the phobic avoidance or dissociation of situations, feelings, or thoughts associated with the traumatic events, 4) numbing of affect, and

5) persistent hypervigilance and autonomic hyperarousal (Furst 1967; Horowitz 1976; Kolb 1987; Trimble 1981). These descriptors were eventually included in DSM-III-R (American Psychiatric Association 1987) as the criteria for the diagnosis of posttraumatic stress disorder.

Terr (1979, 1985) extended the concept of posttraumatic stress. She described how posttraumatic symptoms in children are very similar to those in adults, despite some modifications due to developmental immaturity. Recently, Terr (1991) has distinguished the effect of single-event trauma (e.g., witnessing homicide) from that of multiple traumata (e.g., repeated physical or sexual abuse). Dissociative symptomatology is more likely to be associated with repeated traumata than with single events (Putnam 1989; Terr 1991). The most extreme form of dissociation—multiple personality—is particularly likely to be associated with childhood sexual abuse (Kluft 1985; Putnam 1989; Wilbur 1984). Sexual abuse has also been associated with a variety of trauma spectrum problems, particularly dissociative disorder, somatoform disorder, borderline personality disorder, eating disorder, psychosexual dysfunction, and paraphilia (Asher 1988; Browne and Finkelhor 1986; Gelinas 1983; Kluft 1990). Over the past century, sporadic cases have been described that combine dissociation with psychotic phenomena, particularly audiovisual hallucinosis and the disorganization of goal-directed thought. Anna O. was one such case. Many names have been attached to this condition: hysterical psychosis, hysterical hallucinations, hysterical twilight state, hysterical delirium, hysterical trance, hysterical pseudopsychosis, hysterical pseudoschizophrenia, hysterical pseudodementia, hypnoid state, somnambulistic crisis, psychological automatism, transient psychotic episode, episodic dyscontrol, and dissociative psychosis. In DSM-III-R (American Psychiatric Association 1987) it might be included under the rubric of "brief reactive psychosis." The condition is repeatedly forgotten and continually rediscovered. Recently, for example, Cutting (1992) asserted that hysterical twilight state is a "doubtful entity," despite the fact that it is now at least as prevalent among hospitalized adolescents as is schizophrenia.

In this chapter, the condition is known as "dissociative hallucinosis." The clinical features, epidemiology, differential diagnosis, comorbidity, etiology, and psychopathology of the condition are described. Evidence is presented to link dissociative hallucinosis to posttraumatic stress disorder and to differentiate it from schizophrenia, with which it is often confused. Finally, the treatment of posttraumatic stress disorder is considered. A summary with illustrative case histories ends the chapter.

Definition

Dissociative hallucinosis is a psychiatric condition characterized by the following:

1. Acute onset and brief duration; typically a condition that is recurrent or relapsing, but without subsequent deterioration of personality
2. Episodes of altered consciousness with an abstracted, trancelike, or dreamlike quality
3. Emotional turmoil, fear, anger, and hyperarousal
4. Impulsive aggression, destructiveness, suicide, and self-injury
5. Auditory and visual hallucinations, pseudohallucinations, intrusive mental imagery, and nightmares
6. Disorganization of thinking

Prevalence and Epidemiology

The prevalence of dissociative hallucinosis is uncertain. The diagnosis is likely to be overlooked if dissociative phenomena are not routinely explored in the mental status examination; nevertheless, dissociative disorders are increasingly encountered in adolescent psychiatric inpatient units. As previously described, dissociative disorders are probably more common in adolescents than is schizophrenia, with which they have often been confused. Dissociative disorders are most often recognized in adolescents, although they can also be observed in preadolescents. In hospital practice, the condition is more prevalent among females than males—possibly because males are more likely to exhibit episodic explosions of aggression and to be directed to the correctional system.

Clinical Features

Onset

The onset is often acute and dramatic and may be precipitated by apparent physical or psychological threat (e.g., an impending court appearance for the purpose of testifying against a molester) or by perceived abandonment at the hands of parental figures. In many cases the precipitant remains obscure until psychotherapy uncovers the hidden connections between spell, precipitant, and past history.

Duration

The psychotic episode usually recedes after 1 hour to 1 week. However, it may return repeatedly, particularly if hospitalization provokes regression.

Altered Consciousness

The characteristic state of altered consciousness varies from minor forgetfulness, absences, and abstracted preoccupation to full-blown trance, twilight, or hypnoid states. Some patients deliberately precipitate hypnoid states—by overbreathing, for example, or by rolling their orbits upward under fluttering eyelids. After such an episode, the patient may have complete amnesia or may have no more than a vague memory of what happened during the trance.

Emotional Turmoil

During acute hallucinosis, the patient exhibits autonomic hyperarousal and hyperactivity with fear, terror, or rage, which is congruent with the content of her mental preoccupations. The patient is convinced that she is threatened by imminent attack or loss of control. Following the episode, the patient often expresses relief and appears calm.

Impulsivity

The patient requires close observation for suicidal, self-injurious, destructive, or assaultive impulses. Wrist cutting, wall punching, and the swallowing of foreign objects are common. The patient is readily affected by other self-injurious patients; therefore "epidemics" of wrist cutting ensue. Self-injury is typically painless, and is associated with preceding increase of tension and subsequent relief or numbing of affect. It often carries ideational freight ("It gets the badness out of me"; "It gets the hurt from inside to outside.") Some patients ascribe self-injury to an attempt to counteract emotional numbness or depersonalization ("To show myself that I'm really alive.")

Abnormal Perceptions

The mental content of the trance varies from voiced thoughts and vivid mental imagery, or projected thoughts and visions that the patient realizes are imaginary (pseudohallucinations), to true hallucinations experienced and acted upon with conviction. These mental images are audiovisual reenactments or metaphorical representations of past traumatic experiences. The auditory hallucinations tend to be of the perpetrator threatening or reviling the patient or commanding the patient to hurt himself or herself. Thus the hallucinosis is clearly and directly related to the psychodynamic issues at the root of the disorder. Hypnagogic hallucinations and repetitive nightmares are also common. Like the hallucinations, nightmares are typically direct or metaphorical restatements of the original trauma.

Disorganized Thinking

During the dissociative attacks, thinking is disorganized by terrified preoccupations. Between attacks, careful mental status examination or projective testing sometimes reveals unusual associations, cognitive "slippage," and the dominance of thought by emotional themes of traumatic nature. In many cases, particularly preadolescents, the patient appears vague and subtly disoriented, without manifesting clear evidence of sensorial defect.

Premorbid Personality

In girls, borderline, narcissistic, histrionic, "as-if," or avoidant personalities are the rule. These patients are often strikingly immature, suggestible, dependent, appealing, and vulnerable. The personality type is less clear in boys, but they may have conduct disorder or have antisocial or explosive personalities.

Family Background

Families are often chaotic, with substance abuse, violence, and sexual abuse. Some families are overtly denying, rejecting, and abandoning. Others are well-meaning but strikingly insensitive and unprotective. The child may be unable to convey the nature or depth of his or her distress for fear of disrupting the family, distressing a vulnerable parent, or evoking obtuseness, denial, and rejection.

Etiology and Psychopathology

The etiology of this condition is a matter for speculation. There are probably developmental layers in its evolution—for example: 1) an inherited predisposition to dissociate, 2) severe family dysfunction, with a chaotic early childhood, disrupted and insecure attachment, and the development of a vulnerable personality, 3) failure of the dysfunctional family to protect the already vulnerable subject from sexual or physical abuse during middle childhood or early adolescence, 4) exposure of the subject, over a long period of time, to severe, repeated, inescapable sexual or physical abuse, and 5) psychological entrapment of the child, resulting in a failure to disclose the abuse because of fear of coercion by the perpetrator, parental obtuseness, parental denial, or family disintegration (Summit 1983).

Early attachment disruption, with chronically unmet dependency needs, basic mistrust, and fear of autonomy and individuation, renders the subject vulnerable to later trauma. Repeated, inescapable abuse engenders a chronic traumatic state reactivated and perpetuated by coercion, threat, extortion, and the fear of abandonment.

The child uses dissociation in order to manage trauma, shutting off cognition and shutting down emotion during the abusive experience. Genetic propensity and repeated practice enable the subject to generate a hypnoid state in order to cope with sexual coercion, physical pain, shame, or erotic arousal. Traumatic memories registered during autohypnosis are split from consciousness and remain latent until the subject is threatened with or reminded of assault, abuse, abandonment, or the mother's failure to protect the subject. At such times, hypnoid states are reactivated and dissociated memories emerge with pristine vividness and emotionality. Hypnosis and narcosynthesis have the same effect.

Despite fear of reexperiencing trauma, the subject exhibits trau-matophilia—a compulsion to reenter the abusive situation (van der Kolk et al. 1985). The reason for this compulsion is unclear, but it is germane to the tendency of some survivors to reenact trauma by putting them-selves at risk of being reabused—either by incorporating the trauma into an occupation such as prostitution (James and Meyerding 1977) or writ-ing (Terr 1990), or, in the case of men, by turning the tables and becoming child molesters or rapists themselves (Groth and Birnbaum 1979; Groth and Burgess 1979).

This hypothetical psychopathology of dissociative hallucinosis lo-cates it as a variant of posttraumatic stress disorder in which the clinical picture is dominated by dissociation and intrusive audiovisual reen-actment. The psychopathology described above explains the common overlap between dissociative hallucinosis, borderline personality disor-der, explosive disorder, somatoform disorder, bulimia, and substance abuse.

Differential Diagnosis

Dissociative hallucinosis must be distinguished from schizophrenia and schizophreniform disorder, substance-induced delirium, other organic deliriums, and temporal lobe epilepsy.

Schizophrenia and Schizophreniform Disorder

Schizophrenia and schizophreniform disorder are more likely to be as-sociated with a schizoid, schizotypal, or paranoid premorbid personality. However, only 50% of schizophrenic individuals have this kind of per-sonality. The onset in schizophrenia may be more gradual, though it is not always so. Schizophrenic affect is more likely to be flat or incongru-ent, whereas in dissociative psychosis the emotional turmoil is both char-acteristic of and consistent with the content of thought. In schizophrenia, the process of thought is typically disrupted by tangential or illogical associations, derailment of thinking, or frank blocking. How-ever, some dissociative individuals manifest vagueness and a preoccu-pied perplexity that can be mistaken for schizophrenic thought disorder.

Delusions of influence, reference, thought insertion, thought with-drawal, and somatic change are typical of schizophrenia, not dissociative hallucinosis. Visual hallucinosis is less common in schizophrenia, whereas it is characteristic of dissociative hallucinosis. While the audi-tory hallucinations of dissociative disorder are typically repetitions or fragments derived from traumatic experiences, in schizophrenia the voices are more likely to be a neutral commentary or a conversation between two people. In both conditions, insulting voices and command hallucinations are encountered.

Following the acute episode, and especially after several episodes, the schizophrenic patient's personality tends to deteriorate; the disso-ciative patient's personality does not deteriorate. Finally, whereas people with schizophrenia tend to be opaque, withdrawn, and lacking in rap-port, people with dissociative disorders (if not in trance) are interper-sonally needy, dramatic, and appealing. Unfortunately, psychological testing is not likely to be helpful in differential diagnosis unless the psy-chologist is aware of the diagnosis of dissociative hallucinosis; the minor cognitive slippages and microdissociations manifested by patients with dissociative psychosis are too often misinterpreted by the unwary as evi-dence for schizophrenic thought disorder.

Delirium

Substance-induced delirium (caused by abuse of cocaine, stimulants, or hallucinogens) is typically brief, and can be distinguished by the screen-ing of urine or blood. Other organic deliria (infectious, toxic, electrolytic, hypoglycemic, or hypoxic) are associated with clouding of the sensorium and other signs of an underlying physical illness.

Temporal Lobe Epilepsy

Temporal lobe epilepsy can be associated with a schizophrenia-like psy-chosis characterized by paranoid delusions and auditory hallucinations, but with good rapport and emotional congruence. It is quite rare. Nev-ertheless, biochemical, hematological, drug screening, and electroen-cephalographic investigations should be undertaken in all cases in which alteration of consciousness is suspected.

Brief Reactive Psychosis, Atypical Psychosis, Oneiroid State, Hysterical Pseudodementia, and Transient Psychotic Episode

It is convenient, at this point, to discuss the diagnostic relationship between dissociative hallucinosis and the following conditions: brief reactive psychosis, atypical psychosis, oneiroid state, hysterical pseudodementia, and transient psychotic episode.

In DSM-III-R (American Psychiatric Association 1987), brief reactive psychosis is defined by thought disorder (incoherence, delusions, hallucinations), catatonic or disorganized behavior, and emotional turmoil, lasting from 1 hour to 1 month, in response to severe stress. The description of this condition is sufficiently vague to suggest that some cases of dissociative hallucinosis might fit under its umbrella. The same observation applies to atypical psychosis, which is little more than a diagnostic wastebasket.

The diagnosis of oneiroid state (oneirophrenia) refers to schizophrenic symptoms associated with clouding of consciousness and "multiple scenic hallucinations in which the patient loses all contact with his real surroundings and acts like a dreamer." The fantastic content of the hallucinations is said to include "elements of a semi-realistic melodramatic kind" (Mayer-Gross et al. 1955, pp 261–262). Hysterical pseudodementia (Ganser syndrome) is classified with dissociative disorders in DSM-III-R; however, as described by Ganser (1898), the condition involves loss of memory, the enactment of factitious psychosis, attacks of excitement or stupor, clouding of consciousness, and the phenomenon of vorbeireden (approximate answering presupposing knowledge of the correct response). This dubious entity may be heterogeneous, mixing organic confusion with hysterical twilight states. Adler (1981) described an adolescent with Ganser syndrome.

The concept of "transient psychotic episode" grew out of an appreciation that certain psychoanalytic patients might be vulnerable to a transference psychosis (Knight 1953; Stern 1938). These early observations generated the concept of borderline personality. They also generated a controversy regarding the advisability of including psychotic symptomatology in the diagnostic criteria for borderline personality disorder, thus blurring the boundary between Axis I and Axis II disorders

(Widiger et al. 1992). The clinically apparent association between cluster B personality disorder and dissociative hallucinosis favors the hypothesis that a transient psychotic episode is a variant of dissociative hallucinosis in a traumatized personality.

Dissociative Hallucinosis, Schizophrenia, and Posttraumatic Stress Disorder

In this section, we will examine evidence concerning the distinction between dissociative hallucinosis and schizophrenia and the resemblance between dissociative hallucinosis and posttraumatic stress disorder.

Four senior clinicians reviewed over 800 charts of patients aged 12–17 years who had been hospitalized at Vanderbilt Child and Adolescent Hospital between 1987 and 1990. Three groups of patients were selected. The first satisfied DSM-III-R criteria for a diagnosis of schizophreniform disorder or schizophrenia; the second satisfied the criteria for dissociative hallucinosis, as described above; and the third satisfied DSM-III-R criteria for a diagnosis of posttraumatic stress disorder. Cases upon which agreement could not be reached were discarded. Table 5–1 presents the three groups and their demographic characteristics.

Each chart was classified or rated with regard to the following: 1) family factors (family intactness, family psychiatric disorder, family substance abuse, family antisocial disorder), 2) premorbid history (early developmental history, history of physical abuse, history of sexual abuse, premorbid personality), 3) clinical features (suicidality, eating problems, hallucinations, delusions, thought disorder, mood, relatedness, hyperarousal, avoidance, traumatic intrusions, sleep disturbance, sexual acting out, self-injury, substance abuse), and 4) treatment factors (response to treatment, discharge). The results of a comparison between the three groups were analyzed by the χ^2 method.

No trend ($P < .10$) or significant difference ($P < .05$) was found between the three groups with regard to family intactness, family psychiatric disorder, family substance abuse, family antisocial behavior, patient suicidality, patient eating problems, or treatment outcome. The factors for which trends and significant differences were found are reported in Tables 5–2, 5–3, and 5–4. Table 5–5 compares dissociative hallucinosis to the other three disorders by the significant characteristics listed in

Table 5–1.   Demographic characteristics of three groups of patients
ages 12–17, by disorder

	Disorder		
Characteristic	Schizophrenia ($N = 10$)	Dissociative hallucinosis ($N = 12$)	Posttraumatic stress disorder ($N = 13$)
Age			
Mean (yrs)	16.2	14.0	15.0
SD	2.5	2.0	2.3
Sex*			
M	6	2	3
F	4	11	9
Socioeconomic status (SES)**			
III	9	4	7
IV	0	4	1
V	1	4	5
Race			
White	10	11	11
Black	0	1	2
Hispanic	0	0	0

*$P < .10$. **$P < .05$.

Tables 5–1 through 5–4. It will be seen that dissociative hallucinosis resembles posttraumatic stress disorder and differs from schizophrenia in 15 items, resembles schizophrenia and differs from posttraumatic stress disorder in three items, and differs from the other two conditions in one item (history of physical abuse). Compared to the other two groups, patients with posttraumatic stress disorder appeared more likely to be involved in reckless sexual and drug-taking behavior.

In summary, therefore, dissociative hallucinosis closely resembled posttraumatic stress disorder. Dissociative hallucinosis resembled schizophrenia and differed from posttraumatic stress disorder only in the prevalence of hallucinations and because patients with posttraumatic stress disorder tended to be more adventurous sexually and in the use of illicit drugs.

Table 5–2.   Premorbid history of three groups of patients ages 12–17, by disorder

| | Disorder | | |
| | Schizophrenia | Dissociative hallucinosis | Posttraumatic stress disorder |
Characteristic	(N = 10)	(N = 12)	(N = 13)
Development***			
Normal	3	4	10
Abnormal	7	2	1
Unclear	0	6	2
Premorbid personality***			
Withdrawn	8	0	1
Aggressive	0	8	2
Other	2	5	9
Sexual abuse***			
Positive	0	12	10
Negative	10	0	3
Physical abuse***			
Positive	0	9	3
Negative	10	3	10

***$P < .01$.

Treatment

The definitive treatment of dissociative hallucinosis is unclear. Current clinical practices are derived from experience, not empirical study. The following principles should be regarded as working hypotheses that await testing.

Hospitalization

In most cases, hospitalization is indicated because of the acuity of the patient's condition, with its attendant risk of self-injury, suicide, and reckless self-endangerment. Moreover, initially the patient presents in such turmoil that a rapid, comprehensive diagnostic evaluation is required, supported by intensive nursing care. The patience, nurturance,

Table 5–3. Clinical features of three groups of patients ages 12–17, by disorder

Characteristic	Disorder		
	Schizophrenia ($N = 10$)	Dissociative hallucinosis ($N = 12$)	Posttraumatic stress disorder ($N = 13$)
Hallucinations***			
Present	7	12	3
Absent	3	0	10
Delusions***			
Present	9	1	3
Absent	1	12	9
Thought disorder***			
Present	10	4	3
Absent	0	8	10
Mood***			
Flat	7	0	1
Suspicious	1	0	1
Depressed	2	12	11
Relatedness***			
Intact	0	7	10
Withdrawn	10	3	1
Hostile	0	2	2
Hyperarousal***			
Present	0	7	9
Absent	10	0	0
Unclear	0	5	4
Avoidance***			
Present	2	8	8
Absent	8	4	5
Traumatic intrusions***			
Present	0	11	12
Absent	10	0	0
Unclear	0	2	0
Sleep disturbance*			
Present	3	9	8
Absent	7	3	5
Sexual acting out***			
Present	2	3	10
Absent	8	9	3
Self-injury**			
Present	0	6	5
Absent	10	6	8
Substance abuse*			
Present	2	2	7
Absent	8	10	6

*$P < .10$. **$P < .05$. ***$P < .01$.

Table 5–4.   Treatment of three groups of patients ages 12–17, by disorder

Characteristic	Disorder		
	Schizophrenia ($N = 10$)	Dissociative hallucinosis ($N = 12$)	Posttraumatic stress disorder ($N = 13$)
Discharge*			
Home	9	5	8
Elsewhere	1	7	5

*$P < .10$.

Table 5–5.   Comparison of dissociative hallucinosis with PTSD and schizophrenia in three groups of patients 12–17 (see Tables 5–1 through 5–4)

Resembles PTSD, differs from schizophrenia	Resembles schizophrenia, differs from PTSD	Differs from PTSD, differs from schizophrenia
Demographics		
Sex*	Hallucinosis***	Physical abuse***
Socioeconomic status (SES)***	Sexuality***	
Premorbid history		
Sex abuse***	Substance abuse*	
Development***		
Premorbid personality***		
Clinical features		
Delusions***		
Thought disorder***		
Mood***		
Relatedness***		
Hyperarousal***		
Avoidance***		
Intrusions***		
Sleep disturbance*		
Self-injury**		
Treatment		
Discharge*		

Notes.   Only characteristics for which $P \leq .10$ are listed. PTSD: Posttraumatic stress disorder.
*$P < .10$. **$P < .05$. ***$P < .01$.

and optimism of the nursing staff are crucial to the success of treatment. Often it is to one of them that the patient will first disclose the history of sexual abuse. The aim is to provide security, engender trust, and facilitate disclosure in order to help the patient confront and assimilate fearful memories, and to begin the resolution of trauma. Confrontation and assimilation are never smooth; the staff can anticipate avoidance, divisiveness, manipulation, somatization, self-injury, regression, and episodes of dissociation, even full-blown trances or twilight states. Assisted nutrition and hydration may be required in extreme circumstances.

Individual Psychotherapy

With younger patients, a female therapist may be required. With older adolescents, the therapist's experience is more important than his or her sex. The therapist helps the patient develop trust and a working alliance, partly through the provision of a role model who guides the patient to recover traumatic memories gradually, with abreaction, desensitization, reappraisal, and the consideration of coping options that are preferable to continuing emotional dyscontrol or traumatophilic revictimization. Older patients may be assisted by reading graduated texts such as *The Courage to Heal Workbook* (Davis 1990), in parallel with individual psychotherapy.

Sometimes, the patient presents the embryonic features of multiple personality disorder. Unless this form of psychopathology is well developed, the rudimentary personifications are better ignored, lest inadvertent reinforcement promote their proliferation.

Most difficult of all are those whose severe dissociative symptoms are accompanied by a dependent, manipulative personality. Needy and appealing, feeding the staff with half-truths and partial disclosures, prone to induce hypnoid trances, and liable to injure themselves when threatened, they tax the staff's tolerance for ambiguity and risk. Eating problems (particularly self-induced vomiting) and somatoform symptoms (pseudoseizures, for example) sometimes complicate treatment. Treatment is likely to be further compromised if the patient's parents reject or abandon him or her and if external utilization reviewers press for premature discharge.

Group and Family Therapy

The importance of peer support cannot be overemphasized. Abused adolescents identify with others who have the courage to confront, disclose, and struggle with unresolved trauma. Sexual abuse group therapy, mixing both sexes, and led by male and female cotherapists, is an essential ingredient of therapy.

If the family is prepared to cooperate in treatment, the following goals are appropriate: 1) education in the nature and cause of the problem, 2) avoidance of secrecy and the promotion of more direct communication and listening skills, 3) enhancement of mutual emotional sensitivity, and 4) the alteration of role reversal, enmeshment, and other boundary pathology. Although family members may be limited in what they can achieve, all goals should be addressed. Perpetrators who are motivated to seek help should be referred to an appropriate treatment center.

Confidentiality

Therapeutic confidentiality is diluted by the extent to which the patient is prepared to discuss private matters in group therapy. Complications arise, however, when a disclosure compels the staff to report the abuse to a child protective services agency. The patient should be informed that this is required by law. It commonly blocks therapeutic progress, at least temporarily.

Pharmacotherapy

There have been few empirical studies of the efficacy of pharmacotherapy in posttraumatic stress disorder (see reviews by Friedman 1988 and Davidson and Nemeroff 1989) and only one on its efficacy with children (Famularo et al. 1988). As an adjunct to psychosocial therapies, drugs are prescribed with the following goals in mind: 1) to control acute turmoil, 2) to alleviate intrusive symptoms, 3) to alleviate anxiety and hyperarousal, 4) to improve sleep, 5) to regulate impulsivity and emotional lability, and 6) to counteract depression.

Neuroleptics may be of use during acute turmoil but they are commonly overprescribed, probably as a result of diagnostic confusion with schizophrenia. They should not be used long term.

Antidepressants, particularly heterocyclic antidepressants and serotonin reuptake inhibitors (SRIs), are probably the drugs of choice. There is evidence in adults that heterocyclics and monoamine oxidase inhibitors dampen intrusive thoughts and hyperarousal and alleviate depression, anhedonia, insomnia, and somatization. Benzodiazepines have been recommended because of their purported reduction of neuronal "kindling" in the limbic system. Clonidine, an alpha-2-adrenergic agonist, has been used experimentally, as have propranolol, carbamazepine, and lithium for their hypothetical effect on impulsivity, lability, and aggressive dyscontrol.

Summary

Clinical evidence supports the concept that dissociative hallucinosis is a severe variant of posttraumatic stress disorder and that it is distinct from schizophrenia with which it has often been confused. Among adolescents, it is more common than schizophrenia and is particularly prevalent among adolescent females hospitalized for psychotic turmoil. It is probable that many males with this disorder are admitted to the correctional system.

The distinction from schizophrenia is of more than theoretical significance, for the treatment of the two conditions is quite different. People with schizophrenia are likely to be disturbed by individual and group pressures toward the disclosure and resolution of trauma, a treatment strategy crucial to the therapy of patients with dissociative hallucinosis. Pharmacotherapy is adjunctive in the treatment of dissociative disorder rather than central as it is in schizophrenia. The prolonged use of neuroleptics is inadvisable in dissociative conditions, for it may aggravate this pathological defense mechanism.

The link between this condition and posttraumatic stress disorder explains the prevalence of suicidality, self-injury, and hyperarousal in dissociative hallucinosis, and its frequent association with eating problems, conversion hysteria, cluster B personality disorder, and, in males, episodic dyscontrol and intermittent explosiveness.

Case Reports

Case 1

A 15-year-old girl was in outpatient psychotherapy following the disclosure of sexual abuse perpetrated on her, over a period of 12 months, by the father of a friend. The perpetrator had been charged with rape, and further legal proceedings against him were pending. However, few details of the abuse had been disclosed before the patient became acutely suicidal and was admitted to the hospital. A waiflike ingenue, the patient soon won the hearts of the staff. She formed a close relationship with a borderline youth (who had also been sexually abused), copying his taste in music and imitating his feigned English accent. Alternating between periods of giggling avoidance, depressed withdrawal, and self-injuriousness, she cut her wrists with a variety of sharp objects, surreptitiously made herself vomit after eating, and put antidepressant pills into her cheek. Episodes of dreamy abstraction developed into full-blown trances during which the patient spoke to imaginary figures. The chief imaginary figure was the perpetrator who threatened to make her his own forever, perform oral sex on her (i.e., to "eat" her), rape her, and kill her parents. She found that she could induce trances by hyperventilating and that wrist cutting relieved her anguish: "It gets the hurt from inside to outside where it can heal." She spoke of having been "robbed of her childhood," and she said that she had been made "a wife and mother" before her time (hinting at a past pregnancy).

Following a combination of individual psychotherapy, group therapy, and antidepressant medication, she improved somewhat. She disclosed that the sexual abuse had involved her older brother as well as the neighbor. Nevertheless, her allegations of sexual abuse contained discrepancies. Why had she allowed the older man to abuse her? Purportedly, because he threatened to tell the police that her father had abused her. Why was this threat so persuasive? She would not say. Soon after discharge from hospital to the care of her parents, she telephoned her psychotherapist, saying that she had a gun to her head and would pull the trigger unless the hospital readmitted her. During the first few weeks following readmission, she began again to manifest dissociative trances during which she heard the voice of the perpetrator making obscene threats. Eventually, she disclosed that her father had sexually abused her and that she did not want to return home.

Case 2

The patient was a 15-year-old male. When he was 5 years old, his father deserted the family, and his mother subsequently lived with a series of disreputable boyfriends. For 6 years during his middle childhood, he was physically and sexually abused by one of these boyfriends, an alcoholic man who was apparently resentful of the patient's closeness to the mother. Lurching home drunk at night, the older man would burst into the boy's bedroom, drag him out, beat him about the head, and force him to perform fellatio. At no time did the cowed, drug-addicted mother attempt to protect the child from his assailant. When the patient was 11 years old, he stabbed the perpetrator through the side with a sword and reported him to the police. The man was subsequently removed from the home. The patient was admitted to the hospital 4 years afterward, following repeated episodes, usually at night and without warning, during which he would lose control of his anger and destroy furniture. On one such occasion, in response to a commanding voice, he set fire to a neighbor's house. He said that, although he had the impulse to attack people, he had never actually done so.

On the second day after admission to the hospital, he observed a male peer flirting with a female peer, and he became increasingly tense and withdrawn. Suddenly he became unresponsive, threw furniture around the room, punched the wall, and had to be restrained. The episode lasted about 1 hour. Afterward, he remembered being angered by the way the male patient was "using" the female patient. He recalled that, during the spell, he saw his mother's former boyfriend and heard the man command him to kill somebody and do away with himself. After the patient had psychotherapy and pharmacotherapy, his episodes of explosive dyscontrol, hallucinosis, and self-injury became less frequent and less intense. However, the episodes recurred when, after discharge, the patient rounded the aisle of a local supermarket to come face to face with the person who had originally abused him.

References

Adler R: Pseudodementia or Ganser syndrome in a ten year old boy. Aust N Z J Psychiatry 15:339–342, 1981

American Psychiatric Association: Diagnostic and Statistical Manual of Mental Disorders, 3rd Edition, Revised. Washington, DC, American Psychiatric Association, 1987

Asher SJ: The effects of childhood sexual abuse: a review of the issues and evidence, in Handbook on Sexual Abuse of Children. Edited by Walker LEA. New York, Springer, 1988, pp 30–54

Breuer J, Freud S: Studies on hysteria (1893–1895), in Standard Edition of the Complete Psychological Works of Sigmund Freud, Vol 2. Translated and edited by Strachey J. London, Hogarth Press, 1955, pp 1–319

Browne A, Finkelhor D: The impact of child sexual abuse: a review of the research. Psychol Bull 99:66–77, 1986

Cutting J: Neuropsychiatric aspects of attention and consciousness, in Textbook of Neuropsychiatry. Edited by Yudofsky SC, Hales RE. Washington, DC, American Psychiatric Press, 1992

Davidson JRT, Nemeroff CB: Pharmacotherapy in post-traumatic stress disorder: historical and clinical considerations and future directions. Psychopharmacol Bull 25:422–425, 1989

Davis L: The Courage to Heal Workbook. New York, Harper & Row, 1990

Famularo R, Kinscherff R, Fenton T: Propanolol treatment for childhood post-traumatic stress disorder, acute type. Am J Dis Child 142:1244–1247, 1988

Fenichel O: The Psychoanalytic Theory of Neurosis. London, Routledge & Kegan Paul, 1946

Friedman MJ: Toward rational pharmacotherapy for post-traumatic stress disorder: an interim report. Am J Psychiatry 145:281–285, 1988

Freud S: Beyond the pleasure principle (1920), in Standard Edition of the Complete Psychological Works of Sigmund Freud, Vol 18. Translated and edited by Strachey J. London, Hogarth Press, 1955, pp 1–64

Furst E (ed): Psychic Trauma. New York, Basic Books, 1967

Ganser SJM: Uber einem eigenartigen hysterischen Dammerzustand. Archiven von Psychiatrie und Nervenkrankheiten 30:633–640, 1898

Gelinas DJ: The persisting negative effects of incest. Psychiatry 46:312–333, 1983

Grinker RR, Spiegel JJ: Men Under Stress. New York, McGraw-Hill, 1945

Groth AN, Birnbaum HJ: Men Who Rape: The Psychology of the Offender. New York, Plenum, 1979

Groth AN, Burgess AW: Sexual trauma in the life histories of rapists and child molesters. Victimology: An International Journal 4:10–16, 1979

Horowitz MJ: Stress Response Syndromes. New York, Jason Aronson, 1976

James J, Meyerding J: Early sexual experience as a factor in prostitution. Arch Sex Behav 7:31–42, 1977

Janet P: L'Etat Mental des Hystériques, 2nd Edition. Paris, Alcan, 1911

Kardiner A: The Traumatic Neuroses of War. New York, Hoeber, 1941

Kluft RP (ed): Childhood Antecedents of Multiple Personality. Washington, DC, American Psychiatric Press, 1985

Kluft RP (ed): Incest-Related Syndromes of Adult Psychopathology. Washington, DC, American Psychiatric Press, 1990

Knight R: Borderline states. Bull Menninger Clin 17:1–12, 1953

Kolb LC: A neuropsychological hypothesis explaining post-traumatic stress disorders. Am J Psychiatry 144:989–995, 1987

Mayer-Gross W, Slater E, Roth M: Clinical Psychiatry. London, Cassell, 1955

Putnam FW: Diagnosis and Treatment of Multiple Personality. New York, Guilford, 1989

Sargent WW, Slater E: Acute war neuroses. Lancet 2:1–2, 1940

Stern A: Psychoanalytic investigation and therapy in the borderline group of neuroses. Psychoanal Q 7:467–489, 1938

Summit RR: The child sexual abuse accommodation syndrome. Child Abuse Negl 7:177–193, 1983

Terr LC: Children of Chowchilla: a study of psychic trauma. Psychoanal Study Child 34:547–623, 1979

Terr LC: Psychic trauma in children and adolescents. Psychiatr Clin North Am 8:815–835, 1985

Terr LC: Too Scared to Cry. New York, Harper & Row, 1990

Terr LC: Childhood traumas: an outline and overview. Am J Psychiatry 148:10–20, 1991

Trimble MR: Post-Traumatic Neurosis. New York, Wiley, 1981

van der Kolk BA, van der Hart O: Pierre Janet and the breakdown of adaptation in psychological trauma. Am J Psychiatry 146:1530–1540, 1989

van der Kolk BA, Greenberg M, Boyd H, et al: Inescapable shock, neurotransmitters, and addiction to trauma. Biol Psychiatry 20:314–325, 1985

Widiger TA, Miele GM, Tilly SM: Alternative perspectives on the diagnosis of borderline personality disorder, in Borderline Personality Disorder. Edited by Clarkin JF, Marziali E, Monroe-Blum H. New York, Guilford, 1992

Wilbur CB: Multiple personality and child abuse. Psychiatr Clin North Am 7:3–7, 1984

Chapter 6

Autistic Disorder

Fred R. Volkmar, M.D., Ami Klin, Ph.D.,
Wendy D. Marans, M.S., and Christopher J. McDougle, M.D.

Introduction

In his original description of the syndrome of early infantile autism, Kanner (1943) provided detailed clinical descriptions of 11 children who, in contrast to other developing infants, appeared to present a remarkable lack of interest in other people (autism); this disability appeared congenital in nature. Kanner was careful to frame the lack of social interest developmentally and noted, in contrast, the fascination these children showed with aspects of the nonsocial environment. These children also presented a number of unusual behavioral and developmental features: a marked resistance to change ("insistence on sameness"), stereotyped and self-stimulatory movements, and occasional areas of isolated interest or proficiency. When these children developed language, it was of an unusual type—characterized, for example, by

The support of grants from the National Institute of Mental Health to Dr. Volkmar (MH-30929), National Institute of Child Health and Human Development Grant HD03008, and Mental Health Clinical Research Center Grant 30929 are gratefully acknowledged.

echolalia, pronoun reversal, and problems with the social uses of language. Kanner's description remains a classic contribution to psychiatric taxonomy; it has profoundly influenced the work of several generations of clinicians and investigators in the 50 years since its publication.

At the same time, certain aspects of Kanner's original report proved to be false leads for research. The use of the word *autism* suggested a similarity to schizophrenia. Many early investigators assumed, largely on the basis of severity, a fundamental continuity between autism and schizophrenia (Bender 1947). Kanner's observation of a preponderance of higher-socioeconomic-status parents in the sample led to an assumption that autism was a disorder more common among more educated and successful parents. This observation failed to address the possibility of selective bias in case referral: presumably the most intelligent and affluent parents would be able to find a clinician interested in the very unusual constellation of problems their children exhibited. More recent work, which controls for bias in case detection, does not show any particular social class predominance (Schopler et al. 1980a). Because the children in Kanner's sample performed well on certain portions of IQ tests, Kanner speculated that the children had the potential for normal intelligence; it has become amply apparent that this is not true and that most individuals with autism function in the mentally retarded range (Lockyer and Rutter 1969). Although relative strengths in certain cognitive skills (e.g., block design) are often observed, overall performance is usually quite poor (Rumsey 1992).

One observation unfortunately misled early investigators about the origins of the condition: Kanner observed problems in parent-child interaction and unusual personality features of parents. This was taken to suggest a role of parental psychopathology in production of the syndrome. There was, however, less appreciation than there is now of the potential role of an autistic child in producing impaired interaction (Bell and Harper 1977). Although the notion that parents somehow "caused" autism seemed difficult to reconcile with Kanner's speculation that the disorder was congenital, some clinicians (e.g., Bettelheim 1967) emphasized the role of parental psychopathology in syndrome pathogenesis. Finally, the attractive appearance of the children and an apparent absence of signs of nervous system dysfunction led Kanner to suggest that the disorder was not associated with other medical conditions. However, as autistic children were followed over time and as larger samples of cases could be studied, it became apparent that autism was associated with various medical conditions and that seizures often developed in affected individuals in adolescence (Rutter 1970).

For many years after Kanner's original report there was considerable disagreement about the validity of autism, that is, as a disorder separate from childhood schizophrenia. This disagreement was clarified as several different lines of data became available. Studies of large series of "psychotic" children (Kolvin 1971; Makita 1966; Volkmar et al. 1988b) revealed a bimodal distribution of onset: some children exhibited severe disturbance very early in life, whereas others had a period of several, or many, years of reasonably normal development before the onset of their difficulties (see Figure 6–1). The group that exhibited onset in the first year or two of life had clinical features closely resembling those of Kan-

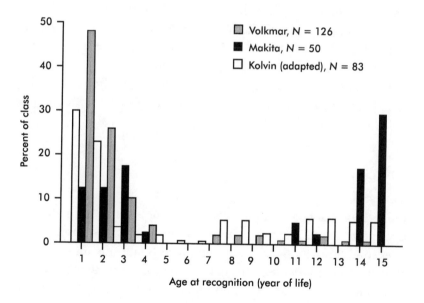

Figure 6–1. Age at recognition of onset in three studies of consecutive series of children with "psychosis."

Source. Kolvin data adapted from Kolvin 1971. Makita data from Makita 1966. Volkmar data from Volkmar et al. 1988b.

ner's description of autism; members of their family did not exhibit a greater than expected frequency of schizophrenia. However, the cases in which onset occurred later in childhood appeared to have delusions, hallucinations, and other features more consistent with those observed in adults with schizophrenia; in this group there was a high frequency of schizophrenia in first-degree relatives. Similarly, the course of the two disorders and their clinical features were markedly different (Rutter 1972).

Other studies suggested important differences between autism and the developmental language disorders as well (Rutter 1978a). Although autism coexisted with mental retardation, the cognitive profile in autism differed from that in mental retardation not associated with autism. In addition, the social and communication skills of children with autism were more delayed and impaired than would be expected based on level of mental retardation alone (Klin and Shephard 1994). The observation of high rates of seizure disorder in samples of autistic individuals as they entered adolescence was similarly a major difference from schizophrenia (Rutter 1970, 1972). Although not included in either the first or second edition of the Diagnostic and Statistical Manual, the large body of data on the validity of autism as a diagnostic category apart from schizophrenia led to its inclusion in DSM-III (American Psychiatric Association 1980).

Definition

Autism is probably one of the strongest examples of a disorder in child psychiatry; features central to its definition are clear and, unlike many other conditions, it does not seem simply to "shade off" into normality (Rutter and Garmezy 1983). Given the general agreement on the validity of autism and of features relevant to its definition, it is not surprising that both categorical and dimensional definitions have been employed; what is somewhat more surprising is the disagreement around important aspects of syndrome definition.

In keeping with Kanner's original (1943) report, Rutter's (1978b) synthesis of it, and subsequent research, four features have usually been emphasized in categorical definitions: 1) the very early onset of the condition, 2) social dysfunction (autism) that is not simply a function of any associated mental retardation, 3) disturbances in communication (not just in language), which also do not simply reflect mental handicap, and 4) a somewhat heterogeneous group of behaviors (stereotypies, resistance to change, and so forth) usually subsumed under the term "insistence on sameness." Other aspects of the disorder—perceptual abnormalities and unusual rates or sequences of development—have sometimes been included in categorical diagnostic systems (e.g., Ritvo and Freeman 1978), although more typically these have been regarded as associated features of the condition.

Although the application of categorical diagnostic criteria has represented an advance in the diagnosis of autism and other disorders (Spitzer et al. 1978), it should be noted that ambiguities can surround the application of categorical diagnostic criteria. More global and broadly framed criteria—for example, pervasive unresponsiveness to others—capture some aspects of underlying diagnostic constructs but do not provide straightforward and truly operational application guidelines to clinicians. On the other hand, DSM-III-R (American Psychiatric Association 1987) tended to overemphasize the examples it uses within criteria. A further problem is introduced by the broad range of syndrome expression in autism over age and developmental level; criteria must therefore encompass both very young children and adults and both very retarded individuals with autism and individuals with above-average IQs (Volkmar and Cohen 1988).

Various dimensional assessment instruments for autism have also been developed and their psychometric properties examined (Parks 1983). Dimensional assessment instruments have certain advantages in that a broader range and number of behaviors can be sampled in relation to underlying diagnostic constructs. For example, rather than relying on a single diagnostic criterion, such as pervasive social unresponsiveness, to capture the nature of autistic social dysfunction, a number of examples of specific social behaviors or of observations of social behavior in standard situations can be employed.

Both categorical and dimensional approaches face similar problems relative to examination of deviant behaviors over a broad range of syndrome expression. Some instruments focus exclusively on historical information, such as parental report of the child's behavior and

development before the fifth birthday, whereas other instruments focus
on contemporaneous ratings—by teachers, for example. Still other instruments focus on contemporaneous examination of the child in a
structured situation by a trained examiner. There are advantages and
disadvantages to each of these approaches. The use of parents to gain
information about early development may not be particularly reliable;
similarly, teacher ratings may be associated with poor reliability and rater
bias because teachers may not have had much experience in evaluating
the kinds of highly unusual behaviors exhibited by autistic children
(Parks 1983). Yet another problem is introduced by the lack, at least until
recently, of metrics for social development (Volkmar et al. 1992a, 1992b).
Diagnostic disagreements, reflecting these problems and broader philosophical issues, are usually most pronounced at the extremes of syndrome expression—in the very young or very old and in individuals with
profound mental retardation or very high IQ. For example, among the
very retarded the frequency of autistic-like behaviors such as stereotypies
increases (Adrien et al. 1987). Given that autism is an uncommon condition, many clinicians have only limited experience with the range of
syndrome expression; not surprisingly, clinician experience is highly important for diagnostic reliability (Volkmar et al. 1994).

Categorical Definitions

DSM-III

Autism was not included as an official diagnostic category until DSM-III,
where it was included in a new class of disorders: the pervasive developmental disorders (PDDs). The name of this class of disorders was meant
to emphasize the severity of the conditions included in the class across
multiple sectors of functioning. The definition of *infantile autism (IA)*
in DSM-III was largely consistent with Rutter's (1978b) synthesis of Kanner's description. The DSM-III definition tended to emphasize the clinical expression of the disorder in its "classic" or "infantile" form. Four
other disorders were included in the PDD class. Residual infantile autism
was to be used when an individual had once met criteria for infantile
autism but no longer did so. Childhood-onset PDD and a corresponding
residual category were included to encompass the presumably very rare
child who developed an autistic-like condition after several years of nor-

mal development, and an atypical PDD category was included for "subthreshold" cases that exhibited features generally similar to those exhibited by individuals with autism but that failed to meet explicit diagnostic criteria (see Chapters 7 and 8 for additional discussion).

To achieve a diagnosis of IA in DSM-III, the patient had to exhibit early onset (less than 30 months) of pervasive social impairment, gross deficits in language development when speech was present, and bizarre responses to the environment. By definition the individual could not present delusions or hallucinations as in schizophrenia, reflecting the general consensus that autism and childhood schizophrenia were not related conditions.

The DSM-III approach was an advance in important ways. The diagnosis of autism could officially be made, the general features outlined in the criteria had historical and conceptual continuity with features generally agreed upon as important in its definition, and the use of explicit criteria was clearly an improvement. Unfortunately, the DSM-III definition proved unsatisfactory in other respects. The definition was indeed most appropriate for younger and more impaired children (e.g., those who exhibited the pervasive unrelatedness). However, by school age many children exhibited some, if highly impaired, social skills so that they would technically no longer exhibit pervasive social unresponsiveness. It seemed unfortunate that the term *residual infantile autism* had to be applied in such cases because the term *residual* seemed to minimize both the continuity of syndrome expression over time and the often major problems that individuals with the disorder continued to exhibit (Rumsey et al. 1985; Schopler and Mesibov 1983; Volkmar and Cohen 1985). The DSM-III definition also failed to address the importance of broader aspects of communicative impairment, not just limited to language as such (Volkmar and Cohen 1988). The approach to diagnosis of autism in individuals with hallucinations and delusions was unsatisfactory; although autism and schizophrenia were apparently unrelated, it was not clear why having autism should act to protect an individual from developing schizophrenia in some instances.

The inclusion of other categories within the PDD class also was problematic. The definition of childhood-onset PDD was highly detailed, in some respects more detailed than that for IA, but children with this condition were rarely seen and this concept was not meant to be analogous to what would otherwise appear to be a similar disorder in ICD-9 (World Health Organization 1977)—disintegrative psychosis (see Chapter 8). Finally, the atypical PDD category was largely congruent with, but unintentionally suggestive of, a previous diagnostic concept— atypical personality development (Rank 1949). Major revisions were made in DSM-III-R to address these issues.

DSM-III-R

The definition of *autistic disorder* in DSM-III-R was, as its name implies, much more developmentally oriented (Volkmar et al. 1992a). This definition was much influenced by the view of Lorna Wing and her colleagues (e.g., Wing and Atwood 1987), who argued for a broader definition. The use of historical information was intentionally avoided. Criteria were framed so as to be applicable to the entire range of syndrome expression, and the onset of the disorder in the first years of life was no longer a necessary diagnostic feature, although onset of the syndrome in childhood was required. The criteria provided in DSM-III-R were much more detailed than previously, examples were included within the criteria, and other aspects of syndrome expression—notably related to deficits in symbolic or imaginative play—were included. The 16 DSM-III-R criteria were grouped in 3 broad categories (impairment in social development, in communication/play/imagination, and in range of interests and activities). Scoring rules for these criteria were established on the basis of a national field trial (Siegel et al. 1990; Spitzer and Siegel 1990). For a diagnosis of autistic disorder, the individual had to exhibit at least 8 of the 16 criteria with a minimum number of criteria specified from each category (at least two from the social category and one criterion from each of the other two clusters).

These changes in the definition of autism meant that the residual category used in DSM-III was no longer needed; similarly the new definition appeared to obviate the need for inclusion of a special category for individuals whose autistic-like disorder developed after age 3. Changes in the name of the subthreshold PDD category (pervasive developmental disorder not otherwise specified, or PDD NOS) clarified that precise overlap with the older term *atypical personality development* was not intended.

Despite the attempts to improve the definition of autism in DSM-III, the new definition of the disorder had several shortcomings. Most prominent among these was the overbroadening of the definition: many individuals who were younger or who were very seriously mentally retarded would, for the first time, receive a diagnosis of autistic disorder (Volkmar et al. 1988a). Several studies (Factor et al. 1989; Hertzig et al. 1990; Szatmari 1992; Volkmar et al. 1988a) suggested that DSM-III-R overdiagnosed the presence of autism relative either to the diagnosis of experienced clinicians or relative to diagnoses based on DSM-III criteria or ICD-10 draft criteria (Volkmar et al. 1992b). In view of the impact of false-negative cases for research, comparisons of studies using different criteria, and the planning and delivery of educational and other interventions, this overdiagnosis was problematic for investigators as well as clinicians.

ICD-10

The ICD-10 (World Health Organization 1990) draft definition of the disorder produced results similar to those generated by DSM-III (if the DSM-III diagnosis was taken in its lifetime sense). The draft definition also appeared to approximate most closely the diagnoses assigned by experienced clinicians (Volkmar et al. 1992b). Another difference between DSM-III-R and ICD-10 was the inclusion in ICD-10 of various other nonautistic PDDs: Rett's disorder, Asperger's disorder, childhood disintegrative disorder, and so forth (see Chapters 7 and 8). The correspondence between DSM-III, DSM-III-R, and ICD-10 PDDs is summarized in Table 6–1. The inclusion of additional disorders with some similarity to autism was meant to foster research on these conditions and made it possible to produce a somewhat more stringent definition of autism. The differences between DSM-III-R and ICD-10 were thus further emphasized, and the potential adverse effects of two markedly different official diagnostic systems were clear (Rutter and Schopler 1992).

DSM-IV

As a result of the concerns about DSM-III-R and its compatibility with ICD-10, a large, multisite, international field trial was undertaken (Volk-

Table 6–1.   Correspondence of categories of pervasive developmental disorder (PDD) in DSM-III, DSM-III-R, and ICD-10

DSM-III	DSM-III-R	ICD-10
Infantile autism	Autistic disorder	Childhood autism
Residual infantile autism	Autistic disorder	Childhood autism
Childhood-onset PDD	?Autistic disorder	?Atypical autism
Residual childhood-onset PDD	?Autistic disorder	?Atypical autism
Atypical PDD	PDD NOS	Atypical autism/ unspecified PDD
?Atypical PDD	?PDD NOS	Childhood disintegrative disorder
?Atypical PDD	?Autistic disorder	Asperger's disorder
?Atypical PDD	?PDD NOS	Rett's disorder

mar et al. 1994). Goals of this field trial included development of a reliable and efficient diagnostic system for autism (and for other disorders that would be included within the PDD class) and achievement of a reasonable balance of sensitivity and specificity (avoiding overdiagnosis of autism in cases with severe retardation and underdiagnosis in individuals with normal IQ levels). The nature of the DSM-III-R overdiagnosis of the condition was to be established, if this indeed was the case, and various alternatives for DSM-IV (American Psychiatric Association 1994) were to be outlined. Issues of criterion and disorder convergence with ICD-10 in the PDD class were also to be explicitly addressed. At the same time, the important differences in ICD and DSM were noted, most notably in the ICD-10 approach of having separate guidelines for clinicians apart from research criteria (Volkmar et al. 1994).

For the DSM-IV field trial, data were collected on a sample of nearly a thousand individuals with a diagnosis of autism or other disorders in a range of settings and sites. Cases were rated by examiners with a range of experience and professional background; cases typically were rated on the basis of contemporaneous examination and past records (not just on record review). Five sites provided ratings on 100 consecutive cases over the period of a year; other sites provided ratings on a smaller number of cases. Comparison cases included those in which the differential diagnosis would reasonably include autism. Certain cases, such as those with a diagnosis of a nonautistic PDD as included in ICD-10, or cases with certain characteristics (e.g., high-functioning females with autism), were intentionally oversampled. Ratings were made of DSM-III, DSM-III-R, and ICD-10 criteria as well as of a range of potential new criteria; basic information was also obtained on the case and rater(s) with due attention to issues such as reliability of ratings.

From the results of the field trial, it did appear that the DSM-III-R definition was too broad and that it tended to overdiagnose autism in individuals with severe mental retardation. The ICD-10 approach was noted to have the best overall agreement with clinician diagnosis. Similarly, the available data provided some support for inclusion of other disorders within the PDD class.

A series of alternatives for DSM-IV were outlined. In addition, based on these analyses and those related to the development of ICD-10, it appeared that several of the 20 detailed ICD-10 criteria could be eliminated with minimal effect on efficiency of the definition. A decision, based both on data and philosophical considerations, was made to establish conceptual convergence of DSM-IV and ICD-10 definitions of autism and related PDD disorders.

The DSM-IV definition of autism consists of 12 criteria equally divided among the 3 clusters of symptoms (social interaction, communication/play/imagination, and restricted patterns of interest and behavior) and an age-at-onset criterion; the definition is conceptually the same as that employed in ICD-10. The DSM-IV definition appears in Table 6–2.

Dimensional Definitions

An alternative approach to diagnosis has used the assessment of the dimensions of function and dysfunction. As noted previously, there are various complications for development and use of such instruments that generally have not been explicitly keyed to categorical diagnostic criteria. Historically, Rimland's E-2 Diagnostic Checklist (see Rimland 1984) was influential. This questionnaire for parents inquired about the presence of autistic-like behaviors during the preschool years. The Autism Behavior Checklist (ABC) (Krug et al. 1980) was designed for teachers; it con-

---

Table 6–2.   DSM-IV diagnostic criteria for autistic disorder

---

A. A total of six (or more) items from (1), (2), and (3), with at least two from (1), and one each from (2) and (3):

(1) qualitative impairment in social interaction, as manifested by at least two of the following:

(a) marked impairment in the use of multiple nonverbal behaviors such as eye-to-eye gaze, facial expression, body postures, and gestures to regulate social interaction
(b) failure to develop peer relationships appropriate to developmental level
(c) a lack of spontaneous seeking to share enjoyment, interests, or achievements with other people (e.g., by a lack of showing, bringing, or pointing out objects of interest)
(d) lack of social or emotional reciprocity

(2) qualitative impairments in communication as manifested by at least one of the following:

(a) delay in, or total lack of, the development of spoken language (not accompanied by an attempt to compensate through alternative modes of communication such as gesture or mime)
(b) in individuals with adequate speech, marked impairment in the ability to initiate or sustain a conversation with others
(c) stereotyped and repetitive use of language or idiosyncratic language
(d) lack of varied, spontaneous make-believe play or social imitative play appropriate to developmental level

(3) restricted repetitive and stereotyped patterns of behavior, interests, and activities, as manifested by at least one of the following:

(a) encompassing preoccupation with one or more stereotyped and restricted patterns of interest that is abnormal either in intensity or focus
(b) apparently inflexible adherence to specific, nonfunctional routines or rituals
(c) stereotyped and repetitive motor mannerisms (e.g., hand or finger flapping or twisting, or complex whole-body movements)
(d) persistent preoccupation with parts of objects

B. Delays or abnormal functioning in at least one of the following areas, with onset prior to age 3 years: (1) social interaction, (2) language as used in social communication, or (3) symbolic or imaginative play.

C. The disturbance is not better accounted for by Rett's disorder or childhood disintegrative disorder.

Source.   American Psychiatric Association, Diagnostic and Statistical Manual of Mental Disorders, 4th Edition. Washington, DC, American Psychiatric Association, 1994, pp. 70–71. Used with permission.

sists of 57 yes-or-no items, each of which is weighted in terms of its relevance to a diagnosis of autism. This instrument is applicable through a wide age range and is readily used. The Childhood Autism Rating Scale (CARS) (Schopler et al. 1980b) provides a more detailed assessment of behavior as completed by a trained examiner in a structured setting. Both the ABC and the CARS provide estimates of the severity of autistic-like behaviors and the probability that an individual is autistic. Two recent instruments are explicitly oriented to categorical diagnostic criteria for autism. The Autism Diagnostic Interview (ADI) (Le Couteur et al. 1989) is administered as a structured interview to parents and the Autism Diagnostic Observation Schedule (ADOS) (Lord et al. 1989) is administered as a structured assessment of the child. These scales are presently being revised to correspond to ICD-10 and DSM-IV criteria.

Instruments designed for screening probably should err on the side of overdiagnosis so that cases can be examined in greater detail, whereas instruments specifically designed to generate reliable diagnoses consistent with official criteria should be more stringent. Generally more is known about the psychometric properties of dimensional assessment instruments in comparison with categorical diagnostic criteria. Of the various instruments available, the recently developed ADOS (Lord et al. 1989) and the ADI (Le Couteur et al. 1989) have the considerable advantage of having been carefully developed and explicitly keyed to ICD-10 and DSM-IV criteria.

The utility of normative assessment instruments—that is, for assessment of intellectual or communication skills—in autism has been well established (D. J. Cohen et al. 1987). Until recently, however, instruments that would measure social skills have been lacking. The Vineland Adaptive Behavior Scales (VABS) (Sparrow et al. 1984) use a semistructured interview to assess social skills on the basis of parental reports of current (not previous) abilities. This instrument, which also provides information on communication, daily living, and motor skills, is very reliable, readily administered, and was nationally standardized on a large sample representative of the United States (based on the 1980 U.S. census). A series of studies using this instrument (e.g., Freeman et al. 1988; Loveland and Kelley 1988; Volkmar et al. 1987, 1993a) have documented that social skills in autism are indeed impaired relative to mental age. The potential use of the VABS as a screening instrument for autism has also been suggested (Volkmar, et al. 1993). In an individual item analysis of social skills that are usually acquired very early, Klin et al. (1992)

demonstrated that children with autism typically fail to exhibit a range of social behaviors that are normatively apparent in the first year of life.

Prevalence and Epidemiology

Predictable problems complicate epidemiological studies of autism and related conditions: the infrequency of the syndrome, issues in case identification and differences in alternative screening or diagnostic procedures, and so forth. However, the available research suggests a frequency of between 1 and 5 cases in every 10,000 children; as expected, more stringent definitions generally produce lower estimates (Bryson, in press; Zahner and Pauls 1987); the condition may be increasing in frequency.

Two important sex differences in the prevalence and expression of autism have repeatedly been noted. First, males consistently outnumber females in epidemiologically based studies on the order of 2 or 3 times to 1 (Wing 1981) and in consecutive-case series on the order of 4 or 5 times to 1 (Lord and Schopler 1987; Volkmar et al. 1993b). Second, when females are affected, it appears that they are more likely to be severely mentally retarded. Higher-functioning females with autism are particularly uncommon (Lord and Schopler 1987; Volkmar et al. 1993b). The preponderance of males is greater than in most other psychiatric and developmental disorders of childhood with the possible exception of attention deficit disorder and the developmental language disorders (Lord and Schopler 1987). In mental retardation not associated with autism higher rates in males are reported among the more severely retarded although sex ratios become more similar in mild and moderately retarded groups. The significance of the observed sex difference is unclear, but it may have some implications for understanding more fundamental pathophysiological mechanisms (Volkmar et al. 1993b).

As noted previously, Kanner's original (1943) impression of higher socioeconomic status in parents of autistic children has not proven to be correct. Studies that control for factors related to bias in case ascertainment find no particular socioeconomic status (SES) distribution; rather, it appears that children with autism come from diverse social classes and cultures (Schopler et al. 1980a).

Clinical Features

Onset and Early Development

Kanner's original (1943) report suggested that the disorder was present from birth—that it was congenital in nature. Subsequent research has slightly modified this notion. In the majority of instances, children with autism indeed have difficulties from very early in life, if not from birth. In a small proportion of cases, perhaps 25%, the child's difficulties are not so apparent and may not be recognized until after the second birthday (Harper and Williams 1975; Short and Schopler 1988; Volkmar et al. 1985) Only very rarely does autism develop after the third birthday. As noted in Chapter 8, the term *childhood disintegrative disorder* has been used for the very rare child who develops an autistic-like condition after a reasonably prolonged (2-year) period of normal development.

Information on the apparent onset of autism in two large consecutive-case series is presented in Figure 6–2. Examination of Figure 6–2 reveals that, as Kanner would have predicted, the vast majority of individuals with autism have a disability that comes to the attention of their parents in the first year of life—even before parents become concerned about delayed speech. Various factors can act to delay case detection and it is important to note that age at onset might more correctly be termed

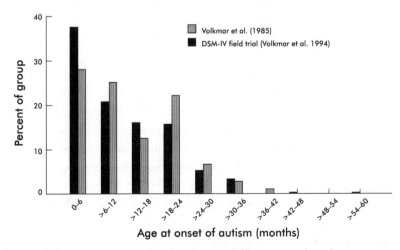

Figure 6–2. Age at onset of autism in two different samples of cases.

age at recognition (Volkmar et al. 1985). Factors intrinsic and extrinsic to the child may tend to delay case recognition. For example, the development of children who are somewhat brighter and higher functioning may be of less concern early in life to their parents (Volkmar and Cohen 1989); certain life circumstances might sometimes be used by parents to account for early developmental delays.

Usually parents become seriously concerned as language fails to develop. A common presenting complaint to physicians when the child is 18–24 months of age is a concern that the child might be deaf. The parent may report an awareness of earlier abnormalities in social development; for example, the infant was "too easy" to care for or seemed relatively uninterested in the social world. Despite any concerns about deafness, parents often report, with some perplexity, that the child is exquisitely sensitive to aspects of the inanimate environment. For example, the child who does not seem aware of his mother's presence responds with panic to the sound of a vacuum cleaner or reacts with disorganization if his or her routine is changed.

The younger autistic child often has interests in nonfunctional aspects of objects—their taste or smell—and may be attached to highly unusual objects, such as a piece of string. Symbolic and imaginative play skills are very impaired (Stone et al. 1990). An object like a truck may not be used for either functional or symbolic play; rather, the younger child with autism may spin the tires for hours on end. Other unusual behaviors develop in the preschool years and include stereotyped motor mannerisms (hand flapping and toe walking) and, occasionally, self-injurious behaviors.

It is somewhat surprising, given the apparent very early onset of autism, that very few studies have actually examined very young autistic children. Although one might expect (consistent with the DSM-III definition) that infants and young children would present the "purest" form of autism (Volkmar and Cohen 1988), in reality, issues in case detection have led to a dearth of studies in children younger than 5 years. Available research on this age range has employed one of several strategies to deal with this issue: inquiring of parents about their child's early development, examining early home movies or videotapes of children, and so forth (Losche 1990; Massie 1978; Ornitz et al. 1977).

Studies using parental retrospection suggest that development in younger autistic children is erratic, with marked unevenness and the emergence of unusual islets of abilities ("splinter skills"). Often development in such children involves periods of some regression or of failure to progress in usual ways (Ritvo and Freeman 1978). Although development between domains often seems to proceed in unexpected ways, sequences of development within a given domain seem to progress in usual ways at, perhaps, a slower rate than would otherwise be expected (Burack and Volkmar 1992).

The nature of early deficits in sensorimotor skills is less clear, again reflecting in large part the paucity of research (see Curcio 1978; Losche 1990; Morgan et al. 1989). Given the generally poor prognosis associated with autism and recent federal mandates for case detection and service, early ascertainment and intervention are a high priority (Simeonson et al. 1987). However, delays in case detection remain very common. Siegel et al. (1988) noted, for example, that a period of 3 years usually elapsed between the time parents became concerned about the child's development and the provision of a definitive diagnosis.

Issues of diagnosis are often most difficult in younger children; on the other hand, provision of an adequate service program can proceed even if the "definitive" diagnosis becomes clear only over time. Delays in referral reflect a lack of awareness on the part of primary health care providers as well as the dearth of simple and readily applied screening techniques. Some attempts have been made to provide simple guidelines for screening, but these have not achieved wide acceptance (see L. R. Watson and Marcus 1988). One recent study reported that examination of very early normative behaviors in a high-risk population could be used to screen for children with autism (Baron-Cohen and Howlin 1993). This study did not, however, employ an appropriate mentally retarded comparison group. Volkmar et al. (1993a) have reported the results of a screening based on the results of the VABS with good sensitivity and specificity; this report has still to be replicated, however. The issue of early screening will likely assume increasing importance in the years ahead.

Social Functioning

Kanner felt that marked lack of social interest (autism) was a central defining feature of the syndrome. It is of interest that all subsequent definitions continued to emphasize the centrality of social deficit and dysfunction in syndrome definition. Studies of diagnostic criteria typically identify social criteria as the most robust predictors of diagnosis (e.g., Siegel et al. 1988). Although there has been general agreement on the importance of social dysfunction for syndrome definition, there has been widespread disagreement as to how this dysfunction is understood. It is just this aspect of the syndrome that has, paradoxically, been least frequently the focus of systematic investigation (Fein et al. 1986). The dearth of studies in this area reflects several issues: 1) an awareness that some limited social skills do develop over time (Volkmar 1987), 2) a tendency to view social factors as secondary to cognitive ones in development (what Cairns [1979] has referred to as the "cognitive primacy hypothesis"), 3) a lack of good metrics of social functioning (Volkmar et al. 1993a), and 4) a general lack of knowledge regarding the neurobiological substrates of social development (Brothers 1989). This tendency to view social factors as secondary to cognitive ones in pathogenesis has also been reflected in recent work on the "theory of mind" hypothesis in autism (Baron-Cohen 1989).

The autistic social dysfunction is fundamentally continuous over the life span in affected individuals, although its manifestations change with age and developmental level (Volkmar 1987). It is clear that more differentiated social skills often develop as children with autism become older, although these skills are neither qualitatively nor quantitatively normal. As infants, children with autism are reported to have displayed a lack of interest in social interaction and in the human face, which, to the normally developing infant, is the most interesting aspect of the environment (Volkmar 1987). Younger children with autism do not exhibit the usual preference for speech sounds (Klin 1993); early nonverbal interactions are impaired and the early imitative games of infancy and other forms of "intersubjectivity" are usually absent (Stern 1987). When sick or injured, younger children with autism usually do not seek comfort from their parents, and when their parents do attempt to hold them, the children may fail to conform to their parents' posture or may actively resist being held (Ornitz et al. 1977). Although some evidence of recognition of and attachment to the parents may be observed, it is of a type highly dissimilar in timing and quality to that seen in normally developing 8- and 9-month-old children (Mundy and Sigman 1989). Younger children with autism may point in order to obtain a desired object but rarely to share an interesting environmental event; often, when they desire an object or action, they may guide the parent's hand to the object or material as if the hand, rather than the person, were responsible for obtaining the desired goal.

As children with autism enter later childhood and adolescence, increases in social skills are often observed, although social interaction remains a major difficulty even for the highest-functioning individuals. Such children have problems with pragmatic communication, with integration of the multiple sources of information in social interaction, with empathy, and so forth. Although they may learn from peers through modeling, normal friendships with peers are very uncommon; usually social relationships are strongest with teachers, parents, and other adults (Schopler and Mesibov 1983).

As adults, even the highest-functioning individuals with autism have tremendous difficulty in reciprocal interaction, in understanding the nuances of social cues, in making friends, and in responding empathically to others (Bemporad 1979; Kanner et al. 1972; Schopler and Mesibov 1983; Volkmar and Cohen 1985). These adults may make extensive use of very elaborate rules for modulating social interaction but often miss the big picture in their struggle to conform by failing to generalize rules to novel situations. For example, one higher-functioning young man was attending college and decided he should have a girlfriend. He reasoned that an appropriate way to do this was to go to a bar and offer to buy a woman a drink. Having gone to the bar and having found a woman willing to accept the offer of a drink, he proceeded to throw the drink on her, which led, much to his puzzlement, to her slapping him and leaving. When asked about the incident, he was perplexed and indicated that he could not understand it, because throwing the drink on her was "very funny." He failed to appreciate that his slapstick humor would not be appreciated by the person who was its target. The young man then decided never to repeat this mistake of throwing a drink on a woman in a bar, but he continued to have similar problems in which he failed to take into account the impact of his actions on other persons.

In many instances, higher-functioning individuals are aware of their disability and develop a number of coping strategies, typically revolving around learning concrete rules for mediating social interaction. An increased awareness of the disability might also result in some degree of depression. Several accounts of such individuals have appeared and are a testament to the desire for and difficulties with social interaction in this population (Bemporad 1979; Schopler and Mesibov 1983; Volkmar and Cohen 1985).

Cognitive Functioning

Kanner's initial (1943) impression that individuals with autism had normal intellectual potential was incorrect. This impression was based on an observation and an assumption, both of which still often lead to inappropriate attribution of high levels of intelligence to autistic children. The observation made by Kanner was that on certain parts of IQ tests children in his sample scored in the normal or near normal range, for example, on tasks involving visual-spatial skills or on tasks that emphasized rote memory. The assumption was then made that if the child scored this well on the rest of the test (which the child did not actually do) the child would not be retarded; in other words, it was assumed that there was homogeneity in cognitive skills and that for various reasons—presumably reflecting motivational or other factors—the child was not willing to participate in other aspects of test procedures.

This and other misattributions led to the early notion that autistic children could not also be mentally retarded, that their behavior was always highly volitional and intentional, and that if only the autistic child could be coaxed out of his or her "shell" the child would then be "normal." Over a period of approximately 20 years it became apparent that the attempt to explain poor test performance on the basis of motivational factors or "testability" was untenable (Alpern 1967). Rather, if tests appropriate to the person's overall level of functioning were used (rather than ones appropriate just to the person's chronological age), the scores obtained on intelligence tests were reliable, reasonably stable, and predictive of ultimate outcome (DeMyer et al. 1981; Klin and Shephard 1994; Lockyer and Rutter 1969; Lotter 1978). Results of full-scale tests of intelligence in a sample of individuals with autism are presented in Figure 6–3.

Although it is clear that most individuals with autism score in the mentally retarded range overall, characteristic patterns or profiles are observed. Usually tasks such as block design or digit span are relatively preserved, whereas tasks involving language comprehension or picture arrangement are depressed (Rumsey 1992). Occasionally very unusual splinter skills, such as the ability to calculate dates, are present (Treffert 1988). However, the overall performance on the test most robustly predicts outcome rather than the presence of splinter skills. Usually nonverbal or performance skills are advanced in comparison with more verbally mediated ones. IQ is also strongly correlated with severity of the social impairment and other aspects of the disorder; in other words, the presence of seizures and other signs of central nervous system (CNS) dysfunction is more common in lower-functioning individuals (Volkmar and Nelson 1990).

The isolated areas of ability or "splinter skills" observed in individuals with autism are occasionally remarkable either because they are out of keeping with the person's overall level of functioning (O'Connor and Hermelin 1988) or because the skill would be prodigious for anyone. Such "savant skills" have included activities such as drawing, musical ability, feats of memory, calendar calculation, and so forth (see Treffert

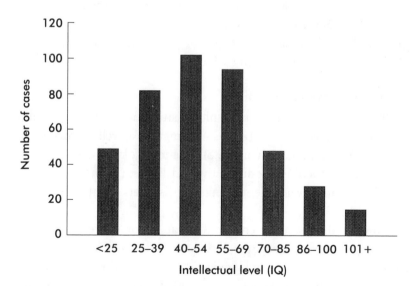

Figure 6–3.   IQ level in a sample of 649 individuals with autism.

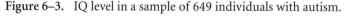

Source.   F. R. Volkmar and A. Klin, unpublished data, October 1995.

1988). Studies of these phenomena have helped clarify the neurocognitive origins of such abilities.

A cognitive theory accounted for the social dysfunction in autism on the basis of a postulated inability to attribute mental states (beliefs, emotions, intentions) to others or to use beliefs about such states to explain behavior. This theory-of-mind hypothesis (Baron-Cohen 1989) arose from a series of elegant experimental studies that have documented the rather circumscribed nature of symbolic difficulties in autism. This hypothesis is of some interest in that it can be used to account for various of the deficits observed in autism as well as those skills that are relatively preserved. The theory remains limited, however, in several important respects. First, it does not account for the time at onset of social dysfunction, which usually is reported, at least retrospectively, well before the time such sophisticated cognitive abilities are evident. Even older autistic children fail to exhibit many social skills that otherwise appear early on in the development of nonautistic children (Klin et al. 1992). Second, the elegant experimental work with this hypothesis has focused almost entirely on the approximately 50% of individuals with autism who are capable of communicative speech. The applicability of this hypothesis to the other 50% of the population remains unclear (Klin et al. 1992). Third, at least one study has suggested that apparent "theory-of-mind" deficits are actually a reflection of developmental level rather than of diagnostic category as such (Prior et al. 1990).

Communicative Functioning

Children with autism invariably exhibit disturbances in communication, including both receptive and expressive language as well as broader communicative activities, such as use of gaze to regulate interaction (Paul 1987). These difficulties are distinctive and different from those observed in children with developmental language disorders (Cantwell and Baker 1984; Paul 1987).

About half of autistic children are largely or entirely mute; those who do speak have language that is remarkable in many ways (Paul 1987). Although certain aspects of language in verbal subjects may be areas of relative strength, such as phonology and syntax (Fay 1983), the pragmatic aspects of communication are typically an area of marked disability (Paul 1987).

In verbal individuals, speech is often monotonic in quality, with a failure to use appropriate inflection—that is, to convey meaning through intonations, as in indicating differences between statements and question. The failure to use intonation may also be characteristic of the vocalizations of preverbal autistic children (Ricks and Wing 1975). Problems such as pronoun reversal and immediate and delayed echolalia (Fay and Schuler 1980) have frequently been described. Pronoun reversal may, however, primarily reflect echoing of the last pronoun heard (Paul 1987). Similarly, although echolalia was once viewed as a maladaptive behavior—that is, as an attempt to avoid interaction—now it appears to have many potentially adaptive functions (Prizant 1987) as it does when it occurs in normally developing children. Semantic difficulties are often reflected in the form of extreme literalness (Fay and Schuler 1980) and in expression of mental states in self or others (Tager-Flusberg 1993). Invariably the pragmatic aspects of language are markedly impaired. Higher-functioning individuals with autism may have difficulties understanding basic conventions of conversation: signaling and turn taking, conversational repair, providing appropriate context for conversational partners, and so forth. This often lends a somewhat odd and eccentrically one-sided flavor to conversational interchange (Paul 1987).

Behavioral Characteristics

Although delays in language and in social development often prompt initial parental concern, various unusual behaviors are also observed early in life. These behaviors, typically subsumed under a term such as *insistence on sameness* or *restricted range of interests* actually encompass a rather diverse group of behavioral features. These include a preferential interest in and responsiveness to the inanimate environment, stereotyped and repetitive movements and mannerisms, difficulties in tolerating even trivial changes in routine or the environment, and a restricted range of interests or preoccupation with some highly idiosyncratic interest.

Deficits in play skills, particularly in symbolic and imaginative play, are characteristic of younger autistic children and have sometimes been included as formal diagnostic criteria. Usually the younger child with autism is more interested in nonfunctional aspects of objects, such as their smell or texture, and often uses materials in highly idiosyncratic ways (Stone et al. 1990).

Course and Prognosis

For purposes of discussion, the course of autism may be arbitrarily divided into four periods: preschool, school age, adolescence, and adulthood. Behavioral and developmental characteristics vary over age and developmental level; both factors must be taken into account in the evaluation of the individual. Similarly, the tasks faced by parents vary depending on the child's age and developmental level and the specific life circumstances the family faces (Morgan 1988).

During the preschool period, children with autism more commonly display the pervasive unrelatedness alluded to in DSM-III criteria (Volkmar et al. 1986). Parents often become seriously concerned within the first year or two of the child's life, but typically several years elapse before a definitive diagnosis (Siegel et al. 1988). Although language and social skills are severely delayed, motor skills are relatively preserved and may indeed be excellent (Klin and Shephard 1994), providing the child with the capacity for engaging in dangerous activities for which good judgment is lacking. Although idiosyncratic responses to the environment are common, severe behavior problems are less frequent in this age group. The child's size also makes behavioral management somewhat easier. Over the preschool years, particularly toward their end, increased social skills may become apparent; for example, the child appears to become more attached to the parents and responds to them more differentially. Tasks for the parents and family members during this period include obtaining an adequate assessment and intervention program and making some accommodation to the diagnosis. Although many services to aid parents and families are theoretically available, the range and intensity of services actually available are often much more limited. Securing an appropriate intervention program is critical during the first years of life.

During the school years, developmental gains are made but behavior problems also increase. Behavioral management of the child may become more of a challenge. During adolescence, some autistic children improve, whereas others exhibit a period of behavioral deterioration (Rutter 1970); the first onset of seizure disorder may be noted during this time. As adults, even the highest-functioning individuals exhibit marked difficulties in social interaction and often remain very isolated (Volkmar and Cohen 1988).

Changes in social interactional style over the course of development have been described. These range from a style of aloofness and indifference to interaction to a style in which interaction is passively accepted although not sought and, finally, to a rather eccentric and odd interactional style in which the individual seeks interaction in idiosyncratic ways (Wing and Atwood 1987). It appears that these styles of interaction are closely related to developmental level (Volkmar et al. 1989).

Although available data on outcome generally suggest a rather grim prognosis, it is important to note that most of these data were collected on individuals first seen in the 1950s and 1960s, before reasonably adequate, early, and intensive interventions were widely available. That notwithstanding, these data would suggest that the outcome for autistic children is quite poor with only about one-third being able to achieve some degree of adult self-sufficiency (DeMyer et al. 1981). The two major predictors of outcome include overall developmental level (IQ) and the ability to use language for communication by age 5 (Lotter 1978). Clearly the importance of IQ to outcome is not limited to autism. Follow-up studies of children seen more recently are critically needed because changes in service provision and in mandates for service and, to some extent, in case detection mean that more children with autism are receiving services earlier and more intensively. At least a few studies, such as Lovaas (1987), suggest that major gains can be made if intervention is started early and if it is intensive.

Etiology and Pathogenesis

Although Kanner's (1943) initial description suggested that autism was a congenital disorder, his description of unusual patterns of parent-child interaction and of the unusual economic and academic success level in the parents studied in his original cases was quickly taken to suggest some role of parental psychopathology in syndrome pathogenesis. Terms such as *refrigerator mother* were used to capture what was felt to be the underlying psychodynamic problem (Despert 1951), and parental psychotherapy and sometimes child institutionalization were suggested to address the presumed deficit in parenting.

Several lines of data argued against these views. First, observation of parents of autistic children failed to reveal specific deficits in child care (Cantwell and Baker 1984). Moreover, usually only the autistic child, and not other siblings, was affected. Similarly, parents did not appear to exhibit unusual psychopathology or extreme personality traits (DeMyer et al. 1981). On the other hand, children reared in institutional settings (Provence and Lipton 1962) or those reared in cultures in which children are largely ignored by adults (Turnbull 1972) did not appear to exhibit high rates of the disorder. As longitudinal data became available, it became apparent that the basis of autism appeared to be some fundamental disturbance in the CNS—as many as 25% of individuals exhibited seizures starting in adolescence (Rutter 1970). It also appeared that deficits in parent-child interaction likely stemmed from problems in the child.

The preponderance of available evidence suggests the centrality of neurobiological factors in syndrome pathogenesis. Children with autism have 1) increased rates of physical anomalies, 2) delayed development of hand dominance, 3) persistence of primitive reflexes, 4) various neurological "soft" signs, 5) various abnormalities in an electroencephalogram (EEG), in computed tomography (CT), or in magnetic resonance imaging (MRI), and 6) increased rates of seizure disorder (Golden 1987; Minderaa et al. 1985; Volkmar and Nelson 1990). They also come from pregnancies that are at greater risk (Tsai 1987). It has also become clear that autism is associated with a host of medical conditions (Coleman 1987). The list of conditions associated with autism is impressive relative both to its length and to the types of other disorders potentially associated with the disorder (see Table 6–3). On the other hand, autism rarely seems to be associated with other conditions, such as Down's syndrome (Bregman and Volkmar 1988).

The variety of conditions associated with autism suggests that the syndrome is the result of one or multiple insults acting on the CNS through some final common pathway. In this sense autism would be analogous to mental retardation in which a host of etiologies have been identified. At the same time knowledge regarding explicit, and testable,

Table 6–3.   Selected medical conditions associated with autism

Type of condition	Example
Structural conditions	Tuberous sclerosis
Chromosome abnormality	Fragile X syndrome
Metabolic abnormality	Phenylketonuria (PKU)
Congenital infection	Congenital rubella
Neurophysiological condition	Infantile spasm

mechanisms of disorder remains highly limited. This reflects the lack of sophistication of current methods in assessing brain function, our limited understanding of CNS correlates of social interaction, and the limited accessibility of brain tissue. Studies have been undertaken in various areas.

Neurochemical Studies

A veritable host of studies has examined neurochemical correlates of autism in relation to neurotransmitters, amino acids, hormones, and so forth (G. M. Anderson and Hoshino 1987). Although no specific biochemical marker has been found, one observation has been repeatedly made. As a group, autistic persons exhibit high peripheral levels of serotonin, and perhaps one-third of the cases exhibit high levels. (Serotonin, a central neurotransmitter involved in various regulatory systems, is also found peripherally in platelets and in the digestive system.) The significance of this observation remains unclear (G. M. Anderson and Hoshino 1987). Reflecting the observation of high levels of stereotyped behavior in autism and the presumption, made by some, of high levels of arousal, other neurochemical studies have focused on the dopaminergic and catecholaminergic neuronal systems (Minderaa et al. 1989).

Neuroanatomical Studies

A range of neuroanatomical models for autism has been proposed with the defect or "site" of the lesion postulated to be at various positions in the CNS—from brain stem to cortex (Golden 1987; Minshew 1992). However, relatively few neuropathological studies have been performed and gross pathology is typically not highly aberrant in autism, although changes at the cellular level have been reported (Bauman and Kemper 1985). Studies using CT scans often revealed mild or equivocal abnormalities that are not diagnostic (Harcherik et al. 1985). One report suggested that higher-functioning individuals with autism had unusual defects in the formation of certain portions of the cerebellum (Courchesne et al. 1988); this observation has not proven easy to replicate. Innovations in technology, particularly with positron-emission tomography (PET) scanning, may, however, provide greater understanding of such factors (Minshew 1992).

Neurophysiological Studies

High rates of EEG abnormalities and frank seizure disorders of various types have been repeatedly noted in individuals with autism. The pattern of seizure onset in autism has been noted to be unusual in that the onset of seizures may occur in adolescence. For example, in Rutter's (1970) follow-up of 53 adolescents with autism, 13 definite and 2 possible seizure disorders were noted; in 10 instances the seizure disorder had developed during adolescence. Deykin and MacMahon (1979) and Volkmar and Nelson (1990) also reported on the frequency of seizure disorders in this population; the results of these two studies and of a comparison based on a large normative sample (Cooper 1975) are presented in Figure 6–4. In both the clinical samples, rates of seizure disorder are increased.

In the Volkmar and Nelson (1990) study, which employed different inclusionary criteria, rates of first seizure (excluding simple febrile seizures) were increased at all age ranges examined. Consistent with this notion, the subjects in the Deykin and MacMahon (1979) study who exhibited only some autistic features were less likely to exhibit seizures than those who were felt to be more truly autistic. Seizure disorders are of diverse types.

Genetic Studies

Initially it appeared that genetic factors had a very limited role in the pathogenesis of autism. However, several factors limited the interpretation of the available data. First, clearly the condition is rare; therefore, large samples might have to be studied to evaluate genetic models adequately. Second, cases apparently failed to reproduce. Finally, early studies did not consider the possibility that some alternative condition in family members, such as language delay or difficulties, might be a manifestation of the same underlying genetic mechanisms (D. J. Cohen et al. 1994). Evidence suggesting the potential importance of genetic factors in autism has come from various sources.

Folstein and Rutter (1977) noted the difficulties in interpretation of early twin study reports in which one twin had autism: the proportion of monozygotic (MZ) twin pairs was much larger than would be expected and many of the fraternal or dizygotic (DZ) twin pairs included opposite-sex siblings. They obtained an unbiased sample of 21 same-sex twin pairs (11 MZ and 10 DZ) in which at least 1 twin exhibited autism; there was increased concordance in MZ twin pairs. Subsequent studies have replicated the increased concordance in MZ twins. Although the data suggested the importance of genetic factors, the observation that MZ twins were not 100% concordant also suggested the importance of nongenetic factors. An additional hypothesis is that the apparent discordance reflects differences in manifestation of the same underlying condition; in other words, that other developmental problems might be

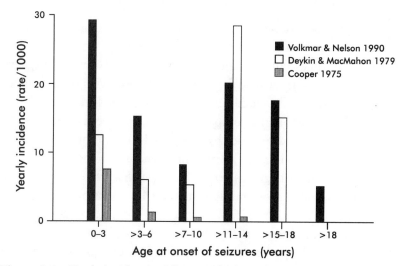

Figure 6–4. Yearly incidence of first onset of seizure disorder in two samples of individuals with autism (Volkmar and Nelson 1990 and Deykin and MacMahon 1979) and a normative sample (Cooper 1975).

observed in the nonautistic co-twin; evidence for this hypothesis was found in the Folstein and Rutter (1977) data.

Additional support for the operation of genetic factors comes from studies of family members of affected children. There is a higher than expected frequency of less severe developmental problems in the relatives of autistic patients. In a study of siblings August et al. (1981) reported that the frequency of autism in siblings was nearly 3%; in other words, the frequency of autism was markedly increased over the expected prevalence in the population. Higher than expected rates of cognitive disorder, as strictly defined, were also present in siblings. Other studies (e.g., Jones and Szatmari 1988; Ritvo et al. 1989) have suggested the importance of genetic factors in autism. On balance the available data suggest some role of genetic factors in syndrome pathogenesis; on the other hand, various problems limit the evaluation of available data, which suggests that alternative hypotheses cannot be ruled out. Support for a multifactorial etiology is also provided by Folstein and Rutter's (1977) study in which the autistic twin in a discordant twin pair was the one at greater obstetrical risk.

Assessment

The term *pervasive developmental disorder* correctly suggests that there are multiple areas of delayed and impaired development exhibited by children and adolescents with autism. A quick perusal of any of the usual categorical diagnostic criteria for autism suggests that children with this condition will have difficulties in the areas of social development, language, and behavior often accompanied by some degree of overall mental retardation and in some cases by associated medical or neurological problems (Rutter et al. 1994). A truly comprehensive assessment usually requires the efforts of various professionals, such as child psychiatrists, psychologists, speech-communication specialists, neurologists, and so forth. Although it is possible for any specialist to work, sometimes quite productively, within the confines of his or her area of expertise, it is often more helpful to the patient and family if an interdisciplinary approach to assessment is undertaken. Such an approach does, however, raise challenges for the members of the team, which must create its own style and pace of working and which must respect the expertise of each discipline represented. There are risks inherent in this approach, such as the potential for fragmentation. Nevertheless, if members of the team work together in a truly collegial fashion, the quality of the evaluation can be significantly enhanced. For example, rather than overwhelming parents with a plethora of individual reports, a single narrative, with input from all involved in the evaluation, may be more accessible to parents. Such an effort also forces the various members of the team to consider discrepancies in the evaluation results and thus may be more likely to provide a truly integrated view of the child.

Various modifications in usual assessment procedures may be needed, reflecting the particular challenges for assessment presented by the child or adolescent with autism (Klin and Shephard 1994). Such modifications may include having more than the usual number of assessment sessions, using behavior modification techniques to elicit the child's attention and cooperation, and conducting the evaluation in an environment that is minimally distracting to the child. In contrast to usual procedures in child psychiatric settings, parental participation in the assessment, preferably through direct observation if this can be arranged, is often helpful. This serves to demystify assessment procedures, lets the parents observe a range of professionals with differing styles as they work with the child, and provides a set of shared observations that can facilitate subsequent discussion. It is important to realize that a major goal of the assessment is to establish a long-term collaborative relationship with parents (Morgan 1988).

Usual assessment instruments and methods relevant to developmentally delayed children are clearly the first choice for administration (Cohen et al. 1987). However, reasonable modifications in assessment procedures or test administration should be made if the clinical judgment of the examiner is that these modifications will provide more reliable estimates of levels of functioning (Klin and Shephard 1994). On the other hand, clinically indicated modifications also imply even greater caution in interpretation of results obtained.

History

Often before the child is actually seen, a careful history will have been obtained. This assists in planning the assessment and provides information helpful in differential diagnosis. For older individuals, parents may be helped to recall information if they are asked to review available records of the child's early development. Sometimes parents, particularly of older children, will have extensive records of previous evaluations or educational interventions that can provide important information. Videotaped recordings are also often useful and can include both recordings of the child when he or she was an infant as well as recordings made of the child at play, in school, and so forth.

In beginning the assessment with the history, the examiner should clarify any ambiguities regarding parental expectations about the nature of the evaluation and their hopes for it and the main reason(s) for the evaluation. Information on the child's early history, including pregnancy, labor, delivery, and early development, should be systematically obtained. Both normative and impaired features should be noted. For example, was the child a very easy baby, was it difficult to get a response from the child, did the child exhibit the social smile, was the child difficult to feed? Discussion of when the parents were first seriously concerned about the child's development often is very helpful for purposes of differential diagnosis.

Medical and family history should be systematically reviewed. The clinician should pay careful attention to any items that suggest the presence of associated medical conditions, such as possible absence spells suggestive of seizures or a family history that might suggest fragile X syndrome.

Psychological Assessment

The psychological assessment should aim to provide measures of cognitive functioning in a structured situation as well as in the child or adolescent's adaptive skills: what the child habitually does without provision of such structure. The purposes of this assessment may vary somewhat depending on the child's age and specific needs. For example, in the United States information on both cognitive (IQ) and adaptive skills is required to establish eligibility for enrollment in programs for the developmentally disabled. Such information is usually also helpful both in differential diagnosis and in the design of intervention programs that address areas of strength and weakness. Various studies have indicated that despite the sometimes formidable difficulties in assessment, results obtained tend to be stable and predictive of ultimate outcome (Klin and Shephard 1994). Experience in testing this population is quite helpful, particularly in interpreting the results of certain tests. For example, single-word vocabulary may appear to be an area of strength when tested through picture-naming and identification tasks, whereas actual use of words for spontaneous communication may be extremely delayed; reading for decoding skills may be very advanced even when reading for understanding is at a very low (and presumably minimally functional) level (Klin and Shephard 1994). As noted previously, interpretation of test results is most readily accomplished when entire batteries of tests can be administered with minimal or no modification in usual procedures. It is always wise to interpret results with appropriate caution and to note various factors that might suggest the results obtained were or were not optimal estimates.

A number of very well-standardized tests of intelligence are available. In the selection of the specific test or tests to be used, appropriate consideration should be given to the primary goals of the evaluation and the apparent strengths and weaknesses of the child. As a practical matter this often implies use of tests originally designed for somewhat younger children or use of tests with minimal verbal requirements. Tests appropriate for the younger or most developmentally delayed individuals include the Bayley Scales of Infant Development (Bayley 1993) and Uzgiris-Hunt Scales using Dunst's norms (Dunst 1980; Uzgiris and Hunt 1975). For children functioning at somewhat higher levels, tests that minimize verbal requirements should be used, such as the Kaufman Assessment Battery for Children (Kaufman and Kaufman 1983). For children who are mute but have nonverbal mental ages over 2 years, nonverbal tests such as the Leiter International Performance Scale (Leiter 1948) may be used. The Leiter was originally developed for individuals with hearing impairment; it requires no verbal instructions and uses a visual matching procedure.

For higher-functioning and/or older children and adolescents, two Wechsler scales, the Wechsler Preschool and Primary Scale of Intelligence—Revised (WPPSI-R) (Wechsler 1989) and the Wechsler Intelligence Scale for Children, 3rd Edition (WISC-III) (Wechsler 1992), should be used in preference to the Stanford-Binet Intelligence Scale,

4th Edition (Thorndike et al. 1986). The Wechsler scales have been extensively evaluated and are well standardized. These scales, in particular, provide a useful division into verbal and performance (visual-perceptual) IQ. The very experienced psychological examiner will also be able to examine aspects of social versus nonsocial information processing. Issues of assessment and specific instruments are discussed in Cohen et al. (1987), L. R. Watson and Marcus (1988), and Klin and Shephard (1994).

No matter which test is chosen, the aim of the testing is to understand how the child solves problems, processes information of various types, understands concepts, responds to different styles of presentation, makes use of memory skills, and so forth. Human figure drawing and tests of visual-motor integration may also provide helpful information.

Adaptive skills are those necessary for personal and social self-sufficiency in real-world situations (Sparrow et al. 1984). These skills are important aspects of the evaluation of the child with autism for several reasons. In addition to being required, along with IQ scores, for diagnosis of any associated mental retardation, they provide a valuable measure of the child's typical skills in day-to-day situations and thus supplement observation of the child's skills in a highly structured assessment. Furthermore, adaptive skills are readily teachable. The existence of major discrepancies between intellectual level and adaptive level, usually in the direction of higher intellectual skills, suggests the real importance of helping the child generalize skills into real life situations in order to increase capacities for adult independence.

The VABS (Sparrow et al. 1984) are the most widely used instruments to assess adaptive skills. These scales were nationally standardized on a large sample representative of the 1980 U.S. census in terms of race and ethnicity, region of the country, parental education, and so forth. The scales are administered as a semistructured interview to parents or caregivers familiar with the child. Adaptive skills are assessed on the basis of current, actual skills. Domains and subdomains of the scales include communication (receptive, expressive, and written language), daily living skills (personal, domestic, and community skills), socialization (interpersonal relationships, play, and leisure time and coping skills), and motor skills (gross and fine). The VABS in their expanded form are particularly valuable, because they are readily translated into goals that are appropriate for inclusion in an individual educational program.

On the VABS a characteristic profile is often obtained for autistic children. This typically consists of relative strengths in the areas of daily living and motor skills and significant deficits in the areas of socialization and, to a lesser extent, communication (Volkmar et al. 1987). The VABS may also have some use as a screening instrument (Volkmar et al. 1993a), and supplementary norms specific to the autistic population should soon be available.

Communication Assessment

The assessment of communication should provide information on the communicative abilities of both verbal and nonverbal children. This part of the evaluation should not be restricted to only selected aspects of language functioning, such as articulation, single-word-receptive, or expressive vocabulary; rather, it should encompass broader issues of communicative intent and activity, turn-taking and protoconversational and conversational skills, use of prosodic features such as intonation to convey meaning, and other pragmatic aspects of language. In the nonverbal or preverbal individual, communicative activity can be assessed around issues of nonverbal communication, gaze behavior, protesting, and so forth. It is important to note how the child's various behaviors may have communicative functions that can be explored by observing antecedents and consequences of even very idiosyncratic, but consistent, behaviors.

For low-functioning or very young children, several scales are available. These include the Sequenced Inventory of Communicative Development—Revised (SIC) (Hedrick et al. 1975); the Receptive-Expressive Emergent Language Scale (REEL) (Bzoch and League 1991); and the Reynell Developmental Language Scales (Reynell and Gruber 1990). Although measures of single-word-expressive or receptive vocabulary can be assessed using instruments such as the Expressive One Word Picture Vocabulary Test—Revised (Gardner 1990) or the Peabody Picture Vocabulary Test—Revised (Dunn and Dunn 1981), results of these tests in this population can be misleading. Individuals with autism may have much greater abilities to name or respond to single words in contrast to their abilities to use words in interaction, to convey more complex meanings, or both.

Observation of the communicative abilities of the nonverbal individual is important, particularly when more traditional assessment methods cannot be used. A number of instruments now being used attempt to provide reliable information on social-communicative behaviors in younger children based on report, elicitation, observation, or all three. An example is the Communication and Symbolic Behavior Scales (Research Edition) (Wetherby and Prizant 1993). Spontaneous and elicited communicative activities can be noted around various situations. Communicative functions such as vocalizing, protesting, sharing a topic or object of interest, pointing, and so forth can be observed. For individuals functioning at a higher developmental level, the Clinical Evaluation of Language Fundamentals—Revised (Wiig et al. 1992) assesses more complex aspects of language, and the Test of Language Competence (Wiig and Secord 1988) assesses nonliteral language skills.

Psychiatric Assessment

The psychiatric assessment of the child should include observation during more and less structured periods. If the psychiatrist is working with other members of a team and if observational facilities are available, it is often valuable to other portions of the child's assessment. This also may be an opportunity to share direct observations with parents, thus creating a common frame of reference, as well as to collect historical and other information. The psychiatrist should ensure that the history taken from parents is adequate and that any features that are unusual or of particular diagnostic significance are explored in detail. Often the psychiatrist will have a major role in coordinating efforts of the various members of a multidisciplinary team and will be concerned with issues of diagnosis, the need for additional medical studies, and program planning and intervention. An awareness of the variations in local service potentials, advocacy organizations, and parental support groups is important.

Areas for direct observation and discussion with parents are summarized in Table 6–4. Both developmentally appropriate and deviant behaviors should be noted. Similarly, attention should be focused both on areas of strength that can be built upon in educational programs and on the presence of problematic behaviors that are likely to impede intervention. In the assessment of areas of strength it is important that the evaluator take a broad and comprehensive view of the child and not become overly entranced with an isolated area of ability. Such areas of ability, when present, should be noted but not confused with the child's general level of functioning. For example, isolated reading for decoding skills is commonly observed (hyperlexia), but usually in the context of limited ability to understand what is read (Klin and Shephard 1994).

Additional Consultations

The services of other consultants—such as pediatric neurologists or geneticists, audiologists, and occupational or physical therapists—may be required, particularly at the time of the first comprehensive evaluation. Examination, the history of the child, or the family history may suggest the need for certain laboratory studies or medical procedures. For example, a family history of mental retardation suggests the need to screen for fragile X syndrome (Bailey et al. 1993). Although it is clear that many different medical conditions are potentially associated with autism, the

Table 6–4. Areas for review and observation in children with autistic disorder

Social development
    Relatedness to people (attachments to parents, siblings)
    Style of interaction with others
    Eye contact (as used to regulate interaction)
    Response to normal affectionate behaviors from others
    Capacities for self/other awareness (e.g., humor)
    Play skills
Communicative development
    Nonverbal communicative abilities
    Verbal (receptive and expressive) communicative capacities
    Communicative intents
    Pragmatic abilities
Responses to the environment
    Response to environmental change or transitions in activities
    Attachments to unusual objects
    Idiosyncratic or highly circumscribed interests
    Stereotyped or self-injurious behaviors

importance of very extensive medical evaluations remains somewhat controversial. Some researchers (e.g., Gillberg 1992) advocate very extensive screening at the time of initial assessment and suggest that a substantial number of cases of autism are associated with some specific and identifiable medical condition. However, others (e.g., Rutter and Schopler 1987) suggest that such cases are in the minority. The latter view argues for more selective use of various tests and procedures, given the relatively low frequency of positive findings and the often considerable costs associated with many of the tests. In a few instances, such as undetected phenylketonuria (PKU), major interventions are possible when the associated medical condition is detected; more frequently the presence of other disorders, such as fragile X syndrome, may have important implications for the parents with regard to future pregnancies.

Given the nature of early parental concerns about delayed language, attempts have been made to evaluate the child's hearing. If behavioral audiometry is inconclusive, brainstem evoked response audiometry should be used (Klin 1993). Periods of apparent unresponsiveness suggest the need for an EEG and neurological consultation. Brain imaging studies using CT, MRI, or PET technology may be appropriate in some cases on clinical grounds and may, on occasion, reveal disorders such as tuberous sclerosis or degenerative CNS disease.

Parent Conference

Results of the evaluation should be presented to parents in a way designed to provide a single, comprehensive, and coherent view of the child. Reports that are written in an easily understood style and that avoid excessive jargon are appreciated both by parents and schools. Such reports should be detailed and should provide realistic suggestions and recommendations. If the results of evaluations of various professionals are available, the report and/or parent conference should attempt to integrate the results and explain any apparent discrepancies.

Differential Diagnosis

The differential diagnosis of autism includes other PDDs (e.g., Asperger's disorder, Rett's disorder, childhood disintegrative disorder, and

PDD NOS) as well as other developmental and psychiatric conditions (language disorders, other specific developmental disorders, deafness, mental retardation, reactive attachment disorder, elective mutism, and very-early-onset schizophrenia).

Probably the differentiation from other forms of PDD is most difficult for the relatively less experienced clinician (Volkmar et al. 1994). Differential diagnostic features for autism in relation to other PDDs and early-onset schizophrenia (EOS) are summarized in Table 6–5. The task of differential diagnosis becomes most complicated when, as is often the case, the child does not exhibit "classical" features of a specific syndrome. At such times it is quite appropriate to frame the discussion of diagnosis in a longitudinal context and to share with the parents the differential diagnosis and a "confidence interval" surrounding the diagnostic impression. In Asperger's disorder the apparent onset of the condition is somewhat later, communication skills (at least early on) are relatively preserved, and a family history of similar problems is common, as are circumscribed interests, whereas cognitive skills are relatively preserved. The diagnosis of this condition has recently become somewhat fashionable, and the concept has often been so broadly applied as to be essentially overlapping with PDD NOS; thus, reasonable stringency should be used in applying this diagnosis in accordance with proposed criteria in ICD-10 (World Health Organization 1990) and DSM-IV (American Psychiatric Association 1994). See also Chapter 7 and Klin (1994).

Differentiation from Rett's disorder is accomplished on the basis of both historical information and the characteristic clinical and developmental features associated with Rett's (e.g., the hand-washing stereotypies, history of early developmental arrest, deceleration in head growth, and so forth—see Chapter 8). In the absence of historical information, differentiation between autism and childhood disintegrative disorder may be difficult because it seems clear that the syndromes are rather similar behaviorally once they are established. Historical information on the nature and type of onset is most helpful in diagnostic differentiation. With the "subthreshold" category of PDD NOS, which, in DSM-IV, includes the use of atypical autism, the nature of the definition is essentially a negative one (problems similar to those in autism that do not meet full criteria). This gives rise to various difficulties. Further complications are introduced by the uses to which diagnostic labels are put

Table 6–5. Differential diagnostic features: autism and nonautistic pervasive developmental disorders

Feature	Disorder				
	Autism	Asperger's disorder	Rett's syndrome	Childhood disintegrative disorder	PDD NOS
Age at recognition (months)	0–36	Usually > 24	5–30	> 24	Variable
Sex ratio	M > F	M > F	F	M > F	M > F
Loss of skills	Usually not	Usually not	Marked	Marked	Usually not
Social skills	Very poor	Poor	Varies with age	Very poor	Variable
Communication skills	Usually poor	Poor to fair	Very poor	Very poor	Fair to good
Circumscribed interests	Variable	Marked	NA	NA	Variable
Family history of similar problems	Uncommon	Frequent	No	No	Unknown
Seizure disorder	Common	Uncommon	Frequent	Common	Uncommon
Head growth decelerates	No	No	Yes	No	No
IQ range	Severe MR to normal	Mild MR to normal	Severe MR	Severe MR	Mild MR to normal
Outcome	Poor	Fair to poor	Very poor	Very poor	Fair to good

Note. PDD NOS: Pervasive developmental disorder no otherwise specified. MR: Mental retardation.
Source. Volkmar FR, Cohen DJ: Nonautistic pervasive developmental disorders, in Psychiatry, Vol 2, Chap 27.2. Edited by Michaels R. Philadelphia, PA, Lippincott, p 4. Used with permission.

in actual practice, such as in entitlement to services.

The differentiation of autism from other forms of developmental disturbance is usually somewhat less problematic. Children with developmental language disorders usually exhibit greater social relatedness than children with autism, even in the face of marked expressive and receptive difficulties. In this group nonverbal communicative abilities are usually relatively preserved and the child may develop a complex set of communicative behaviors.

In children with primary mental retardation (i.e., without autism) it is typically the case that social and communicative skills are at levels that are expected given the child's overall level of intellectual functioning; that is, skills have developed at the same rate in a relatively even way (Burack and Volkmar 1992). Issues of differential diagnosis involving individuals with very marked mental retardation are very complicated and vary, in large part, with the philosophical orientation of the examiner. The tendency in DSM-III-R was probably to overdiagnose autism in this population; both ICD-10 and DSM-IV take a somewhat more conservative view (Volkmar et al. 1994).

Children with hearing impairments may initially exhibit difficulties in social interaction and some stereotyped activities but usually are interested in social interaction. They may also use nonverbal communicative modalities. Children with elective mutism have the capacity for speech and do speak in certain contexts (Klin and Volkmar 1993); not infrequently, an inappropriate diagnosis of elective mutism is made in a child with autism whose parents and evaluators assume that the child could speak if only he or she wished to do so. This is clearly an incorrect use of the diagnostic concept; in autism the issues involved in the major language and communicative deficit are not simply motivational in nature.

Children with reactive attachment disorder have experienced marked psychosocial deprivation; this is not the case in autism. In reactive attachment disorder the social disturbance (either withdrawal or superficial and inappropriate sociability) probably does remit, at least in part, after provision of an appropriate environment (Richters and Volkmar 1994). In EOS, signs of a psychotic illness are, by definition, present.

Although the issue of association between autism and schizophrenia has been somewhat controversial (see Chapter 1) and has reflected previous controversies about continuities of the condition (Petty et al. 1984), recent work suggests that individuals with autism probably are not at increased risk for developing schizophrenia (Volkmar and Cohen 1991). Confusion may, however, surround the exceptional young child who develops schizophrenia and who has an associated change in social relatedness and regression of other developmental skills. Another source of confusion sometimes arises in individuals with Asperger's disorder, in which deficits in conversational and social skills may lead to odd communication styles; this, coupled with sometimes very unusual interests, may lead to an impression of incoherent speech or loosening of associations (Klin 1994).

Differential diagnosis is often very difficult with younger children, particularly those who also have significant developmental delays. This population is often most difficult to assess, autistic-like behaviors are somewhat more common, and associations with other conditions (notably marked mental retardation) pose further complications. Although theoretically it is possible that some children "grow out" of autism, it is much more frequently the case that the course of the disorder is helpful in clarifying the diagnosis—that is, that the very young child with autism goes on to develop the usual clinical picture of autism during the school years. It must also be recognized that, in some instances, a specific diagnosis confers certain rights to mandated services. Generally, regardless of how "classically" autistic a child is, the importance of an appropriately intensive and comprehensive intervention program should be emphasized.

Treatment

The importance of some treatments in the management of individuals with autism is now well established. On the other hand, no treatment has proven to be curative. Apart from studies in a few areas, such as studies of behavior modification procedures or double-blind pharmacological studies, treatments have not been particularly well evaluated. Further complications are introduced by issues of experimental design and methodology. In the absence of rigorously controlled studies, various nonspecific effects of intervention may occur and changes produced may be very short term in nature. These short-term changes may not be truly meaningful or sustained. The occasional report of a "cure" in a single case must similarly be interpreted with great caution. The diagnosis may not have been unequivocally established. The intervention undertaken often has myriad aspects and may, in at least a few cases, be unrelated to what would have been a relatively positive course and outcome in any case. A further complication for interpretation of research studies is the nature of intervention programs for autism. Even before the child's disorder has been recognized, parents often have tried various interventions. Usually, extensive treatments of various types are undertaken, and it becomes difficult to disentangle the effects of changes in syndrome expression with age and the number of interventions.

Behavioral and Educational Treatments

The importance of an intensive, sustained intervention program geared toward the child's needs and employing methods taken from special education and behavior modification has been supported by multiple studies. Simeonsson et al. (1987) reviewed four interventions and noted the importance of intensive, structured intervention starting at a young age and involving the parents. It is clear that more structured programs can more successfully address acquisition of basic skills that are important to long-term outcome (Olley and Stevenson 1989; Prizant and Schuler 1987; Rogers, in press; Rutter and Bartak 1973). Early and intensive intervention may be associated with better outcomes (Lovaas 1987). Intervention programs should include services from special educators, speech-communication disorder specialists, occupational and physical therapists, and so forth. Often, skills may be learned in a very isolated and artificial way; use of naturally occurring and ecologically relevant opportunities for teaching and consistency between home and school settings is important. Advocacy for appropriate educational interventions is an important task for clinicians. Federal mandates for provision of remedial services from birth will likely increase available services and provide a further impetus for early case detection and remediation.

Changing philosophies about intervention and the location of the intervention have produced marked shifts in patterns of service delivery over the past decades. In the 1950s recommendations for institutional placement were common, even for very young children. The isolation of children in large institutions further compounded their difficulties. Over the past 20 years there has been a major shift in social policy in the United States. Residential placements are now avoided at almost all costs; the emphasis is on supporting the child in his or her family and community. The theoretical rationale for this shift is clear as is the potential for much better provision of services to individuals and families. Unfortunately the shift toward community-based services is not always associated with major increases in and support for such services. This issue also arises with respect to mainstreaming children with autism. The rationale for inclusion of children with developmental disabilities is clear; it is based on both a specific philosophical orientation and a small body of research that suggests the potential benefits of including children in regular classroom settings (e.g., Charlop et al. 1983). However, the social deficits associated with autism are a particular problem for attempts at integration (Klin and Cohen 1994). The needs of the individual child should be the highest priority. Advocacy for provision of appropriately intensive educational programs should be a priority for parents and professionals alike.

Pharmacological Interventions

Although drug therapy is not curative, it can be a useful adjunctive treatment in reducing many of the behavioral disturbances of autism with resultant improvements in the quality of life for patient and family members alike (McDougle et al. 1994b). Although research on the pathogenesis of autism suggests various potential pathogenic mechanisms (Rubenstein et al. 1990), both direct and indirect evidence suggests that certain neurochemical systems may be involved in the pathophysiology of the condition (Cook 1990). Clearly, careful consideration of the patient's life circumstances and the potential benefits and risks of pharmacological intervention should be central in considering use of psychotropic agents as one aspect of the individual's treatment program.

The efficacy of the neuroleptics, particularly haloperidol, has been extensively studied in autism. Campbell et al. (1978) conducted a 12-week, double-blind, placebo-controlled study of the dopamine antagonist haloperidol in 40 autistic children (ages 2.6–7.2 years) and noted that this agent was effective in reducing stereotypies and withdrawal, particularly for children above 4.5 years of age. In addition the combination of haloperidol and behavioral language training was more effective in facilitating imitation of new words than either haloperidol or behavioral therapy alone. Other well-controlled studies have produced similar results (L. Anderson and Campbell 1989; Anderson et al. 1984; I. Cohen et al. 1980).

Because longer-term administration of medication is often needed in moderately to severely affected children, Perry et al. (1989) studied the effects of haloperidol given for 6 months to 60 children with autism. Children were randomly assigned either to a group that received haloperidol continuously or to a group that received it discontinuously (5 days of drug treatment and 2 days of placebo) for a 6-month period. Doses of haloperidol ranged from 0.5–4.0 mg/day. At these doses sedation and parkinsonian side effects were not observed. Twelve children developed haloperidol-related dyskinesias, 3 during haloperidol administration and 9 upon discontinuation. The discontinuous drug administration did not reduce the efficacy of haloperidol, and there was no difference in side effects between children receiving continuous versus discontinuous treatment. The authors concluded that because of the emergence of drug-related dyskinesias, safe and more effective drugs needed to be developed for those autistic children who required medication as an adjunct to special education and behavior modification.

In an attempt to define more carefully the occurrence of drug-related dyskinesias, Campbell et al. (1988a) conducted a prospective study of 82 autistic children who ranged in age from 2.3 to 8.2 years at the time the study began. Patients received haloperidol 0.25–10.50 mg/day for 0.8–78.5 months. Twenty-four of the 82 children developed dyskinesias, 21% during haloperidol administration and 79% during drug withdrawal. Although all of the dyskinesias were reversible, the time course for this to occur varied from 7 days to 7.5 months.

Other neuroleptics have been less frequently studied than haloperidol. Pimozide, also a dopamine antagonist, was studied in a multicenter investigation employing a double-blind crossover design using pimozide, haloperidol, and placebo in children with behavior disorders (Naruse et al. 1982). The patients ranged in age from 3 to 16 years and included 34 children with autism. Doses of pimozide ranged from 1 to 9 mg/day. A significant reduction occurred in some types of aggression, although self-mutilation was not significantly decreased. In an open-label pilot study, Ernst et al. (1992) also found pimozide in doses of 3–6 mg/day helpful in management of hospitalized autistic children. Untoward side effects were minimal and transient.

Another line of pharmacological treatment relates to notions of disturbances in arousal in autism and the role of norepinephrine in the condition. Beta-blockers, which block norepinephrine receptors and reduce overall levels of norepinephrine transmission, have been used in several studies. For example, Ratey et al. (1987a, 1987b) described a reduction in aggression, impulsivity, and self-injury as well as improved speech and socialization skills in an open study. The potential side effects of beta-blockers suggest the need for care in its use. Clonidine, an alpha-2-noradrenergic receptor agonist, which decreases norepinephrine neurotransmission, has also been studied. In a double-blind, placebo-controlled crossover study this agent was administered to 8 boys with autism (mean age 8.1 years) who exhibited symptoms of inattention, impulsivity, and hyperactivity (Jaselskis et al. 1992). Clonidine (.15–.20 mg/day) or placebo was given 3 times a day for 6 weeks, and following a 1-week washout, the alternate treatment was given for 6 weeks. Teacher and parent ratings showed modest decrease in hyperactivity and irritability during clonidine treatment. Clinicians' ratings of behavior during videotaped sessions did not, however, reveal significant differences. Sedation and decreased blood pressure were the most frequent side effects. In addition, many of the patients eventually developed tolerance to the therapeutic effects of clonidine. The authors concluded that the use of clonidine to treat symptoms of overactivity in autistic children may be limited.

Another line of research on pharmacological intervention has been stimulated by the repeated observation of high peripheral serotonin (5-HT) in autism. The use of fenfluramine evoked considerable initial interest. This agent, an indirect serotonin (5-hydroxytryptamine [5-HT]) agonist, releases 5-HT presynaptically and blocks its reuptake from 5-HT neurons. Although fenfluramine increases 5-HT neurotransmission acutely, ongoing administration results in a reduction in brain 5-HT. An initial report (Geller et al. 1982) described positive effects of this agent in three boys with autism. Subsequent studies (e.g., Campbell et al. 1988b; Ekman and Miranda-Linné (1989) have not been as positive. In the Campbell et al. (1988) study a double-blind, placebo-controlled, parallel group design was employed and fenfluramine was associated with a significant decrease in fidgetiness and withdrawal. However, no difference between fenfluramine and placebo was found for ratings of stereotype or the core symptoms of autism. Furthermore, fenfluramine interfered with discrimination learning. The most common side effects were weight loss, excessive sedation, and irritability.

Preliminary analysis of a 12-week, double-blind, placebo-controlled trial of fluvoxamine, a potent and selective 5-HT uptake inhibitor, in a sample of 30 adults with autistic disorder suggested that the drug was useful in reducing levels of stereotyped, repetitive behaviors and aggression and in improving social relatedness (McDougle et al. 1994a). Other than mild dyspepsia and sedation in a minority of patients, the agent was well tolerated. In a preliminary open-label study, Cook et al. (1992) reported that fluoxetine, a potent and selective 5-HT uptake inhibitor, led to significant improvement in subjects with autistic disorder and in subjects with mental retardation in autism in doses that ranged from 20 mg every other day to 80 mg/day. Side effects consisted primarily of restlessness, hyperactivity, decreased appetite, or insomnia.

Gordon et al. (1993) found clomipramine, a nonselective 5-HT uptake inhibitor, superior (152 ± 56 mg/day) to the relatively selective norepinephrine uptake inhibitor desipramine (127 ± 52 mg/day) and to placebo in a randomized, crossover study of children with autism. In comparison to placebo, clomipramine was found to be associated with significant decrease in core symptoms of autism: anger and uncooperativeness, hyperactivity, and obsessive-compulsive symptoms. When compared with desipramine, significant changes were observed in all these areas except for hyperactivity. Adverse effects of clomipramine included prolongation of the corrected QT interval, tachycardia, and a grand mal seizure, whereas irritability, temper outbursts, and uncharacteristic aggression were observed with desipramine. Other agents include buspirone, a 5-HT$_{1A}$ partial agonist, which has been marketed in the United States for treatment of generalized anxiety disorder. On one open-label study (Realmuto et al. 1989), 2 children were noted to exhibit a reduction in hyperactivity, 1 had a reduction in stereotypic behavior, and the fourth showed no significant change. No adverse effects were observed. In another open-label study buspirone was administered in 14 developmentally disabled, self-injurious adults (3 of whom exhibited autism), and 9 showed some improvement with the drug (Ratey et al. 1989). The dose of buspirone ranged from 15 to 45 mg/day and of the 9 responders 7 were on concomitant psychoactive medication. The potent and selective 5-HT uptake inhibitor sertraline is presently under study.

Another line of pharmacological work has focused on neuropeptides. In an open-label study, Campbell et al. (1989) evaluated the safety and efficacy of the opiate antagonist naltrexone in 10 hospitalized autistic boys (mean age 5 years). Patients received single oral doses of naltrexone 0.5 mg/kg/day, 1.0 mg/kg/day, and 2.0 mg/kg/day in ascending order, once a week. Seven children showed mild sedation and 1 became hypoactive. Naltrexone resulted in a reduction in withdrawal across all three doses, increased verbal production at the 0.5 mg/kg/day dose, and reduced stereotypies at the 2.0 mg/kg/day dose. The authors' clinical impression was that there was only a slight reduction in self-injurious behavior with naltrexone. However, in a recently published double-blind, placebo-controlled study in 41 autistic children, the same group of investigators (Campbell et al. 1993) found naltrexone useful only for symptoms of hyperactivity with no effect on discrimination learning. The authors reported that there was a suggestion of a positive effect on self-injurious behavior although further study was necessary. Untoward effects of naltrexone were mild and transient. A synthetic analog of adrenocorticotropic hormone (ACTH) has also been studied with mixed results (Buitelaar et al. 1990).

Various claims have been made for the use of megadose vitamins in children with autism (see Raiten and Massaro 1987 for a review). Although this is of considerable interest to parents and although some studies on these agents have been conducted, the utility of such treatments remains to be established.

With all agents the potential benefits and side effects should be carefully discussed with parents and, if appropriate, the child. With the major tranquilizers, sedation is probably the most common side effect. Stimulant medications are rarely used in autism because they are often associated with increased levels of stereotypy and agitation; these agents may be used inappropriately if physicians equate the nonspecific overactivity of younger autistic children with that observed in attention-deficit/ hyperactivity disorder.

Controversial Treatments

In the absence of a definitive cure, a host of other interventions have been attempted. In contrast to the treatments listed in the previous section, these interventions have not usually received any systematic study. These treatments have highly varied theoretical origins and include auditory training, holding therapy, patterning, facilitated communication, vitamin supplementation, and so forth.

Of these, facilitated communication has probably been the object of greatest interest recently on the part of parents. This method, originally developed in Australia for use with students with motor difficulties, entails the use of a facilitator who helps the individual with autism by holding and moving his or her hand over a board with letters and "facilitates" the person as he or she spells out a message. Proponents of the method claim that the child is then able to communicate via the facilitator. Facilitated communication grows out of an established body of research on various methods of augmentative communication; however, the communication obtained is highly suspect in many ways, and emerging validation studies suggest that the message appears to be primarily a function of the facilitator rather than the child (Prior and Cummings 1992).

The efficacy of many of these treatments has yet to be established. Those that are minimally disruptive of the child's educational program and that hold little apparent risk to the child are of less concern than those that entail considerable disruption of the child's educational program or the family's life. In this context it is unfortunate that nonconventional treatments are not subject to the rigorous treatment trials employed in neurobiological treatments (Klin and Cohen 1994).

Summary

Considerable progress in understanding the nature of autism and related disorders has been made over the past 50 years. Given the early onset of the condition it is somewhat paradoxical that our knowledge of autism in infants and very young children remains limited in important respects. Our knowledge of the other PDDs is even more limited. Although it now appears that these conditions arise as a result of some insult to the developing CNS, precise and testable pathophysiological mechanisms have not yet been identified.

Nevertheless, autism remains one of the most studied early childhood disorders. Although much of the biological research to date has been unavailing, continued advances in the neurosciences make elucidation of underlying brain pathobiology more likely. The neurosciences can be put to their best use if one clearly understands the present limits of our knowledge concerning phenotype, neurobiology, and etiology. Advances in the understanding of the psychology of autism, both within and across individuals, as well as along behavioral dimensions and with respect to categorical issues, should serve to better direct and organize the biological research. Such advances together with the recent nosological efforts will hopefully result in a better understanding of the syndrome's pathogenesis, which, in turn, might finally translate into more effective treatment interventions. However, such integration of different lines of research and treatment approaches requires an appreciation of the complexity of the clinical phenomena and the enormous range for each of the salient dimensions. In the process of elucidating such a complex disorder affecting the child's basic capacities for socialization, it is likely that a great deal of light will be shed on the intricacies of every child's development.

Case Report

Jim was the second of two children born to working-class parents following an unremarkable pregnancy. The labor and delivery had been problem free and Jim was noted to be in apparently good condition at birth. His mother reported that, in retrospect, he was "too good" as a baby and generally seemed undemanding and placid. He was not interested in the usual social games of infancy. Motor milestones occurred at, or somewhat before, expected times. His language skills were, however, significantly delayed. Although his parents thought that he might have been saying "mama" by 12 months, his language development did not subsequently blossom. By the time Jim was 18 months of age, his parents were seriously concerned that, compared to his older brother, his language was quite delayed in developing. As a toddler he was forever getting into trouble and seemed not to have either a sense of danger or the usual attachment that most babies exhibit to their parents. He was not upset by strangers and was easily left in a baby-sitter's care. On the other hand certain sounds—such as the videotape rewinding in the VCR—often "set him off."

The parents expressed their concerns to the pediatrician but were initially reassured that he was a "late talker." When Jim was nearly 2 years old, the pediatrician was sufficiently concerned to obtain be-havioral audiometry. Although difficult to test, it did appear that his hearing was probably adequate for development of speech. Shortly after his third birthday he was seen for assessment.

At the time of assessment he was noted to have motor skills at age level. His nonverbal problem-solving skills—for example, with puz-zles—were similarly very close to age level. However, both expressive and receptive language skills were below the 1-year level. He made few sounds and no word approximations. In addition, he did not appear to exhibit many intentionally communicative behaviors such as point-ing, protesting, greeting, and so forth. He had developed a certain be-havioral rigidity and was intolerant of change in the environment. He often seemed to have his greatest behavioral difficulties around the time of transitions. Although he had not previously had a transitional object, he became very attached to the *Reader's Digest* and had to have an issue of this magazine with him at all times. He was interested in the smell and feel of play materials and lined them up but did not use them for symbolic play. There was limited apparent interest in social interaction. He had marked difficulties with tasks that required imi-tation and little evidence of empathy toward others. He generally did not make eye contact. A comprehensive medical examination revealed a normal EEG and normal CT scan; chromosome analysis was simi-larly within normal limits. A diagnosis of autistic disorder was made.

Jim was then enrolled in a preschool intervention program, which was intensive and language based. The efforts of an experienced be-havioral psychologist resulted in reduced levels of off-task behaviors (e.g., self-stimulation and stereotypy). By 48 months of age, Jim was able to say a few words (and to echo many phrases). His speech was not well inflected. He often required prompting to use those language skills that he did have.

By the time he reached school age, Jim had developed some increased relatedness toward his parents, clearly discriminating them
from strangers and approaching them when he was in distress or when
he needed something. Levels of self-stimulatory behaviors increased,
and, if not otherwise occupied, he spent considerable periods of time
body rocking. When frustrated, he engaged in some head banging. He
was exquisitely sensitive to the inanimate environment; for example,
he became very upset when a toilet was flushed in a restroom four
rooms away. He also insisted that his particular routines be adhered
to. Intelligence testing at the age of 8 years revealed marked delays in
language and communication skills, with nonverbal skills close to the
borderline range. As an adolescent, Jim developed seizures and his
behavioral functioning deteriorated. Plans for him as an adult include
placement in a group home and a special vocational program designed
for autistic adults with supported employment in the community.

References

Adrien JL, Ornitz E, Barthelemy C, et al: The presence or absence of certain
     behaviors associated with infantile autism in severely retarded autistic and
     nonautistic retarded children and very young normal children. J Autism
     Dev Disord 17:407–416, 1987
Alpern GD: Measurement of "untestable" autistic children. J Abnorm Psychol
     72:478–496, 1967
American Psychiatric Association: Diagnostic and Statistical Manual of Mental
     Disorders, 3rd Edition. Washington, DC, American Psychiatric Associa-
     tion, 1980
American Psychiatric Association: Diagnostic and Statistical Manual of Mental
     Disorders, 3rd Edition, Revised. Washington, DC, American Psychiatric
     Association, 1987
American Psychiatric Association: Diagnostic and Statistical Manual of Mental
     Disorders, 4th Edition. Washington, DC, American Psychiatric Associa-
     tion, 1994
Anderson GM, Hoshino Y: Neurochemical studies of autism, in Handbook of
     Autism and Pervasive Developmental Disorders. Edited by Cohen DJ,
     Donnellan A. New York, Wiley, 1987, pp 166–191
Anderson L, Campbell M: The effects of haloperidol on discrimination learn-
     ing and behavioral symptoms in autistic children. J Autism Dev Disord
     19:227–239, 1989

Anderson L, Campbell M, Grega D, et al: Haloperidol in the treatment of infantile autism: effects on learning and behavioral symptoms. Am J Psychiatry 141:1195–1202, 1984

August GJ, Stewart MA, Tsai L: The incidence of cognitive disabilities in the siblings of autistic children. Br J Psychiatry 138:416–422, 1981

Bailey A, Bolton P, Butler L, et al: Prevalence of the Fragile X anomaly amongst autistic twins and singletons. J Child Psychol Psychiatry 34:673–688, 1993

Baron-Cohen S: The autistic child's theory of mind: a case of specific developmental delay. J Child Psychol Psychiatry 30:285–297, 1989

Baron-Cohen S, Howlin P: The theory of mind deficit in autism: some questions for teaching and diagnosis, in Understanding Other Minds: Perspectives from Autism. Edited by Baron-Cohen S, Tager-Flusberg H, Cohen DJ. Oxford, Oxford Medical Publications, 1993, pp 466–480

Bauman M, Kemper TL: Histoanatomic observation of the brain in early infantile autism. Neurology 35:866–874, 1985

Bayley N: Bayley Scales of Infant Development, 2nd Edition. San Antonio, TX, Psychological Corporation, 1993

Bell RQ, Harper LV: Child Effects on Adults. New York, Erlbaum, 1977

Bemporad JR: Adult recollections of a formerly autistic child. J Autism Dev Disord 9:179–197, 1979

Bender L: Childhood schizophrenia: clinical study of 100 schizophrenic children. Am J Orthopsychiatry 17:40–56, 1947

Bettelheim B: The Empty Fortress. New York, Free Press, 1967

Bregman J, Volkmar FR: Brief report: autistic social dysfunction and Down syndrome. J Am Acad Child Adolesc Psychiatry 27:440–441, 1988

Brothers L: A biological perspective on empathy. Am J Psychiatry 146:10–19, 1989

Bryson S: Epidemiology of autism. J Autism Dev Disord (in press)

Buitelaar J, van Engeland H, van Ree J, et al: Behavioral effects of Org 2766 in 14 outpatient autistic children. J Autism Dev Disord 20:467–478, 1990

Burack J, Volkmar FR: Development of low- and high-functioning autistic children. J Child Psychol Psychiatry 33:607–616, 1992

Bzoch K, League R: Receptive Expressive Emergent Language Scale. Gainesville, FL, Language Educational Division, Computer Management Corporation, 1991

Cairns RB: Social Development: The Origins and Plasticity of Interchanges. San Francisco, Freeman, 1979

Campbell M, Anderson L, Meier M, et al: A comparison of haloperidol and behavior therapy and their interaction in autistic children. J Am Acad Child Psychiatry 17:640–655, 1978

Campbell M, Adams P, Perry R, et al: Tardive and withdrawal dyskinesia in autistic children: a prospective study. Psychopharmacol Bull 24:251–255, 1988a

Campbell M, Adams P, Small A, et al: Efficacy and safety of fenfluramine in autistic children. J Am Acad Child Adolesc Psychiatry 27:434–439, 1988b

Campbell M, Overall J, Small A, et al: Naltrexone in autistic children: an acute open dose range tolerance trial. J Am Acad Child Adolesc Psychiatry 28:200–206, 1989

Campbell M, Anderson LT, Small AM, et al: Naltrexone in autistic children: behavioral symptoms and attentional learning. J Am Acad Child Adolesc Psychiatry 32:1283–1291, 1993

Cantwell DP, Baker L: Research concerning families of children with autism, in The Effects of Autism on the Family. Edited by Schopler E, Mesibov G. New York, Plenum, 1984, pp 31–55

Charlop MJ, Schreiman L, Tryon AD: Learning though observation: the effects of peer modeling on acquisition and generalization in autistic children. J Abnorm Child Psychol 11:355–366, 1983

Cohen DJ, Paul R, Volkmar FR: Issues in the classification of pervasive developmental disorders and associated conditions, in Handbook of Autism and Pervasive Developmental Disorders. Edited by Cohen DJ, Donnellan A. New York, Wiley, pp 20–40, 1987

Cohen DJ, Pauls D, Volkmar FR: Recent research in autism. Child and Adolescent Psychiatry Clinics of North America 3:161–171, 1994

Cohen I, Campbell M, Posner D, et al: Behavioral effects of haloperidol in young autistic children. J Am Acad Child Psychiatry 19:665–677, 1980

Coleman M: The search for neurobiological subgroups in autism, in Neurobiological Issues in Autism. Edited by Schopler E, Mesibov G. New York, Plenum, 1987, pp 163–179

Cook E: Autism: review of neurochemical investigations. Synapse 6:292–308, 1990

Cook EHJ, Rowlett R, Jaselski C, et al: Fluoxetine treatment of children with autistic disorder and mental retardation. J Am Acad Child Adolesc Psychiatry 31:739–745, 1992

Cooper JE: Epilepsy in a longitudinal survey of 5000 children British Medical Journal 1:1020–1022, 1975

Courchesne E, Yeung-Courchesne R, Press GA, et al: Hypoplasia of cerebellar vermal lobules VI and VII in autism. N Engl J Med 318:1349–1354, 1988

Curcio F: Sensorimotor functioning and communication in mute autistic children. Journal of Autism and Child Schizophrenia 8:281–292, 1978

DeMyer MK, Hingtgen JN, Jackson RK: Infantile autism reviewed: a decade of research. Schizophr Bull 7:388–451,1981

Despert JL: Some considerations relating to the genesis of autistic behavior in children. Am J Orthopsychiatry 21:335–350, 1951

Deykin EY, MacMahon B: The incidence of seizures among children with autistic symptoms. Am J Psychiatry 126:1310–1312, 1979

Dunn LM, Dunn LM: Peabody Picture Vocabulary Test—Revised. Circle Pines, MN, American Guidance Service, 1981

Dunst C: A Clinical and Educational Manual for Use with the Uzgiriz and Hunt Scales. Baltimore, MD, University Park Press, 1980

Ekman G, Miranda-Linné F: Fenfluramine treatment of twenty children with autism. J Autism Dev Disord 19:511–532, 1989

Ernst M, Magee H, Gonzalez N, et al: Pimozide in autistic children. Psychopharmacol Bull 28:187–191, 1992

Factor DC, Freeman NL, Kardash A: A comparison of DSM-III and DSM-III-R criteria for autism. J Autism Dev Disord 19:637–640, 1989

Fay W: Verbal memory systems and the autistic child. Seminars in Speech and Language 4:17–26, 1983

Fay W, Schuler AL: Emerging Language in Autistic Children. Baltimore, MD, University Park Press, 1980

Fein D, Pennington B, Markowitz P, et al: Towards a neuro-psychological model of infantile autism: are the social deficits primary? J Am Acad Child Psychiatry 25:198–212, 1986

Folstein S, Rutter M: Infantile autism: a genetic study of 21 twin pairs. J Child Psychol Psychiatry 18:297–321, 1977

Freeman BJ, Ritvo E, Yokota D, et al: WISC-R and Vineland Adaptive Behavior Scale Scores in autistic children. J Am Acad Child Adolesc Psychiatry 27:428–429, 1988

Gardner M: Expressive One-Word Picture Vocabulary Test—Revised. Novato, CA: Academic Therapy Publications, 1990

Geller E, Ritvo E, Freeman B, et al: Preliminary observations on the effect of fenfluramine on blood serotonin and symptoms in three autistic boys. N Engl J Med 307:165–169, 1982

Gillberg C: Autism and autistic-like conditions: subclasses among disorders of empathy. J Child Psychol Psychiatry 33:813–842, 1992

Golden G: Neurological functioning, in Handbook of Autism and Pervasive Developmental Disorders. Edited by Cohen DJ, Donnellan A. New York, Wiley, 1987, pp 133–147

Gordon CT, State RC, Nelson JE, et al: A double-blind comparison of clomipramine, desipramine, and placebo in the treatment of autistic disorder. Arch Gen Psychiatry 50:441–447, 1993

Harcherik D, Cohen DJ, Paul R, et al: Computed tomographic brain scanning in four neuropsychiatric disorders of childhood: attention deficit disorder, autism, language disorder, and Tourette's syndrome. Am J Psychiatry 146:731–734, 1985

Harper J, Williams K: Age and type of onset as critical variables in early infantile autism. Journal of Autism and Childhood Schizophrenia 5:25–35, 1975

Hedrick D, Prather F, Tobin A: Sequenced Inventory of Communicative Development. Seattle, WA, University of Washington Press, 1975

Hertzig M, Snow M, New E, et al: DSM-III and DSM-III-R diagnosis of autism and PDD in nursery school children. J Am Acad Child Psychiatry 29:123–126, 1990

Jaselskis CA, Cook EHJ, Fletcher KE, et al: Clonidine treatment of hyperactive and impulsive children with autistic disorder. J Clin Psychopharmacol 12:322–327, 1992

Jones MG, Szatmari P: Stoppage rules and genetic studies of autism. J Autism Dev Disord 18:31–40, 1988

Kanner L: Autistic disturbances of affective contact. Nervous Child 2:217–250, 1943

Kanner L, Rodriguez A, Ashenden B: How far can autistic children go in matters of social adaptation? Journal of Autism and Childhood Schizophrenia 2:9–33, 1972

Kaufman AS, Kaufman NL: Kaufman Assessment Battery for Children. Circle Pines, MN, American Guidance Service, 1983

Klin A: Auditory brainstem responses in autism: brainstem dysfunction or peripheral hearing loss? J Autism Dev Disord 23:15–35, 1993

Klin A: Asperger's syndrome. Child and Adolescent Psychiatric Clinics of North America 3:131–148, 1994

Klin A, Cohen DJ: The immorality of not-knowing: the ethical imperative to conduct research in child and adolescent psychiatry, in Ethics in Child Psychiatry. Edited by Hattab J. Jerusalem, Israel, Gefan Publishers, 1994, pp 217–232

Klin A, Shephard B: Psychological assessment of autistic children. Child and Adolescent Psychiatric Clinics of North America 3:53–70, 1994

Klin A, Volkmar F: Elective mutism and mental retardation J Am Acad Child Adolesc Psychiatry 32: 860–864, 1993

Klin A, Volkmar FR, Sparrow SS: Autistic social dysfunction: some limitations of the theory of mind hypothesis. J Child Psychol Psychiatry 33:861–876, 1992

Kolvin I: Studies in the childhood psychoses, I: diagnostic criteria and classification. Br J Psychiatry 118:381–384, 1971

Krug DA, Arick JR, Almond P: Behavior checklist for identifying severely handicapped individuals with high levels of autistic behavior. J Child Psychol Psychiatry 21:221–229, 1980

Le Couteur A, Rutter M, Lord C, et al: Autism diagnostic interview: a standardized investigator-based instrument. J Autism Dev Disord 19:363–388, 1989

Leiter RG: Leiter International Performance Scale. Chicago, IL, Stoelting Co, 1948

Lockyer L, Rutter M: A five to fifteen year follow-up study of infantile psychosis, III: psychological aspects. Br J Psychiatry 115:865–882, 1969

Lord C, Schopler E: Neurobiological implications of sex differences in autism, in Neurobiological Issues in Autism. Edited by Schopler E, Mesibov G. New York, Plenum, 1987, pp 192–212

Lord C, Rutter M, Goode S, et al: Autism Diagnostic Observation Schedule: a standardized observation of communicative and social behavior. J Autism Dev Disord 19:185–212, 1989

Losche G: Sensorimotor and action development in autistic children from infancy to early childhood. J Child Psychol Psychiatry 31:749–761, 1990

Lotter V: Follow-up studies, in Autism: A Reappraisal of Concepts and Treatment. Edited by Rutter M, Schopler E. New York, Plenum, 1978, pp 475–496

Lovaas OI: Behavioral treatment and normal educational and intellectual functioning in young autistic children. J Consult Clin Psychol 55:3–9, 1987

Loveland, KL, Kelley ML: Development of adaptive behavior in adolescents and young adults with autism and Down syndrome. American Journal of Mental Deficiency 93:84–92, 1988

Makita K: The age of onset of childhood schizophrenia. Folia Psychiatrica Neurologica Japonica 20:111–121, 1966

Massie HN: Blind ratings of mother-infant interaction in home movies of prepsychotic and normal infants. Am J Psychiatry 135:1371–1374, 1978

McDougle CJ, Naylor ST, Volkmar FR, et al: A double-blind placebo-controlled investigation of fluvoxamine in adults with autism. Paper presented at the annual meeting of the Society for Neuroscience, Miami, FL, November 13–18, 1994a

McDougle CJ, Price LH, Volkmar FR: Recent advances in the pharmacotherapy of autism and related conditions. Child and Adolescent Psychiatric Clinics of North America 3:71–90, 1994b

Minderaa RB, Volkmar FR, Hansen CR, et al: Snout and visual rooting reflex in infantile autism. J Autism Dev Disord 15:409–415, 1985

Minderaa RB, Anderson GM, Volkmar FR, et al: Neurochemical study of dopamine functioning in autistic and normal subjects. J Am Acad Child Adolesc Psychiatry 28:200–206, 1989

Minshew NH: Neurological localization in autism, in High-Functioning Individuals with Autism. Edited by Schopler E, Mesibov G. New York, Plenum, 1992, pp 65–89

Morgan S: The autistic child and family functioning: a developmental-family systems perspective. J Autism Dev Disord 18:263–280, 1988

Morgan S, Curtrer PS, Coplin JW, et al: Do autistic children differ from retarded and normal children in Piagetian sensorimotor functioning? J Child Psychol Psychiatry 30:857–864, 1989

Mundy P, Sigman M: Specifying the nature of the social impairment in autism, in Autism: Nature, Diagnosis, and Treatment. Edited by Dawson G. New York, Guilford, 1989, pp 1–21

Naruse H, Nagata M, Nakane Y, et al: A multi-center double-blind trial of pimozide (Orap), haloperidol and placebo in children with behavior disorders, using cross-over design. Acta Paedopsychiatr 48:173–184, 1982

O'Connor N, Hermelin B: Annotation: low intelligence and special abilities. J Child Psychol Psychiatry 29:391–396, 1988

Olley JG, Stevenson SE: Preschool curriculum for children with autism: addressing early social skills, in Autism: Nature, Diagnosis, and Treatment. Edited by Dawson G. New York, Guilford, 1989, pp 346–366

Ornitz EM, Guthrie D, Farley AJ: Early development of autistic children. Journal of Autism and Childhood Schizophrenia 7:203–229, 1977

Parks SL: The assessment of autistic children: a selective review of available instruments. J Autism Dev Disord 13:255–267, 1983

Paul R: Communication in autism, in Handbook of Autism and Pervasive Developmental Disorders. Edited by Cohen DJ, Donnellan A. New York, Wiley, 1987, pp 61–84

Perry R, Campbell M, Adams P, et al: Long-term efficacy of haloperidol in autistic children: continuous versus discontinuous drug administration. J Am Acad Child Adolesc Psychiatry 28:87–92, 1989

Petty LK, Ornitz EM, Michelman JG, et al: Autistic children who become schizophrenic. Arch Gen Psychiatry 41:129–135, 1984

Prior M, Cummings R: Questions about facilitated communication and autism. J Autism Dev Disord 21:57–67, 1992

Prior M, Dahlstrom B, Squires T: Autistic children's knowledge of thinking and feeling states in other people. J Child Psychol Psychiatry 31:587–601, 1990

Prizant BM: Language acquisition and communicative behavior in autism: toward an understanding of the "whole" of it. Journal of Speech and Hearing Disorders 48:296–307, 1987

Prizant BM, Schuler AL: Facilitating communication: pre-language approaches, in Handbook of Autism and Pervasive Developmental Disorders. Edited by Cohen DJ, Donnellan A. New York, Wiley, 1987, pp 301–315

Provence S, Lipton RC: Infants in Institutions. New York, International Universities Press, 1962

Raiten DJ, Massaro TG: Nutrition and developmental disabilities: an examination of the orthomolecular hypothesis, in Handbook of Autism and Pervasive Developmental Disorders. Edited by Cohen DJ, Donnellan A. New York, Wiley, 1987, pp 566–583

Rank B: Adaptation of the psychoanalytic technique for the treatment of young children with atypical development. Am J Orthopsychiatry 19:130–139, 1949

Ratey J, Bemporad J, Sorgi P, et al: Brief report: open trial effects of beta-blockers on speech and social behaviors in 8 autistic adults. J Autism Dev Disord 17:439–446, 1987a

Ratey J, Mikkelsen E, Sorgi P, et al: Autism: the treatment of aggressive behaviors. J Clin Psychopharmacol 7:35–41, 1987b

Ratey J, Sovner R, Mikkelsen E, et al: Buspirone therapy for maladaptive behavior and anxiety in developmentally disabled persons. J Clin Psychiatry 50:382–384, 1989

Realmuto G, August G, Garfinkel B: Clinical effects of buspirone in autistic children. J Clin Psychopharmacol 9:122–125, 1989

Reynell J, Gruber C: Reynell Developmental Language Scales-U.S. Edition. Los Angeles, CA, Western Psychological Services, 1990

Richters MM, Volkmar FR: Reactive attachment disorder of infancy or early childhood. J Am Acad Child Adolesc Psychiatry 33:328–332, 1994

Ricks DM, Wing L: Language communication and the use of symbols in normal and autistic children. Journal of Autism and Childhood Schizophrenia 5:191–200, 1975

Rimland B: Diagnostic Checklist Form E-2: a reply to Parks. J Autism Dev Disord 14:343–345, 1984

Ritvo ER, Freeman BJ: National Society for Autistic Children definition of the syndrome of autism. J Autism Dev Disord 8:162–169, 1978

Ritvo ER, Freeman BJ, Pingree C: The UCLA-University of Utah epidemiological survey of autism: recurrence risk estimates and genetic counseling. Am J Psychiatry 146:1032–1035, 1989

Rogers S: Early intervention in autism. J Autism Dev Disord (in press)

Rubenstein JLR, Lotspeich L, Ciaranello RD: The neurobiology of developmental disorders, in Advances in Clinical Child Psychology. Edited by Lahey BB, Krazdin AE. New York, Plenum, 1990, pp 155–177

Rumsey JJ, Rapoport JL, Scerry WR: Autistic children as adults: psychiatric, social and behavioral outcomes. J Am Acad Child Psychiatry 24:465–473, 1985

Rumsey JJ: Neuropsychological studies of high-level autism, in High-Functioning Individuals with Autism. Edited by Schopler E, Mesibov G. New York, Plenum, 1992, pp 42–64

Rutter M: Autistic children: infancy to adulthood. Seminars in Psychiatry 2:435–450, 1970

Rutter M: Childhood schizophrenia reconsidered. Journal of Autism and Childhood Schizophrenia 2:315–338, 1972

Rutter M: Language disorder and infantile autism, in Autism: A Reappraisal of Concepts and Treatment. Edited by Rutter M, Schopler E. New York, Plenum, 1978a, pp 85–104

Rutter M: Diagnosis and definition, in Autism: A Reappraisal of Concepts and Treatment. Edited by Rutter M, Schopler E. New York, Plenum, 1978b, pp 1–25

Rutter M, Bartak L: Special educational treatment of autistic children: a comparative study, II: follow-up findings and implications for services. J Child Psychol Psychiatry 14:241–270, 1973

Rutter M, Garmezy N: Developmental psychopathology, in Handbook of Child Psychology, 4th Edition, Vol 4: Socialization, Personality, and Social Development. Edited by Hetherington EM. New York, Wiley, 1983, pp 775–911

Rutter M, Schopler E: Autism and pervasive developmental disorders: concepts and diagnostic issues. J Autism Dev Disord 17:159–186, 1987

Rutter M, Schopler E: Classification of pervasive developmental disorders: some concepts and practical considerations. J Autism Dev Disord 22:459–482, 1992

Rutter M, Baily A, Bolton P, et al: Autism and known medical conditions: myth and substance. J Child Psychol Psychiatry 35:311–332, 1994

Schopler E, Mesibov G (eds): Autism in Adolescents and Adults. New York, Plenum, 1983

Schopler E, Mesibov G (eds): The Effects of Autism on the Family. New York, Plenum, 1984

Schopler E, Andrews CE, Strupp K: Do autistic children come from upper-middle-class parents? J Autism Dev Disord 10:91–103, 1980a

Schopler E, Reichler RJ, DeVellis RF, et al: Toward objective classification of childhood autism: Childhood Autism Rating Scale (CARS). J Autism Dev Disord 9:1–10, 1980b

Short AB, Schopler E: Factors relating to age of onset in autism. J Autism Dev Disord 18:207–216, 1988

Siegel B, Pliner C, Eschler J, et al: How autistic children are diagnosed: difficulties in identification of children with multiple developmental delays. J Dev Behav Pediatr 9:199–204, 1988

Siegel B, Vukicevic J, Spitzer RL: Using signal detection methodology to revise DSM-III-R: re-analysis of the DSM-III-R national field trials for autistic disorder. Journal of Psychiatric Research 24:293–311, 1990

Simeonson RJ, Olley JG, Rosenthal SL: Early intervention for children with autism, in The Effectiveness of Early Intervention for At-Risk and Handicapped Children. Edited by Guralnick MJ, Bennett FC. New York, Academic Press, 1987, pp 78–88

Sparrow S, Balla D, Ciccheti D: Vineland Adaptive Behavior Scales. Circle Pines, MN, American Guidance Service, 1984

Spitzer RL, Siegel B: The DSM-III-R field trial of pervasive developmental disorders. J Am Acad Child Adolesc Psychiatry 6:855–862,1990

Spitzer RL, Endicott JE, Robins E: Research diagnostic criteria. Arch Gen Psychiatry 35:773–782, 1978

Stern D: The Interpersonal World of the Human Infant. New York, Basic Books, 1987

Stone WL, Lemanek KL, Fischel PT, et al: Play and imitation skills in the diagnosis of autism in young children. Pediatrics 86:267–272, 1990

Szatmari P: The validity of autistic spectrum disorders: a literature review. J Autism Dev Disord 22:583–600, 1992

Tager-Flusberg H: What language reveals about the understanding of minds in children with autism, in Understanding Other Minds: Perspectives from Autism. Edited by Baron-Cohen S, Tager-Flusberg H, Cohen DJ. Oxford, Oxford Medical Publications, 1993, pp 138–157

Thorndike RL, Hagen EP, Sattler JM: Guide for Administering and Scoring the Stanford-Binet Intelligence Scale, 4th Edition. Chicago, IL, Riverside Publishing, 1986

Treffert DA: The idiot savant: a review of the syndrome. Am J Psychiatry 145:563–572, 1988

Tsai LY: Pre-, peri-, and neonatal factors in autism, in Neurobiological Issues in Autism. Edited by Schopler E, Mesibov G. New York, Plenum, 1987, pp 180–187

Turnbull CM: The Mountain People. New York, Simon and Schuster, 1972

Uzgiris IC, Hunt J McV: Assessment in Infancy: Ordinal Scales of Psychological Development. Urbana, IL, University of Illinois Press, 1975

Volkmar FR: Social development, in Handbook of Autism and Pervasive Developmental Disorders. Edited by Cohen DJ, Donnellan A. New York, Wiley, 1987, pp 41–60

Volkmar FR, Cohen DJ: The experience of infantile autism: a first person account by Tony W. J Autism Dev Disord 15:47–54, 1985

Volkmar FR, Cohen DJ: Diagnosis of pervasive developmental disorders, in Advances in Clinical Child Psychology. Edited by Lahey B, Kazdin A. New York, Plenum, 1988, pp 249–284

Volkmar FR, Cohen DJ: Disintegrative disorder or "late onset" autism. J Child Psychol Psychiatry 30:717–724, 1989

Volkmar FR, Cohen DJ: Comorbid association of autism and schizophrenia. Am J Psychiatry 148:1705–1707, 1991

Volkmar FR, Nelson DS: Seizure disorders in autism. J Am Acad Child Adolesc Psychiatry 29:127–129, 1990

Volkmar FR, Stier DM, Cohen DJ: Age of recognition of pervasive developmental disorder. Am J Psychiatry 142:1450–1452, 1985

Volkmar FR, Sparrow S, Goudreau D, et al: Social deficits in autism: an operational approach using the Vineland Adaptive Behavior Scales. J Am Acad Child Adolesc Psychiatry 26:156–161, 1987

Volkmar FR, Bregman J, Cohen DJ, et al: DSM III and DSM III-R diagnoses of autism. Am J Psychiatry 145:1404–1408, 1988a

Volkmar FR, Cohen DJ, Hoshino Y, et al: Phenomenology and classification of the childhood psychoses. Psychol Med 18:191–201, 1988b

Volkmar FR, Cohen DJ, Bregman JD, et al: An examination of social typologies in autism. J Am Acad Child Adolesc Psychiatry 28: 82–85, 1989

Volkmar FR, Cicchetti DV, Bregman J, et al: Developmental aspects of DSM-III-R criteria for autism. J Autism Dev Disord 22:657–662, 1992a

Volkmar FR, Cicchetti DV, Bregman J, et al: Three diagnostic systems for autism: DSM-III, DSM-III-R and ICD-10. J Autism Dev Disord 22:483–492, 1992b

Volkmar FR, Carter A, Sparrow SS, et al: Quantifying social development in autism. J Am Acad Child Adolesc Psychiatry 32:626–632, 1993

Volkmar FR, Klin A, Siegel B, et al: Field trial for autistic disorder in DSM-IV. Am J Psychiatry 151:1361–1367, 1994

Watson LR, Marcus LM: Diagnosis and assessment of preschool children, in Diagnosis and Assessment in Autism. Edited by Schopler E, Mesibov G. New York, Plenum, 1988, pp 271–301

Wechsler D: Manual for the Wechsler Preschool and Primary Scale of Intelligence. San Antonio, TX, The Psychological Corporation, 1989

Wechsler D: Manual for the Wechsler Intelligence Scale for Children, 3rd Edition. San Antonio, TX, The Psychological Corporation, 1992

Wetherby AM, Prizant BM: Communication and Symbolic Behavior Scales. Chicago, IL, Riverside Publishing, 1993

Wiig EH, Secord W: Test of Language Competence, Expanded Edition. San Antonio, TX, The Psychological Corporation, 1988

Wiig EH, Wayne S, Semel E: Clinical Evaluation of Language Fundamentals—Preschool. San Antonio, TX, The Psychological Corporation, 1992

Wing L: Asperger's syndrome: a clinical account. Psychol Med 11:115–130, 1981

Wing L, Atwood T: Syndromes of autism and atypical development, in Handbook of Autism and Pervasive Developmental Disorders. Edited by Cohen DJ, Donnellan A. New York, Wiley, 1987, pp 3–19

World Health Organization: Mental Disorders: Glossary and Guide to Their Classification in Accordance with the Ninth Revision of the International Classification of Diseases. Geneva, World Health Organization, 1977

World Health Organization: International Classification of Diseases, 10th Edition: Diagnostic Criteria for Research [draft]. Geneva, World Health Organization, 1990

Zahner GEP, Pauls DL: Epidemiological surveys of infantile autism, in Handbook of Autism and Pervasive Developmental Disorders. Edited by Cohen DJ, Donnellan A. New York, Wiley, 1987, pp 199–210

Chapter 7

Asperger's Disorder and Atypical Pervasive Developmental Disorder

Peter Szatmari, M.D.

Introduction

Soon after Kanner (1943) first described the syndrome of early infantile autism, clinicians became aware of a large number of children sharing similar characteristics. These children received different labels during the 1950s and 1960s, including atypical development, symbiotic psychosis, and pseudoneurotic schizophrenia. These conditions, along with infantile autism, were considered eventually to be varieties of childhood schizophrenia. Important work by Kolvin (1971), however, demonstrated significant differences between autistic and schizophrenic children. Although this was an important step forward, there remained a sizable group of children who demonstrated many clinical features of autism in milder form.

The epidemiological work of Wing and Gould (1979) and of Lotter

(1966) highlighted these autistic-like children. In both community studies, a nuclear group of autistic or Kanner syndrome children were identified as well as a larger group of children sharing many but not all clinical features. This observation led Wing (Wing 1988; Wing and Gould 1979) to suggest that there exists a triad of impairments in social interaction, communication, and play. The notion of a continuum of autistic characteristics, defined as dimensions, became firmly established. DSM-III (American Psychiatric Association 1980) adopted this idea and proposed that the term *pervasive developmental disorder* (PDD) be used to refer to the triad of disorders. Autism was considered to be one among several subtypes of PDD.

The quantity and quality of empirical data on autism are impressive. There is now reasonably good agreement on the clinical presentation, course, and response to treatment of this disorder. Although a precise understanding of etiology is not yet available, the evidence favors some kind of biological, possibly genetic, causation related to brain structure and function. Many fewer data are available on the other PDDs—those on the spectrum of autistic disabilities. As yet there is no agreement on classification or clinical presentation. Overlapping subtypes such as atypical autism, Asperger's disorder, disintegrative autism, childhood-onset PDD, and atypical PDD (APDD) have been proposed as autistic spectrum disorders. Unfortunately, this lack of agreement has severely hampered efforts to study in more detail the etiology, course, and response to treatment of these various nonautistic types of PDD. In general, it can be said that autistic spectrum disorders differ from autism in one of several ways: by having fewer symptoms, by lacking specific types of behaviors, or by having a different age at onset and course. These differences roughly correspond to the definition of APDD, Asperger's disorder, disintegrative disorder, and Rett's disorder respectively. In this chapter, I review the first two conditions.

Asperger's Disorder

Overview

Hans Asperger, a pediatrician practicing in Vienna, published a paper on "autistic psychopathy" (Asperger 1944) the year after Kanner's influential monograph appeared (1943). Both authors borrowed the term *autism* independently from Bleuler, who used it to describe one of the cardinal features of schizophrenia (Van Krevelen 1971). Asperger described children with "autistic psychopathy" as having profound impairments in two-way social interaction. Speech developed on time but walking was often delayed. Intelligence was usually above average even though the children experienced enormous difficulties at school. He noted that the disorder was almost entirely confined to boys and that many of the children's fathers displayed similar behaviors. Perhaps the most characteristic feature of the disorder was the intense interest the children displayed in unusual subjects such as astronomy, the weather, geology, and chemistry.

Lorna Wing's report (Wing 1981) stimulated interest in the English-speaking literature. In that paper, she described 34 severely impaired individuals with "Asperger Syndrome." Since then, many case reports have appeared (Bowman 1988; C. Gillberg 1985; Tantam et al. 1990). More recently a book containing a translation of Asperger's original paper (Frith 1991) and several studies have provided information on clinical presentation and possible differences from autism (Gillberg 1989; Kerbeshian et al. 1990; Szatmari et al. 1989a, 1990).

Wolff and colleagues in Edinburgh have published over the years a series of papers on schizoid children (Wolff 1991a, 1991b, 1991c; Wolff and Barlow 1979; Wolff and Chick 1980; Wolff et al. 1988; Wolff et al. 1991). She argues that schizoid disorder is conceptually similar to Asperger's disorder even though the former group is less severely impaired than those described by Asperger, Wing, and other authors.

Definition

Asperger's disorder did not appear in the DSM-III (American Psychiatric Association 1980) or in the DSM-III-R (American Psychiatric Association 1987). The term was used more frequently in Europe and the United Kingdom than in North America. It is included in ICD-10 (Rutter and Schopler 1992; World Health Organization 1992) and in DSM-IV (American Psychiatric Association 1994) as a PDD subtype; DSM-IV criteria for the condition are listed in Table 7–1.

For a diagnosis of Asperger's disorder there must be some evidence

---

Table 7–1. DSM-IV diagnostic criteria for Asperger's disorder

---

A. Qualitative impairment in social interaction, as manifested by at least two of the following:

  (1) marked impairment in the use of multiple nonverbal behaviors such as eye-to-eye gaze, facial expression, body postures, and gestures to regulate social interaction
  (2) failure to develop peer relationships appropriate to developmental level
  (3) a lack of spontaneous seeking to share enjoyment, interests, or achievements with other people (e.g., by a lack of showing, bringing, or pointing out objects of interest to other people)
  (4) lack of social or emotional reciprocity

B. Restricted repetitive and stereotyped patterns of behavior, interests, and activities, as manifested by at least one of the following:

  (1) encompassing preoccupation with one or more stereotyped and restricted patterns of interest that is abnormal either in intensity or focus
  (2) apparently inflexible adherence to specific, nonfunctional routines or rituals
  (3) stereotyped and repetitive motor mannerisms (e.g., hand or finger flapping or twisting, or complex whole-body movements)
  (4) persistent preoccupation with parts of objects

C. The disturbance causes clinically significant impairment in social, occupational, or other important areas of functioning.

D. There is no clinically significant general delay in language (e.g., single words used by age 2 years, communicative phrases used by age 3 years).

E. There is no clinically significant delay in cognitive development or in the development of age-appropriate self-help skills, adaptive behavior (other than in social interaction), and curiosity about the environment in childhood.

F. Criteria are not met for another specific pervasive developmental disorder or schizophrenia.

Source. American Psychiatric Association: Diagnostic and Statistical Manual of Mental Disorders, 4th Edition. Washington, DC, American Psychiatric Association, 1994, p. 77. Used with permission.

of impairments in reciprocal social interaction of the type seen in autism: marked impairment in the use of nonverbal behaviors to regulate social interaction, a failure to develop peer relationships, little evidence of seeking to share enjoyment, and lack of social or emotional reciprocity. In addition, there must be evidence of a pattern of restricted, stereotyped activities or behaviors as manifested by abnormal preoccupations, inflexible adherence to nonfunctional routines or rituals, stereotypies, or persistent preoccupation with parts of objects. Again, these are features identical to those for autistic disorder. However, to distinguish Asperger's disorder from autism there can be no clinically significant delay in language acquisition nor a clinically significant delay in cognitive development or age-appropriate self-help skills. Finally, a diagnostic hierarchy is imposed such that if a child also meets criteria for autism, Rett's disorder, or childhood disintegrative disorder this condition takes precedence; this ensures that individuals who meet criteria for Asperger's disorder will have sufficient symptoms of a pervasive developmental disorder without meeting criteria for one of the better-established disorders in the PDD class. The ICD-10 criteria for Asperger's disorder are very similar although the issue of continuity with autism is noted to be debatable. These criteria reflect the available literature on the condition and will encourage both clinical diagnosis and research.

However, some questions remain about the implementation of the criteria. First, there may be very few children with severe social impairment and repetitive patterns of behavior who do not also meet criteria for autism (even if they speak on time and have no clinically significant delay in cognitive development). It seems likely that the vast majority of children with Asperger's disorder described in the current literature would either meet the current DSM-IV criteria for autism or else would fail to meet the criteria for both autism and Asperger's disorder. Second, the literature suggests that not only does language begin on time in Asperger's disorder but also that there is an absence of unusual aspects of language development often seen in verbal individuals with autism, such as delayed echolalia and pronoun reversal. The DSM-IV criteria do not mention these clinical features. Future research will be needed to see which measure of language development proves to be a more robust predictor of differences between groups of children with these conditions.

Prevalence and Epidemiology

Unfortunately, there are no community studies of Asperger's disorder available. Gillberg and Gillberg (1989) have summarized several studies of handicapped children and have extrapolated from these to estimate prevalence rates of the disorder. They suggest that the prevalence of Asperger's disorder is between 10 and 26 per 10,000. According to these estimates, although it is often thought that Asperger's disorder is quite rare, the condition is at least as common, if not more common, than autism. However, it must be emphasized that none of the studies was specifically designed to measure the prevalence of Asperger's disorder and so they await replication.

Clinical Features

Several case reports (Bowman 1988; Gillberg 1985; Tantam et al. 1990) and case series (I. C. Gillberg and C. Gillberg 1989; Szatmari et al. 1989c; Tantam 1988a, 1988b; Wing 1981) have described the clinical features of children, adolescents, and adults with Asperger's disorder. Although there are some differences in content and emphasis, there are also remarkable similarities. The degree and severity of social impairment is striking. Not only are these children socially isolated, but they demonstrate an abnormal range and type of social interaction that cannot be explained by other factors such as shyness, short attention span, aggressive behavior, or lack of experience. These impairments take many forms and include not showing any interest in other children, being a passive participant in other children's play, or interacting with others only in respect to their own obsessive interests. If they do play with other children, those with Asperger's disorder frequently interact with younger children or with girls. They often demonstrate a desire to interact with other children but can be socially intrusive and awkward. They can be quite disinhibited in their interactions with strangers, ask inappropriate questions, come too close to others, and make embarrassing remarks. Children with Asperger's disorder appear to lack the ability to modulate their social behavior to the demands of the social context or the environment.

Many difficulties in nonverbal communication are also apparent. Often, children with Asperger's disorder lack eye-to-eye contact; they do not use gestures to accompany their conversation or their gestures are clumsy and inappropriate. They may lack facial expressions or may demonstrate inappropriate facial expressions, such as laughing or smiling inappropriately. Although it is true that children with Asperger's disorder develop speech on time and lack the impaired language development so commonly seen in autistic children, nevertheless they have enormous difficulties in initiating and sustaining a conversation with others (Szatmari et al. 1989c). Parents describe their conversation as tangential and as not providing essential information. At other times they can be quite mute and uncommunicative, vague and circumstantial. Their voice often lacks appropriate inflection, and they frequently put stress in inappropriate places in conversation (Fine et al. 1991). Their conversations are often one-sided, centering around their own obsessive interests. Rarely do they inquire about the feelings or concerns of others. One of the most characteristic features of these children is their restricted range of interests. These interests often take unusual or bizarre forms. For example, children with Asperger's disorder may demonstrate an extreme interest in subjects such as astronomy, meteorology, subways, or bus timetables. Such children can watch clothes tumbling in a washing machine for hours, or sit fascinated by home furnaces. Sometimes these interests are difficult to separate from normal hobbies and interests. Occasionally adolescents with Asperger's disorder develop intense preoccupations with horror movies, science fiction, wrestling, or certain sports. Older adolescents and young adults may develop a very complex fantasy life. The distinguishing feature is that these interests take up virtually all their leisure time to the exclusion of other social activities. Furthermore, trying to distract children with Asperger's disorder from these interests may result in noncompliant and occasionally aggressive behavior.

Differences From Autism

The clinical features described above bear many similarities to those seen in high-functioning (i.e., nonretarded) autistic children. This has led many experts to conclude that Asperger's disorder represents a mild form of autism (Frith 1991) rather than a type of PDD. Although this may seem, in part, a problem of definition, the key issue is whether there are useful clinical differences between Asperger's disorder and autistic children matched on IQ or another measure of severity.

Using different sets of inclusion criteria (which did not include normal language development), two studies have reported that children with Asperger's disorder lack the impaired language development so characteristic of children with autism (C. Gillberg 1989; Szatmari et al. 1989a).

For example, rates of echolalia and pronoun reversal are found less frequently in children with Asperger's disorder than in high-functioning autistic children. In both studies, there were no differences in IQ between the groups, thus controlling for at least one aspect of severity.

Several differences were also reported with respect to impairments in reciprocal social interaction. For example, parents of children with Asperger's disorder frequently recall that their children did develop a bond with them and were affectionate and responsive in the early years (Szatmari et al. 1989a). Usually the impairments in social interaction were more subtle and appeared when the children began to interact with peers in nursery or preschool. The progression from parallel to cooperative play was severely delayed in children with Asperger's disorder and was characterized by the unusual interactions noted above. In contrast, parents of autistic children described impairments in early mother-infant relationships, in social responsiveness, in social smiling, and in seeking comfort.

Imaginative play was another behavior that distinguished the groups. Typically, autistic children do not develop imaginative play but remain preoccupied with parts of objects or else play with toys in an inappropriate way. For example, autistic children may spend a lot of time spinning wheels and lining up things, or they are fascinated with certain objects, textures, or visual patterns. In contrast, children with Asperger's disorder develop imaginative play. However, their play is stereotypic, repetitive, and lacking in creativity. Often the same scenario is repeated day after day with little variation. Parents or other children may participate in this play; however, they have a rigid script to follow. If the script is not adhered to, the child quickly loses interest.

So far the results have suggested that children with Asperger's disorder consistently have fewer PDD symptoms than autistic children do, even controlling for IQ. The notion that valid distinctions can be drawn between the groups would be strengthened if there were other behaviors or symptoms seen more frequently in children with Asperger's disorder than in autistic children. In fact, C. Gillberg (1989) has reported that children with Asperger's disorder are clumsier and have higher rates of circumscribed interests than autistic children do. Several studies have also reported that comorbid psychiatric symptoms occur more frequently in Asperger's disorder than in high-functioning, or nonretarded, autistic children. For example, parents report more symptoms of anxiety and schizotypal symptoms, such as magical thinking, in those with Asperger's disorder than in those with autism (Szatmari et al. 1989a). The group from Edinburgh (Wolff 1991b; Wolff and Chick 1980) also reported frequent comorbid diagnoses such as elective mutism, attention-deficit disorders, and schizophrenia in schizoid children.

Over the years, several efforts have been made to identify the core deficits associated with autism. Recently, interest has shifted from seeing some kind of language impairment as primary to considering social deficits as essential. Among theories used to understand this social deficit, affect recognition (Hobson 1986) and theory of mind (Baron-Cohen 1989) have received the most attention. There is some evidence that, compared with controls, autistic children have serious difficulties in decoding affective information from others, or alternatively they lack a "theory" of other people's minds. In other words, they cannot ascribe thoughts, feelings, or motivations to other people. One carefully done study tested these two theories with autistic children and children with Asperger's disorder, matched on IQ (Ozonoff et al. 1991). Although both groups, compared with controls, had significant difficulty in decoding affective information, only the autistic group did poorly on measures of theory of mind. If this finding can be replicated, it would be quite useful in suggesting fundamental differences between the groups.

Course and Prognosis

There are several important issues with respect to the outcome of Asperger's disorder: 1) whether the diagnosis is stable over time, 2) how the behaviors change with development, 3) what level of adaptive impairment persists, 4) whether adolescents and adults with Asperger's disorder are at risk for other psychiatric disorders, and 5) how the outcome for children with Asperger's disorder differs from that for children with autism. This last issue is extremely important in helping to decide whether Asperger's disorder is a useful diagnostic label. For example, even though Asperger's disorder and autism may share several clinical features and etiological mechanisms, if outcome and course are different, retaining the label of Asperger's disorder may be useful for clinical practice and research.

Unfortunately, there are few data available on the course of Asperger's disorder and the outcome for children with Asperger's disorder.
The most extensive work is by Wolff and Chick (1980) and Wolff et al.
(1991) on schizoid children. Their work suggests that the diagnosis is
stable over time, that schizoid children are at risk for other psychiatric
disorders during adolescence or adulthood (such as depression and
schizophrenia), and that serious impairments in social and occupational
functioning remain. However, a reasonable level of functioning is possible in some circumstances. Although a comparison with IQ-matched
autistic children was not included, the outcome for schizoid children in
this study does seem to be better than the outcome usually reported for
autistic children (Cantwell et al. 1989; Rumsey et al. 1985; Szatmari et
al. 1989b). These data are certainly interesting and suggest that the diagnosis does carry predictive validity. Future studies will need to have
clear inclusion criteria and will need to include a control group of autistic
children.

Etiology and Pathogenesis

The etiology and pathogenesis of Asperger's disorder are unknown. If
one accepts that the disorder represents a subtype of PDD or a variant
of autism, it would be logical to see whether children with Asperger's
disorder also have abnormalities in serotonin metabolism or structural
abnormalities on brain imaging, electroencephalography, or other
markers of brain dysfunction commonly seen in autistic children.

The markers of organic etiologies that have been studied include
neuropsychological deficits, family history, pregnancy and birth complications, and comorbid disease. Szatmari et al. (1990) compared
neuropsychological deficits of children with Asperger's disorder, IQ-
matched autistic children, and a control group with nonspecific social
problems. No significant differences were observed in cognitive functioning between the autistic and Asperger's disorder groups. However,
these subjects differed strongly from the control group, even matching
closely for IQ. The two PDD subtypes demonstrated very poor motor
coordination, verbal comprehension, and nonverbal problem solving
compared with control subjects. This pattern of deficits is consistent

across several studies and appears to be specific to PDD individuals compared with other dyslexic individuals (Rumsey and Hamburger 1990).

C. Gillberg (1989) has reported on etiological factors in 23 children with Asperger's disorder and a control group of autistic children with normal IQs. Rates of neurological disorder, chromosomal abnormalities, and abnormal electroencephalograms (EEGs) and computed tomography (CT) scans were roughly equal between the groups. The only significant difference was that the autistic children had more prenatal and perinatal complications than did those with Asperger's disorder.

Family history data also suggest that Asperger's disorder and autism share a common etiology. Burgoine and Wing (1983) reported on a set of triplets; one of the three children was autistic and the other two had Asperger's disorder. Indeed, the early report of twins by Folstein and Rutter (1977) suggests that the monozygous co-twins of autistic children often have severe social dysfunction possibly reminiscent of Asperger's disorder. This finding has been replicated for nontwin siblings by Piven et al. (1990) and for cousins by DeLong and Dwyer (1988). C. Gillberg (1989) reports that fathers of children with Asperger's disorder often demonstrate clinical features very similar to those of their sons. This has been reported for fathers of autistic children as well (Wolff et al. 1988). Thus, the bulk of the data suggests that although there may be some differences in pathogenesis between autism and Asperger's disorder, both disorders probably share a common etiology.

Assessment

The objectives of the assessment of a child suspected of having Asperger's disorder are 1) to decide whether there are elements of PDD present (i.e., qualitative impairments in reciprocal social interaction, qualitative impairments in verbal and nonverbal communication, and a pattern of repetitive stereotypic activities), 2) to see whether the child qualifies for a diagnosis of Asperger's disorder as opposed to other subtypes of PDD, 3) to determine if other psychiatric disorders or medical diseases are present, and 4) to identify the major handicaps that require intervention. To accomplish this, information must be obtained from several sources (parents, teachers, and the children themselves) as well as by different methods (interview and direct observation). The clinician must know how PDD behaviors change with development and must understand the normal developmental milestones signaling the emergence of social, language, and play skills. Only then is it possible to decide whether various behaviors are developmentally inappropriate.

Several standardized interviews are available that help in collecting systematic data from parents and children. The most well known are the semistructured Autism Diagnostic Interview (ADI) and the Autism Diagnostic Observation Schedule (ADOS) developed by Rutter and colleagues (Le Couteur et al. 1989; Lord et al. 1989). These instruments have excellent reliability and validity in terms of making a diagnosis of autism. Unfortunately, a diagnostic algorithm for Asperger's disorder has not been worked out. The Structured Interview for Social and Communication Disorders (SISCD) (Szatmari et al. 1989a, 1989c) also has good interrater reliability and was specifically designed to measure the types of behaviors seen in Asperger's disorder and in high-functioning autism.

Another useful instrument is the Vineland Adaptive Behavior Scales (VABS) (Sparrow et al. 1984a, 1984b). This is a semistructured interview that measures competence in socialization, communication, activities of daily living, and motor skills. Norms are available on children up to 18 years of age. The advantage of this instrument is that not only does it provide an estimate of developmental levels, but it also characterizes a child's profile of skills in socialization and communication. Several studies have shown that autistic children score very poorly on the socialization and communication subscales compared with nonverbal IQ (Volkmar et al. 1987). Potentially, this pattern can also be used to help differentiate children with Asperger's disorder from autistic children. Since the diagnostic criteria for Asperger's disorder include normal cognitive and language development, there should be a discrepancy between the socialization and communication subscales of the VABS for children with Asperger's disorder; that is, communication skills should be in the normal range but socialization should be delayed.

Other useful instruments include the Childhood Autism Rating Scale (CARS) (Schopler et al. 1986) and the Autism Behavior Checklist (ABC) (Krug et al. 1980). The ability of these instruments to differentiate children with Asperger's disorder from autistic children, however, has not been evaluated.

Differential Diagnosis

The differential diagnosis of Asperger's disorder includes any child psychiatric disorder that presents with severe and chronic impairments in social functioning. The key features that are helpful in diagnosing Asperger's disorder are the early onset, the presence of specific types of social impairment, normal language and cognitive development, and a pattern of repetitive stereotypic activities and unusual interests from an early age.

Clinical differences from autism have been discussed earlier. Evidence of persistent delayed echolalia, pronoun reversal, jargon speech, and neologisms is a sign of impaired language development that excludes a diagnosis of Asperger's disorder. Phrases should have developed by 3 years of age, and the child needs to have a normal IQ to qualify for a diagnosis of Asperger's disorder. These features should distinguish the Asperger's disorder child from children with autism, mental retardation, and language disorders.

Severe social impairments can also occur in children with attention deficits, elective mutism, anxiety disorders (particularly social phobia), schizotypal personality disorder, and obsessive-compulsive disorder. Differential diagnosis can be particularly difficult if these disorders have an early onset and if they are associated with other developmental disabilities. There are, however, several points in the history that would point to a diagnosis of Asperger's disorder. First, when the child does interact with other children or adults (even though this may occur infrequently), there should be evidence of the types of impairments in reciprocal social interaction seen in PDD (Szatmari et al. 1989c). Second, although language development may be normal, children with Asperger's disorder still present with serious difficulties in the pragmatics of communication—that is, the use of language for social discourse (Bishop 1989). Thus, children with Asperger's disorder have difficulty initiating and sustaining a conversation, and they tend to be verbose, pedantic, tangential, and circumstantial in their speech. Third, one of the most characteristic features of Asperger's disorder is intense interest in a very restricted range of play. This restricted range of play interests may change over time, but it appears early in the preschool years, does not disappear entirely, and is uncommon in other disorders. Finally, children with Asperger's disorder tend to develop problems very early on but then slowly improve with age. Any signs of a deteriorating clinical course would be more consistent with a disorder of somewhat later onset, such as schizotypal disorders or schizophrenia.

Conclusion

It is apparent that there exists a group of children who show a variety of PDD symptoms in the context of normal IQ and language development. The nosological status of this group is unclear, however. Should it be classified as a type of PDD or a mild variant of autism? Although there is some evidence that clinical distinctions can be drawn between the groups, even controlling for IQ (Szatmari et al. 1989c), whether these distinctions are clinically useful has yet to be determined. In addition, these studies were conducted prior to the publication of the ICD-10 and DSM-IV criteria for Asperger's disorder. The use of these criteria, which are more stringent than those used by Szatmari et al. (1989a, 1989c) and C. Gillberg (1989), may lead to greater separation between the groups.

Atypical Pervasive Developmental Disorder

Overview

The literature on APDD is more extensive than on Asperger's disorder. It is generally used as a diagnosis of exclusion; in other words, it is applied to PDD children who do not meet criteria for autism. The definition of APDD depends almost exclusively on the prior definition of autism; as the conception of autism changes, so will descriptions of APDD. As a result, most definitions of this disorder have been quite nonspecific. For example, in the studies reviewed below, there is no stipulation (as there is in ICD-10) that a prerequisite number or type of autistic behaviors be present. In DSM-III, the term *atypical PDD* was used to refer to children who demonstrate disturbances in the development of social skills and language but who could not be classified as having either infantile autism or childhood-onset PDD. In DSM-III-R, these nonautistic forms of PDD were replaced by the term *PDD not otherwise specified* (PDD NOS). In contrast, ICD-10 and DSM-IV take a different approach. Several subtypes of PDD are proposed, including APDD. This latter term is used to refer to children who either have a later onset or have fewer symptoms than are required for a diagnosis of autism. ICD-10 states that there should be a sufficient number of abnormalities in all three areas of reciprocal social interaction, communication, and repetitive behavior to qualify for a diagnosis of autism. In contrast, children with APDD meet criteria for autism in at least one area, but not all three, or the full criteria for autism are met but onset is after 36 months. ICD-10 further states that APDD is most commonly found among children with profound mental retardation who lack the capacity to develop certain autistic symptoms (i.e., rituals or resistance to change) or in those with severe disturbances of receptive language who also show profound social impairment.

Prevalence and Epidemiology

Several community studies of autism have also reported on the prevalence of atypical forms of this disorder. Lotter (1966) screened the entire population of 8- to 10-year-old children in Middlesex, UK, to identify a group of children with "autistic conditions of early childhood." Fifty-four children were identified and divided into three groups: a nuclear autistic group, which demonstrated lack of social responsiveness and insistence on sameness; a nonnuclear autistic group, which showed one or other of these symptoms (but not both); and a nonautistic group with some autistic behaviors (such as echolalia, being solitary, aloofness, and ritualistic play) but milder in degree. The prevalence of nuclear autism was 2.1 per 10,000; the rate of nonnuclear autism was 2.4 per 10,000; and for the nonautistic it was 2.9 per 10,000. This study clearly illustrates the problem in reviewing the literature in atypical autism: which is the atypical group—the nonnuclear group, the nonautistic group, or both?

Wing and Gould (1979), in their classic study, screened 914 children known to local authorities as being handicapped or as having a behavioral disturbance. Seventy-four (a rate of 21 out of 10,000) were identified as having profound impairments in social interaction, language abnormalities, and repetitive, stereotypic behaviors. Seventeen of these 74 children were classified as having "typical" autism, but the majority (16 out of 10,000) were considered to be atypical. This atypical group was characterized by lower nonverbal IQ, an earlier age at onset, and a greater likelihood of being female. They demonstrated lower rates of idiosyncratic speech, pronoun reversal, and ritualistic behavior. However, there were no significant differences between the groups on several other behaviors, although this may have been due in part to small sample sizes.

A third prevalence study was reported by Steffenburg and C. Gillberg (1986). They surveyed clinicians in an urban area and a rural area of Sweden to identify children with a diagnosis of autism, childhood schizophrenia, mental retardation with autistic traits, and related disorders. The children were then clinically assessed by the authors and classified as autistic (according to DSM-III) or autistic-like. The prevalence of autism was estimated to be 4.5 per 10,000, and 2.2 per 10,000 for the autistic-like group. The latter children demonstrated either atypical traits (i.e., clinging behavior) or had an age at onset after 30 months. They contained a higher proportion of girls and higher rates of epilepsy compared with the autistic group, but there were no differences in IQ. In this study, only 12% of the atypical group had an IQ in the normal range.

A similar methodology was used to measure prevalence rates of PDD in North Dakota (Burd et al. 1987). Children ages 2–18 years who had been identified by clinicians as having autistic symptoms were reviewed by the authors and classified according to DSM-III criteria. Twenty-one cases of autism and 36 cases of "atypical PDD" were identified. Given the number of children living in the state, prevalence estimates of 1.16 per 10,000 and 1.99 per 10,000, respectively, were calculated. In this study, there was no difference between the groups in gender ratio, but 22% of the atypical group had normal IQ compared with none in the autistic group. The atypical group also had better language skills, and a higher frequency of accompanying neurological disorder.

Unfortunately, although these studies attempted to estimate prevalence rates, they did not use probability-based sampling. In addition, it is not possible to clearly identify the target population or the sensitivity of the screening procedures. The study authors relied to a large extent on clinicians' judgment and recall for case identification. The rates should probably be seen as underestimates because more mildly affected cases would be missed (see Bryson et al. 1988 for a more systematic approach to case-finding). Nevertheless, there does seem to be some agreement that APDD is at least as common as, if not more common than, autism. Although there is reasonable consistency in the clinical features of autistic children described in these four studies, they report different gender ratios, IQ ranges, and rates of comorbid neurological diseases for those with APDD.

Clinical Features

Two approaches have been used to study the clinical features of APDD. Multivariate techniques such as cluster analysis can be used to generate subgroups of PDD children based on similarities in clinical profiles. Instead of differentiating groups on the basis of diagnostic categories, continuous measures of PDD symptoms are used to compare individual profiles. Alternatively, groups can be initially defined on the basis of diagnostic criteria and then compared on associated clinical features.

Five studies have used cluster analytic techniques to subclassify PDD children. In the earliest study, Prior et al. (1975) used data from the Rimland Diagnostic Checklist on 142 psychotic children as the basis for classifying children. The best classification was one in which two classes were obtained: one contained children with an early onset plus the core behaviors of social isolation and impaired communication; the second (atypical) class had a later onset, fewer impairments in socialization and communication, and fewer stereotypic behaviors.

Two other cluster analytic studies used overlapping clinical samples (Dahl et al. 1986; Rescorla 1988). In the Rescorla (1988) study, 204 boys between 3 and 5 years of age were assessed. Among other diagnostic groups, the sample included 79 autistic and autistic-like children. The developmental quotients between these two groups were significantly different (61.7 versus 85.1 respectively). Items from the Child Behavior Checklist were coded from the charts and subjected first to factor analysis and then to a cluster analysis. Two clusters of PDD children emerged only when 4, 5, or 6 clusters were requested and corresponded to the clinical classification. In general, the autistic-like group was more developmentally mature and had more symptoms of anxiety than did the autistic group.

Siegel et al. (1986) used a sophisticated procedure to cluster-analyze

35 male and 11 female autistic and autistic-like subjects on the basis of behavior coded during a semistructured play situation. Four clusters emerged, three of which roughly correspond to 1) a classically autistic group, 2) a group with mental retardation, and 3) a schizoid group. The classically autistic group was characterized by high scores on preservative play, preoccupations with parts of objects, and noncommunicative language. The low-functioning atypical group showed a high number of stereotypies and was usually without language altogether. The schizoid (or high-functioning atypical) group, on the other hand, was characterized by less preservative play and fewer stereotypies, but the subjects displayed odd speech, unusual ideas, and disjointed play.

Szatmari et al. (1989a) performed a cluster analysis on 53 children with PDD and normal IQ. Dimensional scores of impairments in socialization, communication, and imaginative activities were used to separate the groups. A three-cluster solution was derived. The *autistic* group showed the most impairment in socialization and communication and the most restricted range of imaginative activities. The second *(Asperger)* group had the lowest scores on the three dimensions. A third *(atypical)* group was as impaired in language and imaginative activities as the autistic group, but it was no different from the Asperger group in socialization. This study suggests that among nonretarded PDD children, three groups emerge: one with good language (the Asperger's disorder group), a second group (the atypical group) with children similar to the receptive dysphasic children with autistic features described by others (Bartak et al. 1975; Paul et al. 1983), and a typically autistic group.

Among the studies employing a categorical approach to comparison are the epidemiological studies reviewed earlier and a study by Volkmar et al. (1988) using clinic-identified children. Volkmar et al. (1988) first distinguished autistic, APDD, and schizophreniform children on clinical grounds and then compared them on associated features. There were 228 consecutive cases of children ages 2–15 years who were classified according to DSM-III criteria. The atypical group had a somewhat later age at recognition (4.1 versus 2.9 years) and a higher IQ (91.1 versus 43.8). There was also a trend for the atypical group to have a higher proportion of males. The atypical group was less impaired socially, had less evidence of mutism and peculiar speech patterns such as echolalia and pronoun reversal, and had better nonverbal communication. In ad-

dition, the autistic group had more stereotypies, attachments to inanimate objects, self-mutilation, and insistence on sameness than the atypical group. Once again, the observation is made that the atypical group
had more anxiety and affective disturbance.

These studies suggest that, in general, children with APDD show
fewer PDD behaviors and, possibly, a later age at onset. There may exist
several subtypes of atypical children characterized by different IQ levels.
The epidemiological studies referred to earlier characterize atypical children as quite low functioning with an equal number of males and females. The cluster analysis by Siegel et al. (1986) also identifies this group.
On the other hand, the clinical studies identify a higher-functioning
group of atypical children, with more boys than girls. It is unclear
whether these high-functioning atypical children include children with
Asperger's disorder, those with severe problems in receptive language
and social interaction, or some other group. Future studies need to be
more precise about the types of children described as having APDD and
need to exclude those with Asperger's disorder.

Course and Prognosis

The issues outlined above with respect to the outcome of children with
Asperger's disorder apply as well to APDD. Once again, the issues are
whether the diagnosis is stable over time, how behaviors change with
development, what level of impairment persists, whether APDD children are at risk for other disorders, and how the outcome of APDD
differs from that of autism. Unfortunately, answers to these questions
are limited because there are only three outcome studies of atypical children available (Demb and Weintraub 1989; Gillberg and Steffenburg
1987; Sparrow et al. 1986).

C. Gillberg and Steffenburg (1987) reported on the outcome of the
atypical group from their community-based study. Most of these children continued to be quite low functioning, and there was a trend for
them to have a worse outcome than autistic children (in spite of the fact
that they had fewer autistic symptoms). Sparrow et al. (1986) reported
on the outcome of 11 preschool children with atypical development at
10 years of age. As preschoolers, the atypical group had serious impairments in socialization, a fascination with objects, odd use of language,

and tangential conversation. The atypical group and a normal control group did not differ at the start on measures of language, problem solving, and personal-social skills. At follow-up, roughly 7 years later, there were still no differences between the groups on cognitive tests or measures of academic achievement. However, there were large differences between the groups on domains of the VABS. The largest difference was seen on the socialization domain, suggesting that the impairments in reciprocal social interaction were stable over the 7 years. Furthermore, in spite of normal IQ, the atypical group was functioning between one and two standard deviations below the mean on several VABS subscales, indicating a substantial degree of impairment at follow-up.

Demb and Weintraub (1989) reported on 12 of 18 APDD children followed up after 5 years at a mean age of 11 years, 3 months. At follow-up, the children remained significantly impaired; 10 children received a diagnosis of PDD, 1 had schizotypal personality disorder, and the remaining child was diagnosed as having attention-deficit disorder. In addition, many children experienced symptoms of anxiety and depression and required continuing treatment.

These follow-up studies, although based on very small numbers, indicate that PDD symptoms (if not the actual diagnosis) remain stable over time and that a significant level of impairment persists. The Gillberg and Steffenburg (1987) study suggests that the low-functioning atypical group has a worse outcome than autistic children. On the other hand, if the APDD children are high functioning, they may have a better outcome, judging by interpretations of the findings from Demb and Weintraub (1989) and Sparrow et al. (1986). Clearly, however, a properly controlled follow-up study of autistic, Asperger's disorder, and APDD children matched on IQ is needed.

Etiology and Pathogenesis

Etiological studies of APDD have been hampered by the nonspecific biological markers available for study. Most often, inferences about etiology are made on the basis of gender ratios, prevalence of accompanying neurological disorder, and pregnancy and birth complications. Unfortunately, the one area that has significant potential in elucidating etiology—family history—has not been employed to full advantage.

Volkmar et al. (1988) assessed the frequency of organic involvement in their sample of autistic and atypical children. Almost 50% of the autistic group had some evidence of organicity compared with only 25% of the atypical group. However, this was probably accounted for by the lower IQ of the children with autism, as organicity and IQ below 50 were strongly associated.

From the multivariate studies, Siegel et al. (1986) report that, compared with autistic children, the low-functioning atypical group in their study contained a higher proportion of females and had lower IQ, but no differences in the number of pregnancy and birth complications were observed. The higher-functioning group (schizoid), however, had fewer pregnancy and birth complications compared with the autistic group. The other multivariate studies (Dahl et al. 1986; Rescorla 1986, 1988) found no differences between types of PDD children on either psychosocial or developmental correlates.

The epidemiological studies also provided data on rates of comorbid neurological diseases in atypical and autistic individuals. Steffenburg and Gillberg (1986) reported that, although epilepsy was more common in the atypical group, 28% of the autistic group had specific neurological disorders (such as Martin-Bell syndrome or tuberous sclerosis) compared with 12% of the atypical group. The exact opposite was found in the North Dakota study (Fisher et al. 1987); that is, compared with the APDD group, the autistic group had a slightly higher proportion with seizures (33% versus 19%) but a lower prevalence of associated disorder (29% versus 71%). Wing and Gould (1979) did not find differences between the groups in prevalence of associated medical conditions. The family and twin studies of autism indicate that among twins and first-degree relatives there may be higher rates of severe social dysfunction compared with control subjects. Whether these deficits are severe enough to warrant a diagnosis of APDD remains to be determined, however.

In conclusion, there is little evidence that autism and atypical autism differ on variables of etiological interest. Any differences that are reported may be due, in part, to IQ differences between the groups. Carefully done family studies should be able to provide more definitive data on this subject in the future.

Assessment

The assessment of APDD is similar to assessment procedures in autism and Asperger's disorder. Structured or semistructured interviews, as well as questionnaires, are helpful in collecting systematic data. It is also important to collect information from multiple informants (i.e., parents and teachers) because there might be differences in behavior across settings. Measures of adaptive functioning (i.e., the VABS) and measures of verbal and nonverbal cognitive skills are important in order to have an accurate assessment of developmental accomplishments. Finally, a thorough medical examination is indicated to uncover evidence of specific neurological-medical disorders given the frequency of mental retardation in a subgroup of atypical children. Several studies have reported that high-functioning atypical children appear to have higher rates of comorbid psychiatric disorders such as attention-deficit/hyperactivity disorder (ADHD), anxiety disorder, and tics (Clarke et al. 1989; Demb and Weintraub 1989; Volkmar et al. 1988). Thus, the psychiatric evaluation of these children should be sensitive to these difficulties as well.

Differential Diagnosis

If the differentiation of autism from mental retardation and other developmental disabilities is difficult, then the differentiation of these disorders from APDD is even more problematic. At least with autism, the severity of PDD behaviors can be used to distinguish one disorder from another. With APDD, severity of symptoms is less helpful precisely because of the nature of the disorder. In fact, the differentiation of APDD from other forms of PDD (such as Asperger's disorder) has never been attempted.

Part of the problem is that the diagnostic criteria employed in the studies reviewed above are quite vague and nonspecific. In ICD-10, at least, APDD differs from autism in age at onset, in having fewer PDD symptoms, or both. In contrast to Asperger's disorder, there are no perquisite behaviors that either include or exclude the disorder.

The distinction of APDD from mental retardation is quite difficult. Many developmentally delayed children are mute, lack imaginative play, have stereotypies, and so on. However, to qualify for a diagnosis of

APDD, sufficient PDD symptoms must be present and must constitute an additional handicap over and above the child's developmental level. Thus, an assessment of cognitive skills and adaptive behavior is essential. It is also important to have some knowledge of normal developmental milestones in socialization, language acquisition, and play in order to judge the extent to which a child's PDD symptoms represent a discrepancy from mental age. For example, if a child has a mental age of 5 years, then mutism and lack of imaginative play represent "true" PDD symptoms. If, however, mental age is less than 2 years, these behaviors become noncontributory.

Children with receptive language disorders are often severely handicapped in their social relationships and occasionally demonstrate unusual behaviors (Cantwell et al. 1989). The key issue is that in APDD the social impairment must be a primary problem and not secondary to an inability to communicate. Thus, children with pure language disorders will babble, will use nonverbal means to communicate, and will show an interest in interacting and a desire to interact with other children. Children with APDD will demonstrate these skills less frequently. In addition, the impairment in social responsiveness is usually present prior to the time speech should have developed, and it will persist beyond the point at which speech becomes more fluent. Thus, natural history may be the only way to distinguish APDD from other forms of developmental disability.

The differentiation of APDD from autism, Asperger's disorder, mental retardation, and language disorder is extremely complex. The suggestions outlined above have not been empirically tested. An important issue for future studies, then, is the extent to which APDD can be reliably differentiated from other, related disorders.

Conclusion

These studies indicate that there exists a group of children with a range of impairments in reciprocal social interaction and in verbal and nonverbal communication, along with a pattern of stereotypic, repetitive behaviors. In spite of these common deficits, substantial variation exists in the severity of PDD behaviors across dimensions. Whenever a "typically" autistic group is identified, there usually remains a group with fewer symptoms or a different age at onset. Although the exact boundaries between typical and atypical autism may vary, there does seem to be some agreement that boundaries can be found.

This literature review also highlights the possibility that two subgroups of APDD children can be identified: a low-functioning group with more females, more organicity, and a worse outcome; and a higher-functioning group with more males, less organicity, and (perhaps) a better outcome than autistic children. The extent to which the higher-functioning group overlaps with the Asperger's disorder group is unclear. The cluster analysis by Szatmari et al. (1989a) suggests that perhaps children with Asperger's disorder can be differentiated from atypical children by the presence of impaired language development in the latter group. This finding, however, needs to be replicated.

Thus, although it seems possible to identify subgroups that differ along the PDD dimensions, whether these are meaningful boundaries remains to be determined. Clinically significant differences in etiology, natural history, and response to treatment have not yet been demonstrated.

Directions for Research

This chapter has attempted to review the available data on Asperger's disorder and APDD, two nonautistic forms of PDD. The review indicates that these syndromes can be identified in community and clinic samples, and reasonably consistent differences in clinical presentation are described across studies. In spite of these clinical differences, there is little definitive evidence at this point to conclude that there are also differences in etiology, outcome, or response to treatment. This is largely because the appropriate studies, using clearly defined samples of PDD subtypes, have not yet been completed.

Given this, are any conclusions possible about the nosological status of Asperger's disorder and APDD? Waterhouse et al. (1992) have been the most forceful proponents of the argument that specification of PDD subtypes is unwise. They argue that there is enormous heterogeneity with respect to the clinical presentation, etiology, and outcome in autism. There is, in fact, no such thing as "typical" autism, and, clearly, without typical autism the forms of "nonautistic" PDD represent random, or meaningless, variations in symptomatology. Waterhouse et al. (1992) point, as proof of this view, to the fact that valid distinctions have yet to emerge between autism and these other subtypes.

This conclusion may be both too stringent and premature (Cox 1991; Green 1990; Wolff 1991a). It is possible to argue that without the ability to diagnose autism without error, weak associations will always be found between diagnostic groups and other variables such as etiology and outcome. The same is true for comparisons between other disorders such as conduct disorder and ADHD or between anxiety and depression. Enormous overlap and comorbidity exist for all forms of psychopathology. Given this, absolute validity may be too abstract a notion for the classification of PDD. The key issue is whether useful distinctions—not necessarily valid ones—can be drawn between autism on the one hand and APDD and Asperger's disorder on the other. What may be useful in one context may not be useful in another (regardless of whether one disorder is "truly" different from another). For example, it may be more useful to combine PDD subtypes for genetic studies of etiology (if APDD and autism run in the same families) than to keep them separate. On the other hand, it may be more useful to distinguish them for treatment studies (if autism and Asperger's disorder have a different natural history). Useful distinctions between disorders that convey new information can be made in one context but not in another. For example, Tourette's syndrome and obsessive-compulsive disorder can be distinguished on the basis of clinical presentation and response to treatment, but not on the basis of etiology.

The conclusion of Waterhouse et al. (1992) may also be premature. Definitive studies of etiology, outcome, and response to treatment are not yet available. To say that useful distinctions between subtypes do not yet exist presupposes that adequate studies have been published. Unfortunately this is not yet the case with Asperger's disorder and APDD.

What types of studies are required to resolve these issues? Several questions are in need of clarification.

1. What is the measurement potential of APDD and Asperger's disorder; that is, can operational criteria be specified, can they be reliably diagnosed, and to what extent are the criteria homogeneous and specific to that subtype?

2. What is the prevalence of autism and the other PDD subtypes in an unselected series of cases? (This would be best answered in a community study, but even a clinic-based study would be useful.)
3. To what extent are the "core" deficits of autism (theories of mind, person recognition, and so forth) also present in other PDD subtypes?
4. Are there etiological differences in brain structure, serotonin metabolism, family history, and so on between the subtypes?
5. Are there differences in outcome and natural history, controlling for confounding differences in IQ and severity?
6. Do the different subtypes have a better response to certain treatment strategies? For example, if children with Asperger's disorder have a theory of mind, might they also have a better response to social skills training, which often presupposes an awareness of others' responses to one's behavior?

Clearly a new generation of studies is required to answer these questions. Much remains to be done, and work in this area has the potential not only to deepen our understanding of the nature of autism and PDD but also to help children with significant social and communication impairments regardless of questions of nosological status.

Case Report: An Example of Asperger's Disorder

William, a 5-year-old boy, was referred for evaluation because of poor social skills, social isolation, and a reluctance to speak to other children.

There were no abnormalities during the pregnancy, but William was born weighing 4½ pounds even though he was born at term. He was delivered by cesarean section and had mild fetal distress. After birth William was in an incubator for 2 days but discharged home within 10 days.

William was described as a very good baby, who was somewhat passive and nursed easily. He smiled appropriately and showed good eye contact during breast feeding. William's mother felt that he had a very good strong bond with her and that he enjoyed playing games with her and listening to music. He walked at 14 months and used phrases spontaneously by 36 months. At 5 years of age he did not communicate very often and only in certain contexts. For example, he only engaged in a conversation around his particular obsessions, which included trains, insects, or other items that he enjoyed collecting. At no point during his speech development had there been evidence of delayed echolalia, pronoun reversal, or the use of neologisms.

On examination William was an attractive little boy who always smiled easily, showed anticipatory gestures, and was quite affectionate. He would come for comfort if he was hurt and showed separation anxiety in the company of strangers or when his mother went out for the evening. There were, however, some impairments in his social play in that his mother had to intrude on his game activities or else he would not engage her in his play. His favorite activity had to do with collecting objects such as pins, boats, little toys, and insects. He also showed an intense interest in dinosaurs, trains, space travel, and geography. Virtually all of his conversation consisted of repetitive questions on these topics or else a description of the things he had collected. Psychological assessment showed that William had cognitive skills in the average range with little discrepancy between verbal and performance subscales. A speech and language evaluation did not uncover significant impairments in receptive or expressive language skills.

William was enrolled in an integrated kindergarten setting with an educational program that focused on social and communication skills. He made slow but steady progress and remained in the regular school system. Over time there has been improvement in many areas, but significant impairments persist in his overall level of functioning and socialization.

References

American Psychiatric Association: Diagnostic and Statistical Manual of Mental Disorders, 3rd Edition. Washington, DC, American Psychiatric Association, 1980

American Psychiatric Association: Diagnostic and Statistical Manual of Mental Disorders, 3rd Edition, Revised. Washington, DC, American Psychiatric Association, 1987

American Psychiatric Association: Diagnostic and Statistical Manual of Mental Disorders, 4th Edition. Washington DC, American Psychiatric Association, 1994

Asperger H: Die "autistischen psychopathen" in Kindesalter. Archiv für Psychiatrie und Nerven Krankheiten 117:76–136, 1944

Baron-Cohen S: The autistic child's theory of mind: a case of specific developmental delay. J Child Psychol Psychiatry 30:285–298, 1989

Bartak L, Rutter M, Cox A: A comparative study of infantile autism and specific developmental receptive language disorder: I. The children. Br J Psychiatry 126:127–145, 1975

Bishop DVM: Autism, Asperger's syndrome and semantic-pragmatic disorders: where are the boundaries? British Journal of Disorders of Communication 24:107–121, 1989

Bowman EP: Asperger's syndrome and autism: the case for a connection. Br J Psychiatry 152:377–382, 1988

Bryson SE, Clark BS, Smith I: First report of a Canadian epidemiological study of autistic syndromes. J Child Psychol Psychiatry 29:433–446, 1988

Burd L, Fisher W, Kerbeshian J: A prevalence study of pervasive developmental disorders in North Dakota. J Am Acad Child Adolesc Psychiatry 26:700–703, 1987

Burgoine E, Wing L: Identical triplets with Asperger's syndrome. Br J Psychiatry 143:261–265, 1983

Cantwell DP, Baker L, Rutter M, et al: Infantile autism and development receptive dysphasia: a comparative follow-up into middle childhood. J Autism Dev Disord 19:19–32, 1989

Clarke DJ, Littlejohns CS, Corbett JA, et al: Pervasive developmental disorders and psychoses in adult life. Br J Psychiatry 155:692–699, 1989

Cox AD: Is Asperger's syndrome a useful diagnosis? Arch Dis Child 66:259–262, 1991

Dahl EK, Cohen DJ, Provence S: Clinical and multivariate approaches to the nosology of pervasive developmental disorders. J Am Acad Child Psychiatry 25:170–181, 1986

Demb HB, Weintraub AG: A five-year follow-up of preschool children diagnosed as having an atypical pervasive developmental disorder. J Dev Behav Pediatr 10:292–298, 1989

DeLong GR, Dwyer JJ: Correlation of family history with specific autistic subgroups: Asperger's syndrome and bipolar affective disorder. J Autism Dev Disord 18:593–600, 1988

Fine J, Bartolucci G, Ginsberg G, et al: The use of intonation to communicate in pervasive developmental disorders. J Child Psychol Psychiatry 32:771–778, 1991

Fisher W, Burd L, Kerbeshian J: Comparisons of DSM-III defined pervasive developmental disorders in North Dakota children. J Am Acad Child Adolesc Psychiatry 26:704–710, 1987

Folstein S, Rutter M: Infantile autism: a genetic study of 21 twin pairs. J Child Psychol Psychiatry 18:297–321, 1977

Frith U: Autism and Asperger Syndrome. Cambridge, Cambridge University Press, 1991

Gillberg C: Asperger's syndrome and recurrent psychosis—a case study. J Autism Dev Disord 15:389–398, 1985

Gillberg C, Steffenburg S: Outcome and prognostic factors in infantile autism and similar conditions: a population-based study of 46 cases followed through puberty. J Autism Dev Disord 17:273–288, 1987

Gillberg C: Asperger's syndrome in 23 Swedish children. Dev Med Child Neurol 31:520–531, 1989

Gillberg IC, Gillberg C: Asperger syndrome—some epidemiological considerations: a research note. J Child Psychol Psychiatry 30:631–638, 1989

Green J: Is Asperger's a syndrome? Dev Med Child Neurol 32:743–747, 1990

Hobson RP: The autistic child's appraisal of expressions of emotion. J Child Psychol Psychiatry 27:321–342, 1986

Kanner L: Autistic disturbances of affective contact. Nervous Child 2:217–250, 1943

Kerbeshian J, Burd L, Fisher W: Asperger's syndrome: to be or not to be? Br J Psychiatry 156:721–772, 1990

Kolvin I: Psychoses in childhood—a comparative study, in Infantile Autism: Concepts, Characteristics and Treatment. Edited by Rutter M. Edinburgh, Churchill Livingstone, 1971, pp 7–26

Krug DA, Arik J, Almond P: Behavior checklist for identifying severely handicapped individuals with high levels of autistic behavior. J Child Psychol Psychiatry 21:221–229, 1980

Le Couteur A, Rutter M, Lord C, et al: Autism Diagnostic Interivew. J Autism Dev Disord 19:363–388, 1989

Lord C, Rutter M, Goode S, et al: Autism Diagnostic Observation Schedule: a standardized observation of communicative and social behavior. J Autism Dev Disord 19:185–211, 1989

Lotter V: Epidemiology of autistic conditions in young children I. Prevalence. Social Psychiatry 1:124–137, 1966

Ozonoff S, Rogers SJ, Pennington BF: Asperger's syndrome: evidence of an empirical distinction from high-functioning autism. J Child Psychol Psychiatry 32:1107–1122, 1991

Paul R, Cohen DJ, Caparulo DK: A longitudinal study of patients with severe developmental disorders of language learning. J Am Acad Child Psychiatry 22:525–534, 1983

Piven J, Gayle J, Chase GA, et al: A family history study of neuropsychiatric disorders in the adult siblings of autistic individuals. J Am Acad Child Adolesc Psychiatry 29:177–183, 1990

Prior M, Perry D, Gajzago C: Kanner's syndrome or early onset psychosis: a taxonomic analysis of 142 cases. Journal of Autism and Childhood Schizophrenia 5:71–78, 1975

Rescorla LA: Preschool psychiatric disorders: diagnostic classification and symptom patterns. J Am Acad Child Psychiatry 25:162–170, 1986

Rescorla LA: Cluster analytic identification of autistic preschoolers. J Autism Dev Disord 18:475–492, 1988

Rumsey JM, Hamburger SD: Neuropsychological divergence of high level autism and severe dyslexia. J Autism Dev Disord 20:155–168, 1990

Rumsey JM, Rapoport JL, Sceery WR: Autistic children as adults: psychiatric, social, and behavioural outcomes. J Am Acad Child Psychiatry 24:465–473, 1985

Rutter M, Schopler E: Classification of pervasive developmental disorders: some concepts and practical considerations. J Autism Dev Disord 22:459–482, 1992

Schopler E, Rechler RJ, Renner BR: The Childhood Autism Rating Scale. New York, Irvington, 1986

Siegel B, Anders TF, Ciaranello RD, et al: Empirically derived subclassification of the autistic syndrome. J Autism Dev Disord 16:275–294, 1986

Sparrow SS, Balla D, Cicchetti D: Vineland Adaptive Behavior Scales (Expanded Form). Circle Pines, MN, American Guidance Service, 1984a

Sparrow SS, Balla D, Cicchetti D: Vineland Adaptive Behavior Scales (Survey Form). Circle Pines, MN, American Guidance Service, 1984b

Sparrow SS, Rescorla LA, Provence S, et al: Follow-up of "atypical" children. J Am Acad Child Psychiatry 25:180–185, 1986

Steffenburg S, Gillberg C: Autism and autistic-like conditions in Swedish rural and urban areas: a population study. Br J Psychiatry 149:81–87, 1986

Szatmari P, Bremner R, Nagy J: Asperger's syndrome: a review of clinical features. Can J Psychiatry 34:554–560, 1989a

Szatmari P, Bartolucci G, Bremner R: Asperger's syndrome and autism: comparisons on early history and outcome. Dev Med Child Neurol 31:709–720, 1989b

Szatmari P, Bartolucci G, Bremner R, et al: A follow-up of high functioning autistic children. J Autism Dev Disord 19:213–225, 1989c

Szatmari P, Tuff L, Finlayson MAJ, et al: Asperger's syndrome and autism: neurocognitive aspects. J Am Acad Child Adolesc Psychiatry 29:130–136, 1990

Tantam D: Lifelong eccentricity and social isolation: II Asperger's syndrome or schizoid personality disorder? Br J Psychiatry 153:783–791, 1988a

Tantam D: Asperger's syndrome. J Child Psychol Psychiatry 29:245–255, 1988b

Tantam D, Evered C, Hersov L: Asperger's syndrome and ligamentous laxity. J Am Acad Child Adolesc Psychiatry 29:769–774, 1990

Van Krevelen DA: Early infantile autism and autistic psychopathy. Journal of Autism and Childhood Schizophrenia 1:82–86, 1971

Volkmar FR, Sparrow SS, Goudreau D, et al: Social deficits in autism: an operational approach using the Vineland Adaptive Behavior Scales. J Am Acad Child Adolesc Psychiatry 26:156–161, 1987

Volkmar FR, Cohen DJ, Hoshino Y, et al: Phenomenology and classification of the childhood psychoses. Psychol Med 18:191–201, 1988

Waterhouse L, Wing L, Spitzer R, et al: Pervasive developmental disorders: from DSM-III to DSM-III-R. J Autism Dev Disord 22:525–550, 1992

Wing L: Asperger's syndrome: a clinical account. Psychol Med 11:115–130, 1981

Wing L: The continuum of autistic characteristics, in Diagnosis and Assessment in Autism. Edited by Schopler E, Mesibov G. New York, Plenum, 1988, pp 91–110

Wing L, Gould J: Severe impairments of social interaction and associated abnormalities in children: epidemiology and classification. J Autism Dev Disord 9:11–29, 1979

Wolff S: "Schizoid" personality in childhood and adult life I: The vagaries of diagnostic labelling. Br J Psychiatry 159:615–620, 1991a

Wolff S: "Schizoid" personality in childhood and adult life III: The childhood picture. Br J Psychiatry 159:629–635, 1991b

Wolff S: Asperger's syndrome. Arch Dis Child 66:178–179, 1991c

Wolff S, Barlow A: Schizoid personality in childhood: a comparative study of schizoid, autistic, and normal children. J Child Psychol Psychiatry 20:29–46, 1979

Wolff S, Chick J: Schizoid personality in childhood: a controlled follow-up study. Psychol Med 10:85–100, 1980

Wolff S, Narayan S, Moyes B: Personality characteristics of parents of autistic children: a controlled study. J Child Psychol Psychiatry 29:143–153, 1988

Wolff S, Townshend R, McGuire RJ: "Schizoid" personality in childhood and adult life II: Adult adjustment and the continuity with schizotypal personality disorder. Br J Psychiatry 159:620–629, 1991

World Health Organization: F84.5, Asperger's syndrome, in ICD-10: The ICD-10 Classification of Mental and Behavioural Disorders, Clinical Descriptions and Diagnostic Guidelines. Geneva: World Health Organization, 1992, pp 258–259

Chapter 8

The Disintegrative Disorders: Childhood Disintegrative Disorder and Rett's Disorder

Fred R. Volkmar, M.D.

Introduction

Over the past century a number of diagnostic concepts were proposed to account for the severe developmental and behavioral disturbances of childhood. Of these, Kanner's syndrome of early infantile autism has received the greatest recognition and widest acceptance. His classic description (Kanner 1943) noted the very early (presumably congenital) disturbances in social interaction, communication, and environmental responsivity associated with this condition. Early controversies regarding the validity of this syndrome—apart from schizophrenia—were resolved (Rutter 1972). For the past decade this condition has been included in DSM-III (American Psychiatric Association 1980) and DSM-III-R (American Psychiatric Association 1987) in the pervasive developmental disorder (PDD) class. At the same time, it has been recognized that some children exhibit similar disorders that, for various reasons, are not readily encompassed within the autism category.

For example, in DSM-III a category termed *childhood-onset pervasive developmental disorder* (childhood-onset PDD) was proposed for the presumably rare child who developed an autistic-like condition after 30 months of age. Inclusion of such a category reflected a desire for comprehensive coverage because the limited available data suggested that an autistic-like condition very occasionally was observed after a reasonably prolonged period of normal development. In Kolvin's (1971) studies on the phenomenology of childhood psychoses, a very small number of children developed such a severe disorder rather later than children with autism and earlier than children with schizophrenic disorders. The inclusion of the childhood-onset PDD concept was unsatisfactory for several reasons and it was dropped from DSM-III-R. On the other hand, ICD-9 (World Health Organization 1978) included a somewhat similar concept (disintegrative psychosis or Heller's syndrome), which was described many years before the syndrome of early infantile autism.

Childhood Disintegrative Disorder

In 1908 Theodor Heller, a Viennese educator, reported six cases of children who exhibited severe developmental regression at 3–4 years of age after a period of previously normal development. Heller initially termed this condition *dementia infantilis.* Subsequently, the concept has been variously referred to as Heller's syndrome, disintegrative psychosis, and, more recently, childhood disintegrative disorder (CDD) (Volkmar 1992). Although most investigators would now question the appropriateness of the term *psychosis* to describe this condition, the term *disintegrative* seems remarkably appropriate.

Recent reviews of published cases (Kurita 1988a; Volkmar 1992) suggest that perhaps 100 cases have been reported in the world literature since Heller's first description. It is also possible that cases were reported prior to Heller's description (e.g., de Sanctis 1906), which, as noted subsequently, was underrecognized in recent years. The available data suggest that the condition, once established, behaviorally resembles autism (Volkmar and Cohen 1989). Accordingly, the critical issue for inclusion of the diagnostic concept in official taxonomies is the establishment of significant points of difference from autism, such as in natural history, outcome, and so forth. Given the small number of cases reported, the available data are clearly limited but childhood disintegrative disorder does appear to differ from autism in various important respects.

The onset of childhood disintegrative disorder condition is distinctive and generally much later than that observed in autism (Harper and Williams 1975; Kurita 1988a; Volkmar 1992; Volkmar et al. 1985). Moreover, although a range of outcomes has been noted, it appears that, in general, the outcome in this condition is generally much worse than that in autism (Volkmar and Cohen 1989).

It appears likely that both autism and childhood disintegrative disorder arise as the result of some insult to the developing central nervous system. Precise etiological mechanisms have not been established for either disorder. In both DSM-III and DSM-III-R the presumption was that most cases of apparent childhood disintegrative disorder represented the overt behavioral and developmental manifestation of some specific and presumably identifiable underlying neurodegenerative disorder. As noted subsequently, the available data question this assumption. The disorder is included in both ICD-10 (World Health Organization 1990) and DSM-IV (American Psychiatric Association 1994).

Rett's Disorder

The description of this diagnostic concept is relatively recent. Cases were first reported in 1966 by an Austrian physician, Andreas Rett, who originally noted two girls with remarkably similar features in his waiting room; he then collected and reported a series of cases (Rett 1966). The initial report of this progressive syndrome described the presence, once the syndrome was established, of autistic-like behaviors, which were accompanied by various features not typical of autism (Olsson and Rett 1985, 1987, 1990; Trevathan and Naidu 1988). These behaviors less typical of autism included ataxia, characteristic stereotyped hand movements (hand washing and wringing movements), very severe retardation, and a history of an early (brief) period of relatively normal or near normal development.

Until a series of cases was published in English (Hagberg et al. 1983), this condition received little attention in the United States. A body of research on this condition has now appeared, and there seems little doubt about the validity of the syndrome (Tsai 1992). The question of its placement, as a neurological versus a psychiatric condition, has been somewhat more controversial. The placement of the condition in the PDD class in ICD-10 and DSM-IV appears justified on the basis of some shared features with other conditions in the class (Rutter and Schopler 1992; Tsai 1992). Although the clinical features and course of Rett's disorder are distinctive, there may be some confusion with autism in the preschool years (Olsson and Rett 1987).

Definition

Childhood Disintegrative Disorder

Following Heller's (1908) initial report of the condition, other cases were reported and some general guidelines to diagnosis identified (Heller 1930; Zappert 1921). These features include 1) a distinctive pattern of syndrome onset after some years of normal development, 2) progressive (either gradual or abrupt) deterioration in developmental skills in multiple areas (including cognition, language, social, and self-help skills), 3) various associated affective and behavioral symptoms, and 4) no other apparent signs of gross neurological dysfunction (apart from the obvious regression and developmental deterioration, patients have normal physical examination and appearance). The term *disintegrative psychosis* implied the presence of hallucinations and delusions; there is now reason to question this assumption, which in part reflected earlier notions about the continuities of psychotic processes across the life span (Rutter 1972).

Disintegrative psychosis was included in ICD-9 and defined on the basis of "normal or near normal development in the first few years followed by a loss of social skills and of speech together with a severe disorder of emotions, behavior, and relationships" (World Health Organization 1978, p. 318). The disorder is included in both ICD-10 and DSM-IV, and the definition in both systems is convergent. The DSM-IV diagnostic criteria are provided in Table 8–1.

Rett's Disorder

Various criteria for Rett's disorder have been described (Hagberg 1985; Hagberg et al. 1983; Trevathan and Moser 1988; World Health Organization 1990). Certain features are essential for diagnosis, and others are supportive of the diagnosis—that is, are associated features or argue against its presence (Tsai 1994). The DSM-IV and the ICD-10 definitions of the condition are convergent. DSM-IV criteria for the condition are summarized in Table 8–2.

Early development (both prenatal and perinatal) is, by definition, normal. Head circumference at birth is normal and psychomotor development initially proceeds appropriately. The clinical onset of the syndrome is usually in the last 6 months of the first year (although

---

Table 8–1.   DSM-IV diagnostic criteria for childhood disintegrative disorder

A. Apparently normal development for at least the first 2 years after birth as manifested by the presence of age-appropriate verbal and nonverbal communication, social relationships, play, and adaptive behavior.

B. Clinically significant loss of previously acquired skills (before age 10 years) in at least two of the following areas:

   (1) expressive or receptive language
   (2) social skills or adaptive behavior
   (3) bowel or bladder control
   (4) play
   (5) motor skills

C. Abnormalities of functioning in at least two of the following areas:

   (1) qualitative impairment in social interaction (e.g., impairment in nonverbal behaviors, failure to develop peer relationships, lack of social or emotional reciprocity)
   (2) qualitative impairments in communication (e.g., delay or lack of spoken language, inability to initiate or sustain a conversation, stereotyped and repetitive use of language, lack of varied make-believe play)
   (3) restricted, repetitive, and stereotyped patterns of behavior, interests, and activities, including motor stereotypies and mannerisms

D. The disturbance is not better accounted for by another specific pervasive developmental disorder or by schizophrenia.

Source.   American Psychiatric Association: Diagnostic and Statistical Manual of Mental Disorders, 4th Edition. Washington, DC, American Psychiatric Association, 1994, pp. 74–75. Used with permission.

Table 8–2.   DSM-IV diagnostic criteria for Rett's disorder

A. All of the following:

    (1) apparently normal prenatal and perinatal development

    (2) apparently normal psychomotor development through the first 5 months after birth

    (3) normal head circumference at birth

B. Onset of all of the following after the period of normal development:

    (1) deceleration of head growth between ages 5 and 48 months

    (2) loss of previously acquired purposeful hand skills between ages 5 and 30 months with the subsequent development of stereotyped hand movements (e.g., hand wringing or hand washing)

    (3) loss of social engagement early in the course (although often social interaction develops later)

    (4) appearance of poorly coordinated gait or trunk movements

    (5) severely impaired expressive and receptive language development with severe psychomotor retardation

---

Source. American Psychiatric Association: Diagnostic and Statistical Manual of Mental Disorders, 4th Edition. Washington, DC, American Psychiatric Association, 1994, pp. 72–73. Used with permission.

sometimes later) and includes deceleration in head growth, the loss of purposeful hand movements, and development of the characteristic hand-washing and hand-wringing stereotypies. Expressive and receptive language skills become severely impaired and are associated with marked mental retardation. In the preschool years, gait apraxia, truncal apraxia, and ataxia develop. A loss of social interactional skills is frequently observed during the preschool years but social interest often increases later.

Other features support the diagnosis when they are present. These features are not necessary, however, and are not included in the definition of the disorder in ICD-10. These associated features include breath-holding spells, periodic hyperventilation, periodic apnea, growth retardation, electroencephalogram (EEG) abnormalities and seizures, dystonia, spasticity, scoliosis, and peripheral vasomotor problems (Harrison and Webb 1990; Perry 1991). The presence of features such as demonstrable prenatal growth retardation or postnatal central nervous system trauma, or the presence of other identifiable progressive neurological disorders, such as storage diseases, argues against the diagnosis.

Prevalence and Epidemiology

Childhood Disintegrative Disorder

As expected, given the apparent infrequency of the condition and the small number of cases reported over the past century, epidemiological data are quite limited. In the consecutive-case series reported by Volkmar and Cohen (1989), the disorder would appear to be perhaps one-tenth as common as autism. Another study employing a more epidemiologically based sample suggested prevalence rates of .11 out of 10,000 (Burd et al. 1989). Given the lack of familiarity with the diagnostic concept it is very likely that the condition has been underrecognized; when clinicians who see large numbers of autistic-like cases first become acquainted with the diagnostic concept they typically recall one or more cases consistent with a childhood disintegrative disorder diagnosis.

The earlier impression of an equal sex distribution of cases in childhood disintegrative disorder now appears to be incorrect. In a recent review of reported cases (Volkmar 1992), an overall male to female ratio of 4 to 1 was noted, similar to the ratio observed in autism (Lord et al. 1982). It is probable, however, that at least some females reported in early-case series may actually have exhibited Rett's disorder (Burd et al. 1989; Millichap 1987; Volkmar 1992). If cases of childhood disintegrative disorder reported only since 1977 are examined, the male to female ratio (8 to 1) is even higher than the ratio reported in autism.

Rett's Disorder

Prevalence estimates of approximately 1 out of 15,000 have been reported (Kerr and Stephenson 1985; Tsai 1994), and the syndrome has been observed in various countries and cultures. To date the condition has been reported only in females, although the possibility that males might exhibit the disorder cannot definitely be excluded (Philippart 1990; Tsai 1994).

Higher rates of Rett's disorder in monozygotic twins have been noted (Hagberg 1989; Percy 1992) as have been some cases in extended family members. Possible modes of genetic transmission have been identified (Tsai 1994). However, familial cases account for only a small proportion of affected individuals and the data available suggest that most cases appear to be sporadic in nature.

Clinical Features

Childhood Disintegrative Disorder

Onset

The onset of the condition is highly distinctive and is a major diagnostic feature. By definition the disorder develops following a relatively prolonged period (several years) of normal development. In contrast to autism, this period of normal development is relatively unequivocal: the child has the capacity to speak in sentences by age 2 (World Health Organization 1990). Heller (1930) reported that the onset was often in the third or fourth year of life, and this still seems to be the case. On the other hand, there is the potential for some confusion with autism, given the occasional report of an individual with autism whose difficulties are recognized after the first year or two of life (Volkmar et al.1985)

Volkmar and Cohen (1989) reviewed a series of cases of early-onset and late-onset autism and childhood disintegrative disorder. In that study, individuals with late-onset autism (in which the disorder was recognized after 24 months) usually were rather higher functioning, and in such cases, detection of the disorder was apparently delayed by the relative preservation of cognitive skills. It appears likely, although not certain, that such patients had previous unrecognized abnormalities in social interaction that were not sufficiently severe to be a major concern to parents. On the other hand the onset of Rett's disorder seems very early and much different from that in childhood disintegrative disorder (Tsai 1992; Volkmar 1992). Data related to age at onset of autism and childhood disintegrative disorder are summarized in Figure 8–1.

There is a clear difference in the distribution of onset of the two conditions. Although lack of knowledge among primary health care providers may delay recognition of the seriousness of the autistic child's developmental delay (Siegel et al. 1989), it appears that in only a handful of cases does autism develop after age 3. In contrast, in cases of childhood disintegrative disorder, onset is much more likely to be after age 2 with a small number of cases reported after school entry (see Volkmar 1992 for a review of cases reported to that date and Malhotra and Singh 1993, for five additional cases). Diagnostic problems may, however, arise in some instances.

Clearly the selection of a precise length of time for the period of normal development before the onset of childhood disintegrative disorder is arbitrary and it is possible that the condition does in rare cases develop before age 2. Kurita (1988a) noted that in some instances there is a history of preexisting, although mild, developmental delay. When information on early development is lacking or when the timing or pattern of developmental regression differs from that specified in criteria for the condition, a diagnosis of atypical autism may be the most appropriate one.

Sometimes childhood disintegrative disorder develops gradually over a period of some weeks or months. In other instances the onset is more abrupt (days to weeks). A premonitory phase is sometimes observed; during this time the child may become agitated, anxious, or dysphoric (Heller 1930).

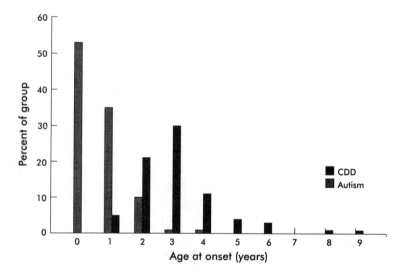

Figure 8–1.   Age at onset in 103 cases with clinical diagnoses of autism and 76 cases of childhood disintegrative disorder.

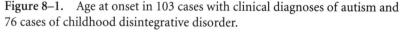

Source.   Data adapted from Volkmar et al. 1985 and Volkmar 1992. Figure reproduced with permission from Volkmar FR: Childhood disintegrative disorder. Child and Adolescent Psychiatry Clinics of North America 3:122, 1994.

Behavioral and Developmental Features

Once established, childhood disintegrative disorder clearly resembles autism in terms of its behavioral and developmental manifestations (Volkmar 1992). Clinical features of the cases reported in a literature review of the condition (Volkmar 1992) are summarized in Table 8–3.

Usually, social skills are markedly impaired and are similar to those observed in autism, although some reports suggest that social skills may be somewhat less impaired in childhood disintegrative disorder (Kanner 1973; Kurita 1988b; Makita et al. 1960). Either total mutism or marked deterioration in verbal communication skills is usual, and it appears that even those individuals who regain some speech have problems in communication similar to those observed in autism (Volkmar and Cohen 1989). Unusual behaviors of the type seen in autism also typically develop; these include stereotypies, problems in dealing with change and transitions, and overactivity. Various unusual affective responses have also been noted, such as a general dysphoria and agitation.

In contrast to autism, deterioration in self-help and motor skills is often marked in childhood disintegrative disorder. Previously acquired bowel and bladder control may be lost (Kurita 1988a; Volkmar 1992).

Table 8–3. Characteristics of childhood disintegrative disorder cases

Variable	Cases 1908–1975 ($N = 48$)	Cases 1977–1990 ($N = 29$)	Entire sample ($N = 77$)
Sex ratio (M/F)	35/12[b]	26/3	61/15
Age at onset (yrs)[a]	3.42 ± 1.12	3.25 ± 1.61	3.36 ± 1.32
Age at follow-up (yrs)[a]	8.67 ± 4.14	14.25 ± 5.35	10.91 ± 5.39
Symptoms, % of (N cases)			
Speech deterioration/loss	100 (47)	100 (29)	100 (76)
Social disturbance	100 (43)	96 (28)	99 (71)
Stereotypy/resistance to change	100 (38)	100 (25)	100 (63)
Overactivity	100 (42)	89 (19)	97 (61)
Affective symptoms/anxiety	100 (17)	94 (17)	97 (17)
Deterioration in self-help skills	94 (33)	90 (20)	92 (53)

Note. Results are based on available data.
[a]Values are means ± SDs. [b]Some reports did not give sex of subjects.
Source. Adapted from Volkmar 1992.

Rett's Disorder

Onset

The condition usually has its onset in the latter half of the first year of life but sometimes later. As noted previously the very early prenatal and perinatal development of the child is normal. After some months of normal or relatively normal development a period of developmental stagnation may be observed (Hagberg and Witt-Engerstrom 1986; Moeschler et al. 1988; Tsai 1994). Often the onset is insidious and only gradually is the presence of developmental delay, decelerated head and body growth, and diminished interest in the environment appreciated. The relative lack of parental sophistication about very early child development may, briefly, delay recognition of developmental loss (in contrast to childhood disintegrative disorder, in which the loss of language skills is quickly of major concern).

In Rett's disorder subsequent developmental deterioration increases, in contrast to the more usual pattern in childhood disintegrative disorder. Previously acquired abilities are lost, including purposeful hand movements (Hagberg and Witt-Engerstrom 1986; Moeschler et al. 1988). Subsequently an apparent plateau may be observed before another phase of more pronounced motor deterioration is noted (Hagberg and Witt-Engerstrom 1986).

Behavioral and Developmental Features

Although the course and aspects of the clinical presentation in Rett's disorder are generally different from those observed in autism, the differential diagnosis of the conditions can be problematic during the preschool years. During that period autistic-like behaviors, such as the stereotyped hand movements as well as deteriorating language, social, and motor skills (Olsson and Rett 1987), often appear most pronounced in Rett's disorder and may be confused with autism.

Course and Prognosis

Childhood Disintegrative Disorder

Three relatively distinctive patterns of course have been noted in the literature (Volkmar 1992). In approximately three-fourths of cases the child's behavior and development deteriorate to some much lower level of functioning. At that point no further deterioration occurs but, on the other hand, developmental gains are then usually minimal (Volkmar and Cohen 1989). In some instances the marked developmental regression is followed by limited recovery; for example, a child who had become totally mute regains the capacity to say single words (Volkmar and Cohen 1989). In perhaps 40% of cases the child may become able to speak in single words; in half of these cases the child is able to regain the capacity to speak in sentences (Volkmar 1992; Volkmar and Cohen 1989). In a small number of cases the developmental deterioration is followed by noteworthy recovery. In other cases the developmental regression does not plateau and is progressive. This appears to be particularly true in instances in which some identifiable progressive neurological process is present; death may eventually then result (Corbett 1987). Otherwise, life expectancy apparently is normal. EEG abnormalities and seizure disorders are frequently observed (Volkmar 1992), as they are in autism.

Rett's Disorder

The course of Rett's disorder is essentially one of progressive neurological deterioration interspersed with an occasional period of plateau and stabilization. Following the relatively brief period of normal early development, a period of developmental stagnation is observed, followed by a period of developmental regression (usually by 18 months of age) (Hagberg and Witt-Engerstrom 1986). The period of "pseudostagnation" following this period may persist for some time; it is during this period that differentiation from autism may be most difficult. Olsson and Rett (1987) noted that the characteristic hand-washing stereotypies of Rett's were helpful differential features, as were the characteristic motor difficulties and hyperventilation. The marked and apparently active social disinterest of autistic children was, on the other hand, not typical of Rett's disorder.

By the time the child reaches school age, autistic-like features are usually less prominent and a developmental plateau is attained. During this time the characteristic severe mental retardation, seizures, and motor problems are a major focus of concern. During this plateau or "pseudostationary" phase, breathing difficulties, bruxism, motor problems, and early scoliosis are observed (Hagberg and Witt-Engerstrom 1986). Episodes of apnea may alternate with hyperventilation. Although motor problems are pronounced, the majority of children remain ambulatory until the final period of late motor deterioration (Hagberg 1989). Seizures of various types commonly develop, and EEG examinations are frequently abnormal. In the final phase of the disorder, motor difficulties and scoliosis often limit mobility, and many patients become nonambulatory. There is an increased risk of sudden death (Hagberg 1989). Typically, adults with the condition require very high levels of support and supervision.

Etiology and Pathogenesis

Childhood Disintegrative Disorder

Given the often very dramatic nature of the developmental regression and the usually very intensive medical investigations conducted, it is surprising that, in most cases, the etiology of the condition remains unknown (Volkmar 1992). In this regard it should be noted that the implicit assumption, in DSM-III and DSM-III-R, that the condition was associated with some specific (and identifiable) neuropathological process is not supported by the available data. In Volkmar's (1992) review of published cases, specific neuropathological conditions were identified in only a small number of cases. Very late onset of the condition does, however, appear to be more frequently associated with some specific neuropathological process. Reported associations have included various neuropathological processes, such as the neurolipidoses, metachromatic leukodystrophy, Addison-Schilder's disease, and subacute sclerosing panencephalitis (Volkmar 1992). It appears, however, that in most instances no such process is identified.

As is likely the case with autism, multiple pathogenic mechanisms, acting through one or a few final pathways, may ultimately be identified. Various data suggest the importance of neurobiological factors and central nervous system dysfunction in syndrome pathogenesis: the association, in a few instances, with clearly identified conditions that might reasonably account for the developmental deterioration, the high frequency of EEG abnormality and seizure disorder, the onset and course of the disorder, and so forth (Corbett 1987; Corbett et al. 1977; Darby 1976; Evans-Jones and Rosenbloom 1978; Hill and Rosenbloom 1986; Kurita 1988a, 1988b; Volkmar and Cohen 1989). As is also true of autism, the absence of clearly identified neuropathological mechanisms likely reflects more on current research techniques than on the absence of such factors (Golden 1987; Rivinus et al. 1975; Wilson 1974).

The observation that the condition sometimes has its onset shortly after certain psychosocial stressors has been repeatedly made (Evans-Jones and Rosenbloom 1978; Kurita 1988a; Volkmar 1992), but the significance of stressful events in syndrome pathogenesis is unclear. Although a diverse group of such stressors has been noted, such as the birth of a sibling or the death of a grandparent, they share the similar feature of being relatively common in the preschool-age group. It appears likely that such associations do not have etiological significance (Rutter 1985).

Rett's Disorder

The pathogenesis of Rett's disorder also remains to be elucidated. In his original report, Rett (1966) speculated on a possible association with high peripheral ammonia levels. However, neither this nor subsequent apparent associations with specific biological markers have been confirmed. As noted previously, there has been some suggestion of a potential genetic contribution. Studies of the central nervous system have suggested decreased brain weight and loss of neurons, and neuropathological and imaging studies often have showed mild brain atrophy (Krageloh-Mann et al. 1989; Tsai 1994). As with autism and childhood disintegrative disorder, seizure disorders of various types are common in Rett's disorder (Hagberg 1985; Hagberg et al. 1983). Although the EEG is frequently abnormal, no specific pattern of abnormality is consistently observed, although the nature of the EEG abnormality may correlate to the stage of the illness (Glaze et al. 1987). The results of neurochemical studies of various substances such as endorphins, cortisol, and dopamine have been contradictory (Brase et al. 1989; Echenne et al. 1991; Perry 1991; Tsai 1994; Wenk et al. 1991).

Assessment

The clinical assessment of a child with childhood disintegrative disorder or Rett's disorder is often most effectively accomplished by an experienced interdisciplinary team because delays and impairments in multiple areas of functioning are often observed. On the other hand, it is important that the assessment team work effectively together to avoid fragmentation and duplication of effort. The efforts of various professionals may be needed, such as child psychiatrists and psychologists, speech pathologists, pediatric neurologists, occupational and physical therapists, orthopedists, and so forth. Parental involvement in the assessment and a long-term collaborative relationship between the parents and evaluation team should be encouraged.

A careful history should be obtained. This should include information related to the pregnancy and neonatal period, early developmental history, and medical and family history. Information on the pattern and apparent age at onset of the condition is critical for differential diagnosis because the course of both childhood disintegrative disorder and Rett's disorder is often distinctive. Although usually even extensive medical investigations fail to reveal the presence of a specific neurodegenerative disorder, a search for such conditions is indicated, particularly if aspects of the history or presentation are unusual. For example, the very late (older than 6 years) onset of childhood disintegrative disorder should prompt extensive evaluation for the presence of a neuropathological condition. Unfortunately, the diagnosis of such conditions can be difficult (Wilson 1974). Initial consultation with a pediatric neurologist is indicated. Given the severity of these conditions, an electroencephalogram (EEG) and a computed tomography (CT) or magnetic resonance imaging (MRI) scan will also usually be obtained. For individuals with Rett's disorder, physical and occupational therapy is needed. The services of other specialists, such as specialists in treating scoliosis or respiratory difficulties, may also be needed.

Psychological and communicative assessment should include various measures chosen to be appropriate to the child's level of functioning. The goal of such assessments is to obtain a reasonably valid indication of current levels of functioning for purposes of programming and intervention, against which subsequent gains or deterioration can be measured; similarly, areas of relative strength can be identified (Fontanesi and Haas 1988).

For both childhood disintegrative disorder and Rett's disorder, the choice of traditional tests of intelligence may be less appropriate than instruments more typically employed with much younger children. Instruments that may be appropriate include 1) the Bayley Scales of Infant Development (Bayley 1993), 2) the Uzgiris and Hunt Scales with Dunst's norms (Dunst 1980; Uzgiris and Hunt 1975), 3) the Leiter International Performance Scale (Leiter 1948), and 4) the Merrill-Palmer scale (Stutsman 1948). Modifications in usual assessment procedures may be indicated, particularly with individuals with Rett's disorder, given the associated motor difficulties. For very-low-functioning children, several communication scales are available, including 1) the Receptive-Expressive Emergent Language Scale (REEL) (Bzoch and League 1971), 2) the Sequenced Inventory of Communicative Development (SICD) (Hedrick et al. 1975), and 3) the Reynell Developmental Language Scales (Reynell and Gruber 1990).

The Vineland Adaptive Behavior Scales (expanded form) (Sparrow et al. 1984) should be administered. This instrument, administered as a semistructured interview to parents, can be used to document levels of functioning of adaptive behaviors in the areas of communication, daily living skills, socialization, and motor skills. Results can be used for program planning and to monitor developmental gains or losses.

The assessment examination should include observation during more and less structured periods. This can often be accomplished by observing the child during developmental or communication assessment and while he or she is interacting with parents. In addition to historical information, areas for observation and/or inquiry with parents include the following: 1) social skills (e.g., interest in social interaction, patterns of gaze and eye contact, differential attachments), 2) communication (e.g., receptive, expressive, and nonverbal language, presence of preverbal communicative intents, and so forth), and 3) responses to the environment and motor behaviors (e.g., difficulties with transitions and resistance to change, nature of stereotyped behaviors observed, other self-stimulatory behaviors, ambulation). The child's capacity for play provides helpful information regarding the child's fine motor abilities, nature of play activities, and so forth. Problem behaviors likely to interfere with intervention (e.g., aggression) or characteristic of certain conditions should be noted (e.g., the hand-washing stereotypies associated with Rett's disorder).

Differential Diagnosis

The differential diagnosis of these conditions includes autism and other PDDs as well as other conditions. Historical information is critical in differentiating autism from childhood disintegrative disorder and Rett's disorder. As noted previously, the autistic-like phase of Rett's disorder is most pronounced during the preschool years, and many females with autism are also severely retarded; however, the history and characteristic findings of Rett's should alert the clinician to this diagnosis. The differentiation of childhood disintegrative disorder and late-onset (after age 2 years) autism may be problematic, although careful inquiry will usually reveal that the child with apparent late-onset autism had some abnormalities that, for various reasons, were not of sufficient concern for parents to seek assessment. Usually, such children tend to have relatively more preserved intellectual and communicative functioning. In childhood disintegrative disorder the early development should be essentially normal with the child able to speak in sentences prior to the onset of the condition. The use of aids to the parents' memory, such as baby diaries, home movies, or home videos, may be helpful in elucidating important historical information. The choice of precise guidelines for diagnosis, as in ICD-10 and DSM-IV, does raise issues of syndrome boundaries. For example, it might be difficult to make a diagnosis of childhood disintegrative disorder in a child who has multiple episodes of otitis media and whose language was, as a result, somewhat delayed but who otherwise seemed communicative and whose development was proceeding normally before a marked regression. Similarly, in Asperger's disorder early language development may seem to have been normal or near normal and diagnosis may be delayed as a result. In this condition, however, intelligence is relatively preserved and there is not a marked loss or regression in functioning of the type seen in childhood disintegrative disorder. Cases in which the diagnosis of childhood disintegrative disorder is questionable usually should receive a diagnosis of atypical autism.

In some instances other psychiatric conditions may be confused with these conditions. For example, the very abrupt onset of childhood schizophrenia, particularly in the rare younger child who is affected, may be confused with the onset of childhood disintegrative disorder; usually the nature of the difficulties in childhood schizophrenia will clarify any confusion. A question of developmental deterioration might similarly arise regarding a child with elective mutism who does not speak on entering school but who is reported to speak at home.

A careful search should be made for any associated neurological or other medical conditions that might account for any of the observed developmental regression. Both childhood disintegrative disorder and Rett's disorder can be diagnosed in the presence of such conditions, which should, if present, be specified on Axis III of the multiaxial diagnostic system. A range of genetic disorders have their manifestation after some period of normal or near normal development. These include gangliosidosis, metachromatic leukodystrophy, Niemann-Pick disease, and so forth. Apparent developmental deterioration may similarly follow the onset of unrecognized seizure disorder—the syndrome of acquired aphasia with epilepsy—following central nervous system infection, and so on (Bishop 1985).

Usually the diagnosis of Rett's disorder can be made on the basis of the characteristic clinical features and history, although the diagnosis may be more difficult with younger children in whom the autistic-like features are more pronounced. Other problems for the differentiation of Rett's disorder from autism include the broadened DSM-III-R definition of autistic disorder, which would likely diagnose many Rett's disorder patients as autistic (Volkmar et al. 1994); furthermore, it is clear that females with autism tend to be more severely retarded (Lord et al. 1982). However, in autism the history of early normal development is less common, and the degree of motor involvement in autism is much less than in Rett's disorder. Changes in head growth and loss of purposeful hand movements are not observed in autism. Differentiation of Rett's disorder from childhood disintegrative disorder is made on the basis of the timing and pattern of the developmental regression but may be difficult in some instances. The history of a prolonged period of normal development (with the capacity to speak in sentences) argues in favor of childhood disintegrative disorder, whereas a shorter period of normal development with characteristic motor features of Rett's disorder argues in favor of Rett's disorder.

The differential diagnosis of childhood disintegrative disorder most commonly includes late-onset autism and the presence of specific neurodegenerative conditions. Historical information is helpful in differential diagnosis. In autism careful inquiry often reveals early abnormalities in social development and communication; patients with apparent late-onset autism often appear to be rather higher functioning, and the pattern of marked developmental regression is not typically observed (Volkmar and Cohen 1989). In childhood disintegrative disorder the onset of the condition is later than in Rett's disorder and in autism. A period of reasonably normal development is required to make the diagnosis. Once established, it does appear that autism and childhood disintegrative disorder share many behavioral features. As noted previously, a thorough search for any associated medical conditions is indicated.

Treatment

Treatment of childhood disintegrative disorder and Rett's disorder shares many similarities to treatment for autism. Special education, behavior modification, pharmacotherapy, and other treatment modalities may be employed to encourage acquisition, or reacquisition, of basic adaptive skills. For Rett's disorder the services of other professionals, such as occupational, physical, and respiratory therapists, have greater prominence. Provision of information to teachers and special educators about these conditions is often helpful.

No specific pharmacological treatments for these conditions, per se, is available. The presence of seizures clearly requires appropriate intervention. Individuals with childhood disintegrative disorder may, at times, profit from use of neuroleptic or other agents of the type used in autism; such intervention should always include a careful consideration of potential risks and benefits.

Consideration should also be given to supporting the parents and siblings of affected individuals. The prognosis for both Rett's disorder and childhood disintegrative disorder is apparently worse than for autism and the stresses on parents and siblings of affected individuals may, if anything, be even greater than on the parents and siblings of individuals with autism. Although research data are limited, at least one study has documented the marked stress experienced by family members and by parents of patients with Rett's disorder (Perry et al. 1992). The evaluation of the child should set the stage for long-term support of parents and siblings as well.

Directions for Research

Knowledge of the pathophysiology of the disintegrative pervasive developmental disorders remains quite limited. Comparatively more work has been done on Rett's disorder than on childhood disintegrative disorder, but basic studies in the phenomenology, epidemiology, and natural history of these conditions are needed. Given the infrequency of these conditions, multicenter collaborative studies may be helpful in recruiting larger case samples.

These conditions are of research interest for various reasons. One reason is that the human and monetary costs of these conditions are clearly very high. Children and adults with these conditions present major challenges for intervention and require very high levels of supervision and support. Research on these conditions may shed important light on pathophysiological mechanisms with relevance to other disorders as well. For example, the delineation of precise (and testable) pathophysiological mechanisms in childhood disintegrative disorder might provide greater insight into the role of similar factors in autism. At the same time it must be noted that despite points of clear phenomenological similarity, the relationships of these disorders to autism at a more basic level remain unclear. The relationship of Rett's disorder and childhood disintegrative disorder also may prove an important topic for future research (Burd et al. 1989; Tsai 1992; Volkmar 1992).

Summary

Childhood disintegrative disorder and Rett's disorder share the general feature of some degree of developmental loss or "disintegration" (Fitzpatrick 1987). Although described nearly 100 years ago, the syndrome of childhood disintegrative disorder has been extensively studied. Once established this condition behaviorally resembles autism. The condition appears to differ from autism in the nature and timing of onset and in terms of long-term outcome. Rett's disorder was described more recently and has attracted more attention in the research literature. This syndrome, so far observed only in females, is characterized by developmental deterioration following a relatively brief period of normal development. Both conditions may be confused with autism. Information on the pathogenesis of these conditions may provide insight into mechanisms of syndrome development in autism.

Case Reports

Childhood Disintegrative Disorder

Donald was the youngest of three children born to college-educated parents. Pregnancy, labor, and delivery and early development were unremarkable. He appeared to be a normally active and sociable baby. He was smiling at 6 weeks, sitting at 7 months, crawling at 9 months, and walking without support at 15 months. He had several ear infections in the first year of life but said first words by 12 months and was speaking in full sentences shortly after his second birthday. Videotapes provided by his parents confirmed his apparently normal developmental status.

Shortly after his third birthday, Donald's parents became concerned about his development because over the course of several weeks he lost both receptive and expressive language and became progressively less interested in interaction and the inanimate environment. He developed various self-stimulatory behaviors and lost the ability to use the toilet independently. No apparent reason for the regression was identified. Extensive medical investigations were undertaken. Although he was noted to have a borderline abnormal EEG, no specific medical condition that might account for his developmental deterioration was identified. Subsequent evaluations at other centers and by other specialists (including pediatric neurologists and geneticists) similarly failed to identify such a condition. There was no family history of similar problems or developmental difficulties in members of the immediate or extended family.

Although he had previously been in a regular nursery school setting, his behavioral and developmental deterioration warranted his placement in a special educational setting. At the age of 4 years, comprehensive evaluation revealed that his cognitive skills were at about the 18-month level, with language and social skills at an even lower level. Over the course of many months, some, although highly limited, expressive language skills returned as he was able to say an occasional single word. His social unrelatedness, lack of interest in the environment, and unusual behaviors continued. At the time of follow-up, at age 6, he continues to be severely impaired.

Rett's Disorder

Donna was born at term after an uncomplicated pregnancy. She was the youngest of four children. Amniocentesis had been obtained because of maternal age, and no abnormalities had been detected. Donna was in good condition at birth; her weight, height, and head circumference were around the 40th percentile. During the first months of life she appeared to be developing normally, smiled responsively, was interested in the environment, and so forth. Early patterns of grasp were reported to be within normal limits.

In the 3 months before her first birthday Donna's development seemed to slow notably. Her interest in the social world markedly diminished. Developmental milestones became so markedly delayed that by 18 months she was not yet walking and was not producing words. When she was evaluated shortly after her second birthday, her pediatrician noted that head growth had decelerated and that she engaged in some self-stimulatory behaviors. A referral for comprehensive evaluation was eventually made, and at that time the possibility of Rett's disorder was raised. At the time of that evaluation (at age 35 months) Donna was noted to have cognitive and communicative skills more typical of 6- to 8-month-old infants. Self-stimulatory behaviors were prominent and sometimes included an unusual hand-washing stereotypy. Neurological consultation revealed nonspecific findings; an EEG and MRI were done and were negative. Affectively, she was often unhappy and engaged in prolonged periods of screaming. By the time she was 6 years of age, her EEG was abnormal and purposeful hand movements were markedly impaired. Subsequently, she developed truncal ataxia and breath-holding spells, and motor skills further deteriorated.

References

American Psychiatric Association: Diagnostic and Statistical Manual of Mental Disorders, 3rd Edition. Washington, DC, American Psychiatric Association, 1980

American Psychiatric Association: Diagnostic and Statistical Manual of Mental Disorders, 3rd Edition. Revised. Washington, DC, American Psychiatric Association, 1987

American Psychiatric Association: Diagnostic and Statistical Manual of Mental Disorders, 4th Edition. Washington, DC, American Psychiatric Association, 1994

Bayley N: Bayley Scales of Infant Development, 2nd Edition. San Antonio, TX, Psychological Corporation, 1993

Bishop DVM: Age of onset and outcome in 'acquired aphasia with convulsive disorder' (Landau-Kleffner syndrome). Developmental Medicine and Child Neurology 27:705–712, 1985

Brase DA, Myer EC, Dewey WL: Possible hyperendorphinergic pathophysiology of the Rett syndrome. Life Sci 45:359–366, 1989

Burd L, Fisher W, Kerbeshian J: Pervasive disintegrative disorder: are Rett syndrome and Heller demential infantilies subtypes? Dev Med Child Neurol 31:609–616, 1989

Bzoch K, League R: Receptive-Expressive Emergent Language Scale. Gainesville, FL, Language Educational Division, Computer Management Corporation, 1971

Corbett J: Development, disintegration and dementia. Journal of Mental Deficiency Research 31:349–356, 1987

Corbett J, Harris R, Taylor E, et al.: Progressive disintegrative pyschosis of childhood. J Child Psychol Psychiatry 18:211–219, 1977

Darby JK: Neuropathologic aspects of psychosis in children. Journal of Autism and Childhood Schizophrenia 6:339–351, 1976

de Sanctis S: On some variations of dementia praecox. Revista Sperimentali di Frenciatria 32:141–165, 1906

Dunst C: A Clinical and Educational Manual for Use With the Uzgiris and Hunt Scales. Baltimore, MD, University Park Press, 1980

Echenne B, Bressot N, Bassir M, et al: Cerebrospinal fluid b-endorphin and cortisol study in Rett syndrome. Journal of Child Neurology 6:257–262,1991

Evans-Jones LG, Rosenbloom L: Disintegrative psychosis in childhood. Dev Med Child Neurol 20:462–470, 1978

Fitzpatrick C: Rett syndrome and Heller Dementia (letter). Dev Med Child Neurol 29:834, 1987

Fontanesi J, Haas RH: Cognitive profile of Rett syndrome. Journal of Child Neurology 3:20–24, 1988

Glaze DG, Frost JD, Zoghbi HY, et al: Rett's syndrome: correlation of electro-encephalographic characteristics with clinical staging. Arch Neurol 44:1053–1056, 1987

Golden G: Neurological functioning, in Handbook of Autism and Pervasive Developmental Disorders. Edited by Cohen D, Donnellan A. New York, Wiley, 1987, pp 133–147

Hagberg B: Rett's syndrome: prevalence and impact on progressive severe mental retardation in girls. Acta Paediatrica Scandinavica 74:320–325, 1985

Hagberg B: Rett syndrome: clinical peculiarities, diagnostic approach, and possible cause. Pediatric Neurology 5:75–83, 1989

Hagberg B, Witt-Engerstrom I: Rett syndrome: a suggested staging system for describing impairment profile with increasing age toward adolescence. Am J Med Genet 224:47–59, 1986

Hagberg B, Aicardi J, Dias K, et al: A progressive syndrome of autism, dementia, ataxia, and loss of purposeful hand use in girls: Rett Syndrome: report of 35 cases. Ann Neurol 14:471–479, 1983

Harper J, Williams S: Age and type of onset as critical variables in early infantile autism. Journal of Autism and Childhood Schizophrenia 5:25–35, 1975

Harrison DJ, Webb PJ: Scoliosis in Rett syndrome: natural history and treatment. Brain Development 12:154–156, 1990

Hedrick D, Prather F, Tobin A: Sequenced Inventory of Communicative Development. Seattle, WA, University of Washington Press, 1975

Heller T: Dementia infantilis. Zeitschrift für die Erforschung und Behandlung des Jugenlichen Schwachsinns 2:141–165, 1908

Heller T: Uber Dementia infantilis. Zeitschrift für Kinderforschung 37:661–667, 1930 [Reprinted in Modern Perspective in International Child Psychiatry. Edited by Howells JG. New York, Brunner/Mazel, 1969, pp 610–616]

Hill AE, Rosenbloom E: Disintegrative psychosis of childhood: teenage follow-up. Dev Med Child Neurol 28:34–40,1986

Kanner L: Autistic disturbances of affective contact. Nervous Child 2:217–250, 1943

Kanner L: Dementia infantilis, in Childhood Psychosis. Edited by Kanner L. Washington, DC, V Winston & Sons, 1973, pp 279–281

Kerr AM, Stephenson JBP: Rett's syndrome in the west of Scotland. BMJ 291:579–582, 1985

Kolvin I: Studies in the childhood psychoses, I: diagnostic criteria and classification. Br J Psychiatry 118:381–384, 1971

Krageloh-Mann I, Schroth G, Niemann G, et al: The Rett syndrome: magnetic resonance imaging and clinical findings in four girls. Brain Development 11:175–178, 1989

Kurita H: Infantile autism with speech loss before the age of thirty months. J Am Acad Child Psychiatry 24:191–196, 1985

Kurita H: The concept and nosology of Heller's syndrome: review of articles and report of two cases. Japanese Journal of Psychiatry and Neurology 42:785–793, 1988a

Kurita H: A case of Heller's syndrome with school refusal. J Autism Dev Disord 18:315–319, 1988b

Leiter RG: Leiter International Performance Scale. Chicago, IL, Stoelting, 1948

Lord C, Schopler E, Revicki D: Sex differences in autism. J Autism Dev Disord 12:317–330, 1982

Makita K, Nakamura M, Takahashi T: A case report of Heller's disease. Japanese Journal of Psychiatry 1:377–386, 1960

Malhotra S, Singh SP: Disintegrative psychosis of childhood: an appraisal and case study. Acta Paedopsychiatr 56:37–40, 1993

Millichap JG: Rett's syndrome: a variant of Heller's dementia? (Letter.) Lancet 1:440, 1987

Moeschler JB, Charman CE, Berg SZ, et al: Rett syndrome: natural history and management. Pediatrics 82:1–10, 1988

Olsson B, Rett A: Behavioral observations concerning differential diagnosis between the Rett syndrome and autism. Brain Development 7:281–289, 1985

Olsson B, Rett A: Autism and Rett syndrome: behavioural investigations and differential. Dev Med Child Neurol 29:429–441, 1987

Olsson B, Rett A: A review of the Rett syndrome with a theory of autism. Brain Development 12:11–15, 1990

Percy AK: The Rett syndrome: recent advances in genetic studies in the USA. Brain Development (suppl) 14:S104–105, 1992

Perry A: Rett syndrome: a comprehensive review of the literature. American Journal of Mental Retardation 96:275–290, 1991

Perry A, Sarlo-McGarvey N, Factor DC: Stress and family functioning in parents of girls with Rett syndrome. J Autism Dev Disord 22:235–248, 1992

Philippart M: The Rett syndrome in males. Brain Development 12:33–36, 1990

Rett A: Uber ein eigenartiges hirntophisces Syndrome bei Hyperammonie im Kindersalter. Wein Medizinische Wochenschrift 118:723–726, 1966

Reynell J, Gruber C: Reynell Developmental Language Scales—U.S. Edition. Los Angeles, CA, Western Psychological Services, 1990

Rivinus TM, Jamison DL, Graham PJ: Childhood organic neurological disease presenting as a psychiatric disorder. Arch Dis Child 50:115–119, 1975

Rutter M: Childhood schizophrenia reconsidered. Journal of Autism and Childhood Schizophrenia 2:315–338, 1972

Rutter M: Infantile autism and other pervasive developmental disorders, in Child and Adolescent Psychiatry—Modern Approaches. Edited by Rutter M, Hersov L. London, Blackwell, 1985, pp 545–566

Rutter M, Schopler E: Classification of pervasive developmental disorders: some concepts and practical considerations. J Autism Dev Disord 22:459–482, 1992

Siegel B, Pliner C, Eschler J, et al: How children with autism are diagnosed: difficulties in identification of children with multiple developmental delays. Developmental and Behavioral Pediatrics 9:199–204, 1989

Sparrow S, Balla D, Cicchetti D: Vineland Adaptive Behavior Scales Expanded Form. Circle Pines, MN, American Guidance Service, 1984

Stutsman R: Merrill-Palmer Scale. Los Angeles, CA, Western Psychological Services, 1948

Trevathan E, Moser HW: Diagnostic criteria for Rett syndrome. Ann Neurol 23:425–428, 1988

Trevathan E, Naidu S: The clinical recognition and differential diagnosis of Rett syndrome. Journal of Child Neurology (suppl) 3:6–16, 1988

Tsai L: Is Rett syndrome a subtype of pervasive developmental disorder? J Autism Dev Disord 22:551–561, 1992

Tsai L: Rett syndrome. Child and Adolescent Psychiatric Clinics of North America 3:105–118, 1994

Uzgiris IC, Hunt JMcV: Assessment in Infancy: Ordinal Scales of Psychological Development. Urbana, IL, University of Illinois Press, 1975

Volkmar FR: Childhood disintegrative disorder: issues for DSM-IV. J Autism Dev Disord 22:625–642, 1992

Volkmar FR: Childhood disintegrative disorder. Child and Adolescent Psychiatric Clinics of North America 3:119–130, 1994

Volkmar FR, Cohen DJ: Disintegrative disorder or "late onset" autism. J Child Psychol Psychiatry 30:717–724, 1989

Volkmar FR, Stier DM, Cohen DJ: Age of recognition of pervasive developmental disorder. Am J Psychiatry 142:1450–1452, 1985

Volkmar FR, Klin A, Siegel B, et al: Field trial for autistic disorder in DSM-IV. Am J Psychiatry 151:1361–1367, 1994

Wenk GL, Naidu S, Casanova MF, et al: Altered neurochemical markers in Rett's syndrome. Neurology 41:1753–1756, 1991

Wilson J: Investigation of degenerative disease of the central nervous system. Arch Dis Child 47:163–170, 1974

World Health Organization: Mental Disorders: Glossary and Guide to Their Classification in Accordance with the Ninth Revision of the International Classification of Diseases. Geneva, World Health Organization, 1978

World Health Organization: International Classification of Diseases, 10th Edition (Draft Version: Diagnostic Criteria for Research). Geneva: WHO, 1990

Zappert J: Dementia infantilis Heller. Monatsschrift für Kinderheilkunde 22:389–391, 1921

Chapter 9

Issues for Research

Donald J. Cohen, M.D., and Fred R. Volkmar, M.D.

Introduction

Over 50 years have now passed since Leo Kanner's classic description of the syndrome of early infantile autism. This phenomenologically based definition marked a major turning point in the field. Kanner's attempt to integrate developmental, psychological, and neurobiological factors in his work set a high standard for subsequent research (Cohen et al. 1993). In the five decades following Kanner's report, considerable prog-ress has been made in our understanding of those conditions we presently consider the childhood psychoses and pervasive developmental disorders (PDDs). Important aspects of syndrome definition have been clarified; basic knowledge of clinical features, course, and treatment and of associated psychological and biological processes has been gained. The substantial body of research on these conditions over the last several decades, and particularly over the last decade, is a testament to the many areas in which knowledge has been advanced. At the same time we must also recognize that the remarkable vision of Leo Kanner's original report has not always been sustained. Progress in research has, at times, been impeded by a narrowness of theoretical or clinical vision; by a tendency for the research enterprise to be swayed by exciting, but unreplicable, reports; and by our continued lack of ignorance regarding basic pathogenic mechanisms.

In this chapter we review the progress that has been made and identify areas where we believe further work is needed. We also note those areas that presently appear to have been false leads for research. Given the large body of work that has accumulated in recent years, our coverage must be selective and somewhat arbitrary. The inconsistencies in research coverage pose further problems for a chapter of this kind. With some conditions, such as autism, the disorder is relatively uncommon but has been the subject of very intensive research efforts. With other conditions, such as borderline conditions and hallucinatory states in childhood, the state of the research enterprise is not as well advanced, and basic issues such as diagnosis and definition have yet to be resolved. In the case of disorders such as childhood schizophrenia, changes in the conceptualization of the disorder complicate interpretation of research studies. Over the past 50 years we have moved from the situation in which childhood schizophrenia was the only generally recognized childhood "psychosis" to the present situation, in which the condition, much more narrowly defined than previously, appears to be even less common than autism.

This chapter is organized into five broad areas: classification and diagnosis, clinical phenomenology, psychological processes, biological processes, and treatment studies. Although this division is useful for purposes of organization, it must be emphasized that in this area, perhaps more than in most other areas, of child and adolescent psychiatry a multidisciplinary and developmental point of view is required.

Classification and Diagnosis

Psychotic conditions have clearly been recognized since antiquity, but interest in these conditions is a relatively modern phenomenon. Although precursors to this interest are seen, for example, in studies concerned with effects of experience on child development (such as the "wild boy" [Lane 1977]), it was not until the mid-nineteenth century that Maudsley (1867) suggested that children could exhibit "insanity." With Kraepelin's description of dementia praecox (see Kraepelin 1919), interest in the psychotic conditions increased markedly, although then, as now, theoretical bias prevented recognition of conditions that were probably rather similar to those seen today. For example, as noted in Chapter 2, the recognition of depression in children was delayed by a theoretical bias on the part of clinicians and investigators (see Akiskal and Weller 1989). Research on classification and diagnosis of these conditions has been critically important in advancing research. Of the various reports of putative diagnostic entities, that of Leo Kanner (1943) remains a pivotal event in our understanding of severe psychiatric disturbance of childhood onset.

Both before and after Kanner's description, other clinician-investigators had proposed various diagnostic concepts, some of which have survived or had a resurgence in recent years. An example would be Heller's description of what is now called childhood disintegrative disorder (see Chapter 8); other diagnostic concepts, such as "symbiotic psychosis" (Mahler 1952), are now largely of historical interest. It is noteworthy that all of the diagnostic concepts proposed in the area of what now would be called the childhood-onset psychoses and pervasive developmental disorders came from clinician-investigators who managed to see regularities and commonalities in patients within the broader and much more complicated pattern of individual differences exhibited. None of these concepts originated from an epidemiologist or clinical researcher sitting down with a large multivariate data set and "discovering" some syndrome as a result of some complicated statistical analysis. Indeed, even if all the modern statistical techniques had been available it seems unlikely, given the relative infrequency of these conditions, that they would ever be "discovered" through analysis of data derived even from large normative samples.

For various reasons Kanner's description of autism provides a benchmark against which previous and subsequent descriptions must be evaluated. Several factors account for the profound influence of Kanner's description. First, it was phenomenologically based. Although Kanner was misled by certain characteristics of his initial sample, such as the predominance of more educated parents (Schopler et al. 1980), his description of the autistic syndrome stuck to the facts. It was not couched

either in highly technical or in theoretical terms. Rather, Kanner emphasized what continues to be a central definition, if not the central definition, of the syndrome of autism: the marked impairment in social
relationships (Volkmar 1987). Second, as befits an early pioneer of
American child psychiatry, Kanner was careful to place his description
of this impairment within a developmental context, citing Gessel's work
on the normative development of social skills in infants. In other words,
the stark absence of social interest in young autistic children was viewed
against the backdrop of the rich pattern of very early social reciprocity
in normally developing children (see Volkmar 1987). Kanner's emphasis
on the congenital nature of the disorder also served to highlight its probable biological origins in a way analogous to the emerging study of in-
born errors of metabolism in pediatrics.

Syndromic Issues

Before Kanner's description the assumption was one of general continuity between adult schizophrenia and severe psychiatric disturbance
in children: continuity based on severity. This assumption was based on
several different factors. First, it was clear (e.g., Kraepelin 1919) that
a certain number of individuals with schizophrenia appeared to have
developed this disorder as children, and certainly some children appeared to exhibit schizophrenia even if relatively strict diagnostic methods were used (see Potter 1933 for an outstanding example of such
research). Second, despite various attempts at diagnostic stringency and
conservatism, views of the diagnostic concept of schizophrenia tended
to be rather broad. Finally, there was a failure to appreciate the importance of a developmental perspective. For example, although the term
psychosis was commonly used in relation to children, normative changes
in the development of children's notions of reality were not appreciated.
As Piaget's work suggests (e.g., Piaget 1955), children's views of the nature of reality change over the course of development with marked discontinuities in cognitive processes over time. Apart from certain aspects
of psychoanalytic theory, most of American psychiatry tended to deemphasize the importance of developmental factors in the expression
of psychopathology (see Volkmar et al., 1995, for a review). Attempts

such as the one by Heller (1908) to note important potential differences between severe childhood disturbance and typical adult schizophrenia as well as attempts by researchers like Potter (1933) to provide narrower definitions of schizophrenia in childhood proved to be not particularly successful at the time (see Eisenberg 1957).

Subsequent to Kanner's classic description of autism, other diagnostic concepts were proposed. These included Asperger's (1944) description of autistic psychopathy (now known as Asperger's disorder or syndrome), Rank's (1949) description of atypical personality development, and Rett's (1966) description of a highly distinctive mental retardation syndrome observed only in girls. Rank's description of atypical personality development largely, if unintentionally, overlapped with pervasive developmental disorder not otherwise specified (PDD NOS), which is listed as a subthreshold category in DSM-III-R (American Psychiatric Association 1987) and DSM-IV (American Psychiatric Association 1994).

The origins and uses of the term *pervasive developmental disorder* deserve special note. This term was coined in DSM-III (American Psychiatric Association 1980) as a new, theoretically neutral term for the class of disorders to which autism (included in the DSM for the first time) would be assigned. The utility of the term *pervasive developmental disorder* has itself been the topic of some debate (e.g., see Gillberg 1991b and Volkmar and Cohen 1991b), and it certainly is possible that, with the wisdom of hindsight, some more apt term could have been chosen. This term did, however, capture something essential about autism and closely related conditions and it has endured through DSM-III-R into DSM-IV and has made its way into the *International Classification of Diseases, 10th Edition* (ICD-10), as well (World Health Organization 1990).

The term *pervasive developmental disorder* has always referred to the class of disorder to which autism belongs; that is, *pervasive developmental disorder* was and is a handy way of referring to the range of conditions characterized by marked disturbances in the development of social and other skills in ways that are distinctive and not just attributable to associated mental retardation. It is sometimes the case that clinicians incorrectly equate PDD with the subthreshold diagnostic concept of *pervasive developmental disorder not otherwise specified.* This is unfortunate because it only adds to the confusion of parents. It is not uncommon to read reports that conclude that the child "meets criteria for PDD" when it is clear 1) that there is no diagnosis of PDD per se and 2) that the PDD NOS category has, by definition, no specific criteria but only the general feature of bearing some similarity to other conditions in the PDD class without, however, meeting full criteria for any such explicitly defined condition. Similar confusion has surrounded the concept of autistic psychopathy or, as it is now more commonly known, Asperger's disorder (or syndrome).

Asperger's description of the syndrome of autistic psychopathy appeared the year after Kanner's, and Asperger was not aware of Kanner's work at the time his description appeared (see Frith 1991 for a review). For many years, interest in the syndrome described by Asperger was confined to continental Europe. With Wing's (1981) highly influential review, interest in this condition and its possible convergence with or divergence from autism became the topic of increasing debate.

As noted in Chapter 7, the absence of "official" or even "semiofficial" definitions of Asperger's disorder presented marked problems for conducting and interpreting research on this condition. In the United States this condition was generally considered to be a synonym for high-functioning autism (see Frith 1991, Gillberg 1991a, and Schopler 1985 for divergent views on this issue). The lack of official definitions led to various inconsistencies in the use of the term so that eventually it came to be used in markedly different ways, such as 1) to refer to high-functioning individuals with autism, 2) to refer to individuals with some but not all features of autism (PDD NOS, in DSM-III-R terms), 3) to refer to adults with autism, or 4) to refer to individuals whose development, course, and clinical features differed from those of individuals with autism in important ways (see Ghaziuddin et al. 1992a, 1992b; Klin 1994; Pomeroy 1991). Only in this last sense is the concept of particular interest from a taxonomic point of view. That is, the convention of referring to cases of "subthreshold" autism (PDD NOS) by use of the eponymous term *Asperger's disorder* (or *syndrome)* can be debated, but the convention does not add to the existing nomenclature. It is also of some interest that, in the area of learning disabilities, cases with features similar to those described by Asperger were also observed. Two examples are nonverbal learning disability (Rourke 1989) and semantic-pragmatic processing disorder (Bishop 1989). The observation of similar cases within this different tradition of research emphasizes the importance of conducting truly multidisciplinary research and of integrating various perspectives to facilitate our understanding of serious psychiatric disturbance in children (Rumsey 1992).

With regard to Rett's disorder, the most recently described of these conditions, the issues of syndrome validity have seemed much less critical than the issue of where the condition is placed diagnostically (Tsai 1994). There seems little doubt that this highly distinctive condition (see Chapter 8) probably has a very specific neurobiological basis (or bases). A cogent argument could be made for inclusion of this condition as a neurological rather than a psychiatric condition (Gillberg 1994). On the other hand, the decision of placement must to some extent be arbitrary. Placement within the PDD class is suggested, given the potential confusion with autism, particularly during the preschool years, and given the importance of including the condition within the classificatory system (Rutter 1994). Although one could argue for placement as a neurological condition—that is, as a specific form of dementia—one could make a similarly cogent argument for placement of autism as a neurological condition, given the clear association of autism with seizure disorder, abnormal findings on neurological examination, and so forth. As Rutter and Schopler (1992) note, these issues are complex and must take into consideration not just the evident "organicity" of the condition but also aspects of case detection and service delivery.

Somewhat paradoxically, what is probably the most common of all these PDDs is also the least frequently studied. In its use in the DSM-IV or "subthreshold" sense, the concept of PDD NOS is used for cases in which a child's disorder has important similarities to other PDDs without meeting full criteria for any of the more explicitly defined conditions (see Chapter 7 and Towbin 1994). Although there is general agreement that impaired social development is a hallmark of this condition, there is much less agreement on what other features are essential for its diagnosis (Mayes et al. 1993). As with Asperger's disorder (which is sometimes equated with PDD NOS), the absence of explicit operational definitions has made for major problems in conducting and interpreting research. On the one hand, funding for research is highly limited if the condition is not truly definable; on the other hand, the few attempts to derive explicit definitions or to identify specific diagnostic features have not resulted in generally accepted diagnostic conventions (see Cohen et al. 1987; Dahl et al. 1986; Towbin 1994). Considerable overlap is likely to exist with other categories, such as with schizotypal personality disorder in DSM-IV (see Towbin 1994). The absence of longitudinal studies, of epidemiological data, and of possible neurobiological concomitants of the condition severely complicates our knowledge of this condition. Significant delays in case detection and diagnosis remain common even for autism, which is the most intensively studied of these disorders (e.g., Siegel et al. 1988).

Categorical Classification Systems

The ability to classify psychiatric conditions has many advantages as well as some inherent limitations. It provides a method for rapid communication of information among clinicians and investigators. Classification schemes vary depending on their purpose (see Werry 1985). As noted elsewhere in this volume, the advent of the research diagnostic criteria (RDC) approach significantly facilitated research on all psychiatric conditions in both children and adults. The advantages of the multiaxial approach (Rutter et al. 1975) and of recognizing developmental issues relative to classification (Volkmar and Cohen 1991b) are important for childhood disorders and have tended to facilitate the recognition that comorbidity tends to be the rule rather than the exception.

As noted in the other chapters in this book, the two rival systems of psychiatric taxonomy have important areas of similarity and difference; both share many strengths as well as some limitations. Although American psychiatrists tend, not surprisingly, to be more familiar with the *Diagnostic and Statistical Manual* (now in its 4th edition), the *International Classification of Diseases* manual (now in its 10th edition) provides a comprehensive diagnostic system used in much of the rest of the world. For the psychoses and pervasive developmental disorders of children, both systems share many similarities—in terms of disorders that are officially recognized and the definition of such disorders. Despite some usually minor differences, the general thrust of both classification systems is rather similar (see Schwab-Stone et al. 1991 for a review). For certain disorders, notably autism and the other PDDs, definitions are conceptually the same in both systems; this is particularly important because vastly different classification systems would impede, rather than facilitate, research on these conditions. Similarly, a multiaxial approach is common to both these categorical systems. On the other hand, important areas of difference and limitations of these systems should be noted.

In contrast to the DSM-IV, the ICD-10 exists in two versions—one for clinical work and the other for research. The pros and cons of these approaches are a matter of debate. The ICD-10 two-version approach is somewhat more flexible, whereas DSM-IV has the advantage of existing in one version for both research and clinical work and is somewhat more oriented around specific symptom constellations.

Particularly for autism, the DSM-IV and ICD-10 definitions have drawn heavily on empirical data. For the revision of DSM-IV an international field trial was conducted (see Volkmar et al. 1994) and data were collected on nearly 1,000 individuals. The results of the field trial suggested 1) that the DSM-III-R definition of autism was overly broad—particularly among more severely retarded individuals and 2) that there was some justification for inclusion of other disorders within the PDD class, in addition to autism. As a result of the various data analyses undertaken, modifications in the ICD-10 and DSM-IV definitions were made so as to make for conceptual identity of these two systems.

The increasing reliance on empirical data, both in DSM and in ICD, is clearly an advantage. Similarly, the commitment to development of definitions on the basis of actual research is also a marked advance. It is, however, also important to note that the shifting boundaries of these conditions reflect a fundamental issue for research interpretation. There are no behavioral or laboratory tests for these conditions; no specific chromosomal pattern or pathogenic agents have been uniquely attributed to them. Thus clinical judgment, hopefully as modified by experience, continues to guide the diagnostic process. Changes in diagnostic convention are sometimes more than amply supported by empirical data but may also have important, if unintended, implications for eligibility for service and for service delivery. This is particularly important here in the United States where early intervention services are mandated.

One of the most striking aspects of autistic disorder is its very broad range of syndrome expression, both over age and developmental level.

There is now little debate about the validity of autism apart from schizophrenia (Volkmar and Cohen 1991a). There also is relatively little debate about central aspects of the definition of autism (Volkmar et al. 1994), although the merits of a relatively broad versus a narrow conception of this condition will continue to be debated (Rutter and Schopler 1992). As noted in Chapter 1, the preponderance of opinion has now swung to the narrower view of childhood schizophrenia, although some investigators, notably those continuing in the tradition of Bender, have continued to advocate a broader conceptualization of childhood schizophrenia (e.g., Cantor 1988). With the affective psychoses, general agreement about the applicability of diagnostic concepts in the childhood and adult forms of the disorder is reasonably well established (see Chapters 2 and 3).

Dimensional Approaches to Classification

Dimensional classifications offer several potential advantages over categorical approaches, although it should be noted that dimensional and categorical systems are not necessarily incompatible (see Volkmar and Cohen 1991b). The dimensional approach is embodied in such diverse assessments as those relating to intellectual ability, degree of thought disorder, or time-sampled behavior ratings. Potential informants for such approaches range from the clinician to the parent or teacher and to the affected individual. Various statistical techniques may be used to analyze data derived from dimensional instruments; the statistical properties of such instruments, such as interrater reliability, often have been extensively studied.

The development, validation, and use of such instruments with the psychoses and PDDs have many advantages as well as some inherent limitations. The development of various rating scales, checklists, and semistructured interviews for many, but not all, of these disorders in the last decade has been a major accomplishment. The statistical sophistication of these instruments has markedly increased over the last few years. For example, Andreasen and Olsen (1982) observed both similarities and differences in the presence and nature of thought disturbance in the adult psychoses; patients with schizophrenia were more likely to have symptoms of negative thought disorder, whereas manic patients were more likely to have positive symptoms.

As might be expected, given the normative changes in concepts of reality (Piaget 1955), disturbances of thought content and process are more difficult to diagnose in preschool children (Green et al. 1984; Russel et al. 1989; Volkmar et al. 1988). However, as children enter the school years, the similarities, rather than the differences, are more striking (Bettes and Walker 1987; Garralda 1984). Although developmental differences in apparent psychotic phenomena have been recognized for some time (Despert 1951), assessment instruments specifically designed to encompass developmental aspects of syndrome expression have only relatively recently been developed (Volkmar et al. 1995).

In autism a number of different approaches have been employed (see Parks 1983 for a review). These include use of teacher and/or parent report, observation and examination in structured or semistructured settings, and so forth. The attempt (Le Couteur et al. 1989; Lord et al. 1989) to develop observational methods and parental interviews for autism that are explicitly "keyed" to categorical diagnostic criteria is important. Similarly, Volkmar et al. (1993) reported a novel method for screening for autism using a widely available, developmentally based assessment instrument—the Vineland Adaptive Behavior Scales. In the Volkmar et al. (1993) study, ratios of observed skills in the areas of communication, daily living, and socialization were calculated relative to those expected given the individuals' mental or chronological age. Consistent with Rutter's (1978) definition of autism, individuals with autism had much lower social skills on the Vineland than would be expected given their mental age. Delays and impairments in specific social skills, such as in relation to play and imitation, are also observed (Stone et al. 1990).

Similar measures have been developed relative to childhood schizophrenia. Caplan et al. (1989, 1990) developed the Kiddie Formal Thought Disorder Rating Scale (K-FTDS). With this instrument, illogical thinking and loose associations were noted to differentiate children with schizophrenia from children without schizophrenia. Caplan (1994) has noted that loose associations are not observed after age 7 in normally developing children and illogical thinking decreases markedly in childhood after that time.

Clinical Phenomenology

Clinical Features

Despite earlier presumptions of continuity within all the "psychotic" conditions of childhood, various lines of research have suggested that meaningful distinctions may be made between diagnostic groups on the basis of specific clinical features, course, and so forth. Similarities with the "corresponding" disorder in adult life appear to be greater if the onset of the condition is somewhat later in childhood. Thus, in mania, depression, or schizophrenia, differences in presentation appear in large part to reflect developmental factors. Thus hallucinations may be less vivid and elaborate in children. On the other hand, in conditions with a very early onset, such as autism, disruption of basic developmental processes is a central aspect of the condition with consequent implications for subsequent development. In various studies (Kolvin 1971; Makita 1966; Volkmar et al. 1988) age at onset has consistently been noted as critical in the differentiation of autism and childhood schizophrenia.

Age at onset was included in the definition of autism in DSM-III but not in DSM-III-R. The decision in DSM-III-R to avoid use of age at onset reflected practical as well as philosophical concerns. For example, there were concerns about the reliability of historical information and about the importance of such information in the diagnostic process. On the other hand, there is some evidence that within a given diagnostic category age at onset of the condition may be an important prognostic feature and one associated with severity of disorder; for example, children with very-early-onset schizophrenia (VEOS) tend to have the worst prognosis (Werry, in press) and tend to have higher levels of apparent thought disorder (Caplan 1994). As noted by Caplan et al. (1992), it is also possible that early onset of schizophrenia is associated with impaired acquisition of pragmatic and cognitive skills. Given the usually major impact of these conditions on developmental processes, the use of detailed, quantitative, and standard measures is to be greatly desired but such data are not uniformly obtained.

The onset of both Rett's disorder and childhood disintegrative disorder is highly distinctive and different from that observed in autism. In Rett's disorder the onset is, by definition, in the first months of life, with a characteristic progression of disability. In contrast to Rett's and autism, the onset of childhood disintegrative disorder follows a prolonged period of normal, or very near normal, functioning. Videotapes of children with childhood disintegrative disorder taken both before and after the developmental regression dramatically document the marked developmental and behavioral decline.

Epidemiology

Studies on the epidemiology of all the conditions reported in this volume have been complicated by the infrequency of these conditions, the limitations of available studies (e.g., differing ascertainment methods, diagnostic criteria, and so forth), and the lack of basic support for research in this area. Autism, the best studied of all these conditions, is clearly uncommon, having rates varying from 1 to 5 or more per 10,000 children; the lower rates result from narrower definitions of the syndrome.

It appears certain that both Rett's and childhood disintegrative disorder (see Chapter 8) are much less common than autism. The epidemiology of Asperger's disorder is very uncertain; studies differ markedly, and prevalence estimates likely reflect the major differences in syndrome definition employed. Interestingly, it now appears that childhood schizophrenia is even less common than autism (see Chapter 1).

Epidemiological studies continue to be critically needed for all the PDDs and psychotic disorders of childhood. The limitations of consecutive-case series are clear (see Werry, in press, for a discussion). Unfortunately, existing screening methods, through use of structured interviews, have major limitations so that even more epidemiologically based studies may be difficult to interpret. Even relatively small-scale epidemiological studies need to have access to large populations. Changes in syndrome expression with age complicate both epidemiological and outcome research.

Course and Outcome

Information on course and adult outcome of these conditions has implications for classification, research, and service delivery. Probably the most extensive data are available relative to autism (e.g., DeMyer et al. 1981), although even here the interpretation of available data is complicated, given the changes in the definition of the condition and, more important, given the changes in mandates for intervention and service delivery. Thus, individuals with autism who were diagnosed in the 1950s and followed up in the later 1970s or early 1980s were not, in the United States, legally entitled to the same kinds of services provided to children identified in the 1980s after the passing of the Education for All Handicapped Children Act of 1975 (Public Law 94-142), which mandated appropriate educational intervention for all children with handicaps. There is some suggestion (e.g., see Lovaas 1987) that earlier and more intensive intervention may be associated with markedly improved outcome in autism, although the preponderance of the available literature suggests that most individuals with autism (probably 80%–90%) remain severely handicapped by the condition as adults. Smaller proportions of cases either improve or, somewhat less frequently, deteriorate in adolescence and adulthood (McClellan and Werry 1991; Rumsey et al. 1985).

Outcome information on the other PDDs is more limited. In general, it appears that Asperger's disorder has a better outcome than autism, although this may well be a function of the higher IQ in the former condition. There is some suggestion (e.g., Tantam 1989; Wolff 1991) that individuals with Asperger's are at increased risk for other psychiatric conditions during adolescence and adulthood. The relationship of this condition to other boundary conditions (notably schizoid personality disorder) remains an area for future work (see Asarnow et al. 1991; Petti and Vela 1990; Wolff 1991). In childhood disintegrative disorder and in Rett's disorder the outcome appears to be significantly worse than the outcome in autism, although a few cases of marked recovery in childhood disintegrative disorder have been noted (Tsai 1994; Volkmar 1994). However, it is possible that the relative lack of information on childhood disintegrative disorder may have resulted in a systematic bias in follow-up (i.e., more severe cases may have been more likely to have been reported) (Volkmar 1994).

The dearth of recent outcome research in childhood-onset schizophrenia is unfortunate. Available information suggests that outcome is likely worse than in the adult-onset form of the disorder (Werry, in press). On the other hand, although affective disorders in childhood have probably been underdiagnosed (Weller et al. 1986), outcomes appear to be rather similar in the childhood and the adult-onset forms (Werry et al. 1991). Information on outcomes in children with apparent borderline personality disorder and with hallucinatory and dissociative states is even more limited than that on childhood schizophrenia (Lofgren et al. 1991; Petti and Vela 1990; Putnam 1991).

Continuities of Child and Adult Forms of Disorders

In DSM-IV the introduction to the section of disorders usually first diagnosed in infancy, childhood, or adolescence notes that this section is included only as a matter of convenience; in other words, disorders listed usually present during childhood or adolescence. Conversely, criteria for other conditions that usually do not present during the developmental period are listed elsewhere in the manual. Thus for schizophrenia, the affective psychoses, and borderline personality disorders the description of the disorder and diagnostic criteria are placed outside the child section of the manual. This placement rests on the relatively substantial body of research suggesting that adult presentation of these conditions is typical, although not, of course, invariant and that essential features of the condition are rather similar in children, adolescents, and adults.

As the diagnostic concept of childhood schizophrenia has become increasingly narrow, studies of this condition have similarly become relatively uncommon. This is particularly true, as Werry notes (Chapter 1), of VEOS. However, the studies available do tend to support the position (employed in both ICD-10 and DSM-IV) that, with some modifications based on developmental factors, the definitions of schizophrenia and the affective psychoses are best placed outside the childhood disorders section (see Chapters 1 to 3). This approach has the advantage of being based on a body of research and is scientifically the most parsimonious. It has the disadvantage, unfortunately, of tending to bias clinicians against recognition of these syndromes when they do present in childhood. In other words, such a placement intrinsically tends to deemphasize potential childhood presentation.

Although there has been general consensus that childhood, adolescent, and adult forms of schizophrenia represent fundamentally the same condition, it remains unclear whether developmental differences observed, such as the relatively worse outcome of VEOS, can be attributed to some biological factor or factors (e.g., heavier genetic loading) or whether such differences should be attributed to the greater disruption of psychological processes, in relation to the earlier onset and possible absence of mitigating psychological factors. The basic neurobiological and psychological substrates and precursors of this disorder in childhood remain an important topic for research. Similarly, the applicability of usual adult typologies to childhood schizophrenia remains an important area for research (King 1994).

Although there has been general agreement that separate diagnostic criteria for schizophrenia diagnosed in children are not warranted, specification of the nature of psychotic disturbance in childhood remains problematic. Caplan and her colleagues have conducted extensive research on the nature of psychotic symptomatology in childhood and have noted similarities and differences between children and adults (see Caplan 1994 for a review). In contrast to the growing literature on positive versus negative symptomatology in adult schizophrenia, only one study has addressed this phenomenon in the developmental period (Bettes and Walker 1987).

Psychological Processes

In American psychiatry, interest in the effects of early experience on child development in general, and in the pathogenesis of psychiatric conditions in particular, increased markedly in the years shortly before and following the Second World War. Thus it is not surprising—despite Kanner's initial suggestion that autism was congenital in nature—that much speculation in the late 1940s and 1950s centered on the possibility that some psychological process, or processes, might account for the pathogenesis of conditions such as autism and childhood schizophrenia (e.g., Bettelheim 1967 and Despert 1951). Such notions converged with similar theoretical models of adult psychotic conditions in which regressions to earlier and more "primitive" modes of intrapsychic functioning were posited. Thus, Kanner's (1943) observation of unusual styles of parent-child interaction and of the high levels of educational and professional attainment in parents was taken to suggest a role for experience in the production of autism and childhood schizophrenia. Impaired parenting was presumed to be the main source of unusual patterns of parent-child interaction and the presumed source of the disability in the child. This view led to use of pejorative terms, such as *refrigerator mothers,* and the use of intensive, prolonged psychotherapy to remediate the presumed deficit (Riddle 1987). Little consideration was then given to the equally plausible alternative: that impairment in parent-child interaction must arise from the child rather than the parent. Multiple lines of evidence now suggest that the latter view is correct for autism and other PDDs and probably for childhood schizophrenia as well. With changes in nomenclature and the increasing sophistication of the research enterprise, it does seem that, in certain disorders, such as the borderline syndrome, experiential factors probably play a much larger role (see Chapter 4).

Somewhat paradoxically, given the early and sustained interest in psychological processes, early theoretical biases led investigators and clinicians either to overlook or to minimize data suggesting disturbances in other aspects of psychological functioning. For example, Kanner (1943) initially believed that children with autism were of normal intellectual potential. This attribution reflected his observation that on some parts of intelligence tests the children did rather well. In this view the otherwise poor performance of the children was attributed to factors in the child such as noncompliance or negativism; in other words, the child was selectively deciding not to cooperate (see Klin and Shepherd 1994).

It took nearly three decades to establish that a majority of children with autism also exhibited mental retardation (Klin and Shepherd 1994). Moreover, if assessments of cognitive ability are appropriately selected and administered, the results can be used for purposes of programming, are reasonably stable over time, and predict ultimate outcome. For all the psychoses and PDDS, the early tendency to focus on a single disorder appears to have been fundamentally mistaken because multiple, rather than single, diagnoses are the rule in these conditions. Again somewhat paradoxically, the early notion seems, in retrospect, to have been that having a single disorder tended to "immunize" a child against other conditions rather than, as now seems more likely, to increase the probability of the child's exhibiting other disorders.

In autism, studies of psychological functioning have moved from the issue of associated mental retardation to examination of aspects of particular strengths and weakness. Areas of relative strength are often observed in tasks related to visual-perceptual or memory skills; areas of weakness usually involve the ability to sequence information and to reason conceptually. In contrast to most children with mental retardation, significant scatter is usually observed (Klin and Shepherd 1994). On tests of intelligence that use measures of both verbal and nonverbal or performance abilities, it is typical in autism for verbal IQ to be less than nonverbal or performance IQ (Klin and Shepherd 1994). Unusual islets of ability or splinter skills may be observed; for example, in tasks that focus on rote memory or visual detail such as block design. A few individuals with autism exhibit truly unusual "savant" abilities, in terms of feats of memory, or mathematical or calendar calculation, or musical or drawing ability. Occasionally such skills are remarkable even relative to the rest of the population (Treffert 1988); usually such skills are, if present, very narrow and of minimal practical importance to the individual (O'Connor and Hermelin 1988).

The pattern of intellectual skills in individuals who have autistic-like conditions and IQ scores in the normal range has been controversial. It has been suggested that in Asperger's disorder, verbal skills are more typically an area of strength, whereas among the individuals with strictly defined autism and full-scale IQs in the normal range, performance or nonverbal skills are typically higher (Klin 1994). Other investigators fail, however, to find distinctive neuropsychological patterns (Szatmari et al. 1990). The literature on both Rett's and childhood disintegrative disorder clearly suggests that intellectual skills are markedly impaired; studies on the nature of this impairment are, however, much less advanced than those in autism and, to a lesser extent, Asperger's disorder.

In childhood schizophrenia there is a small but interesting literature on information processing deficits. It does appear that children with schizophrenia have difficulties with distractibility and with processing of visual information (Asarnow et al. 1991; Caplan et al. 1990). A measure of loosening of association has been related to distractibility indices in children with schizophrenia (Caplan et al. 1990). The issue of how such difficulties become manifest in the characteristic symptoms of schizophrenia remains an area for future research (King 1994).

Over the years various attempts have been made to identify or isolate specific cognitive processes or deficits that are presumed to be central in the production of autism and similar disorders. One of the recurrent lessons to be learned from such efforts is the importance of appreciating the degree of developmental delay associated with the syndrome. Various specific processes have initially been posited to be unique to individuals with autism but, on closer examination, are observed to be more parsimoniously explained by developmental delay. For example, the notion of stimulus overselectivity (Lovaas et al. 1971) attracted considerable interest. The idea was that autistic children responded to only one part of a stimulus, thus accounting for the apparent tendency of children with autism to become "stuck" on certain idiosyncratic, and often quite minor, aspects of an object or task. A series of studies have suggested that such deficits are not, however, specific to autism and are more parsimoniously accounted for by general developmental delay (see Frith and Baron-Cohen 1987). Other initially attractive concepts, such as perceptual inconstancy (Ornitz and Ritvo 1968), proved difficult to operationalize empirically.

As Yule (1978) notes, the issue of appropriate control groups is critical because apparent deficits that often initially appear specific to autism are more likely the result of general developmental delay. To further complicate research in this area, the issue of which appropriate control group to use is often very complicated: should the research match on nonverbal IQ, on performance IQ, on verbal IQ, or on social skills? The answers to these questions are highly dependent on the nature of the tasks under study. The ready and commonly employed solution of following "quick and dirty" matching procedures—such as on receptive language abilities—may prove to be highly inappropriate in actual practice. In children with autism, receptive vocabulary skills may be more preserved than skills relative to actual language use (Klin and Shepherd 1994). The recent trend for investigators to employ multiple comparison groups is clearly an advance in this regard. Other approaches have focused on other psychological processes such as deficits in self-awareness and self-recognition or theory-of-mind problems.

The role of cognitive deficits in the pathogenesis of autism has been controversial. It is true that the social disturbances are central aspects of syndrome definition, but the relationship of social deficits to cognitive and communicative ones remains unclear (Volkmar 1987). Attempts to identify specific pathognomonic psychological processes related to deficits in learning, such as overselectivity, or related to deficits in social-perceptual skills, such as self-recognition, have often been more parsimoniously explained by overall levels of cognitive functioning. On the other hand, studies of social development in autism do suggest that delays in social skills are much greater than those predicted by overall cognitive abilities (Volkmar et al. 1993). It is true that the social disturbances seen in autism are primary, at least in terms of syndrome definition.

Recent attempts have been made to account for the social deficits in autism on the basis of a very specific cognitive disability related to deficits in capacities for attributions of wishes and feelings to others (the theory-of-mind hypothesis) (Baron-Cohen 1989). Although attractive in many respects (Tager-Flusberg 1993), this hypothesis does not appear to explain adequately the severity and nature of the social deficit in autism. Although it has generated considerable research, it fails to account for the severity and early onset of social deficits in autism and is essentially inapplicable to the large proportion of autistic individuals who are largely or entirely mute (Klin et al. 1992).

The cognitive development of very young autistic children has been less frequently studied. The available data on aspects of sensorimotor intelligence in this age group are conflicting (Curcio 1976; Losche 1990). Given the importance of the issues of possible cognitive contributions to syndrome pathogenesis, research in this area should be a priority.

The pattern of intellectual skills in individuals with PDDs whose IQ scores fall within the normal range has been controversial. It now appears likely that there are at least two subgroups within the broader autistic spectrum of conditions; these appear to correspond to high-functioning autism and Asperger's disorder (Klin 1994). In Asperger's disorder, verbal skills may, as expected, be an area of strength, whereas among the more capable individuals with autism (strictly defined), performance or nonverbal skills are typically advanced relative to verbal abilities (Klin 1994).

Biological Processes

Interest in possible psychogenic etiologies of these conditions initially impeded research on neurobiological aspects of these conditions. The initial controversies about syndrome boundaries and theoretical issues, such as the ability of a child to experience depression, also complicated early research studies. It is noteworthy that, although early views of childhood schizophrenia emphasized the importance of neurobiological factors (Bender 1947), during the 1950s such factors were less emphasized. This situation changed markedly during the 1960s and 1970s as it became clear that valid distinctions could be drawn within the group of childhood psychoses. For example, it became clear that individuals with autism were at markedly increased risk for development of seizure disorder during childhood and especially during adolescence (Rutter 1970). Subsequently, it became apparent that autism could be observed in association with a host of medical conditions of rather diverse types (Chapter 6). Given that autism is, if strictly defined, relatively rare, it was important to establish whether any such associations were greater than would be expected. It became apparent that this was so for some of these conditions: the frequency of congenital rubella and autism occurring in association is greater than would be expected on chance alone (Chess et al. 1974). These observations helped to refocus research attention on neurobiological factors and provided convincing evidence that autism and disorders that are closely related to it are organically based. Similar although less extensive work has supported the role of neurobiological factors in disorders such as childhood schizophrenia and affective psychoses. Relative to other disorders autism has been, by far, the target of the most extensive and systematic study.

Associations With Other Conditions

Autism has now been linked with a host of associated medical conditions, ranging from chromosomal disorders such as fragile X syndrome (Hagerman et al. 1986) to structural brain disorders such as tuberous sclerosis (Gillberg 1992) and to infections such as congenital rubella (Chess et al. 1974). It is also clear that autism is associated with a markedly increased risk for development of seizure disorders of diverse types throughout the developmental period but very often during adolescence (Deykin and MacMahon 1979; Volkmar and Nelson 1990). Various nonspecific neurological signs are also observed, such as persistence of primitive reflexes (Minderaa et al. 1985). Although there is now little doubt that autism is sometimes associated with these diverse medical conditions, there is disagreement about the degree to which such asso-ciations are observed. This issue has implications for research and clinical services relative to the extent of associated laboratory and other medical studies.

Methodological problems pose substantial difficulties for interpre-tation of many reports of associations between medical conditions and autism and other disorders. The report of a single case obviously may simply reflect chance factors. The issue is whether rates of autism are increased over those in the population. Issues in case ascertainment and especially in the stringency of the diagnostic criteria used may account for sometimes very marked differences between studies. Thus, early studies that reported high degrees of association between autism and the fragile X syndrome have not been replicated, and it appears that fragile X is observed in perhaps 1%–2% of individuals with autism (Bailey et al. 1993; Watson et al. 1984). Although this rate clearly is an increase over the base rate of autism in the population, it also does not account for more than a small proportion of cases. Gillberg and his col-leagues (see Gillberg 1992) have reported especially high rates of autism in association with a known medical condition. Thus, they recommend extensive medical investigations including lumbar puncture. On the other hand Rutter and colleagues, in a comprehensive review of the topic, noted that the rate of known medical conditions and autism is probably about 10% and that apart from screening for fragile X and other chromo-somal disorders, other studies should be guided by history and physical examination (Rutter et al. 1994). It does appear that rates of associated medical conditions rise among individuals with the most severe associ-ated mental retardation; this is also the group in which diagnostic un-certainty is the greatest (Volkmar et al. 1994). The nature and meaning of medical conditions associated with autism remain an important topic for research both from the viewpoint of practical implications for screen-ing and from the viewpoint of research on mechanisms of pathogenesis.

Although information on other PDDs and psychotic conditions is more limited than that for autism, these conditions are sometimes as-sociated with other medical conditions. In childhood disintegrative dis-order in particular, progressive neurological disorders, such as subacute sclerosing panencephalitis, may present with progressive deterioration in functioning. It is also clear, however, that in most cases such conditions are not observed. Similarly, a variety of toxic and metabolic conditions and central nervous system (CNS) infections may produce psychotic symptoms (King 1994).

Associations of these various conditions with each other and with other psychiatric conditions have been the topic of some controversy. It appears, for example, that autism and schizophrenia are occasionally observed together, although at no greater rate than would be expected given the base rates of the disorder in the general population (Volkmar and Cohen 1991a). The association of autism with possible obsessive-compulsive disorder is more controversial (McDougle et al. 1994).

Central Nervous System Abnormalities

The higher rates of psychotic and PDDs associated with various medical conditions have suggested the importance of CNS dysfunction in syndrome pathogenesis (King 1994). Various methods have been used to study CNS dysfunction in these medical conditions: studies of electroencephalograms (EEGs), of neuroimaging, of various neurotransmitters and possible toxins, and so forth. As in other areas of research, early studies were hampered by inconsistencies in diagnostic practice and other methodological problems, such as the need to rely on peripheral measures of CNS neurochemical activity. Autopsy studies (e.g., Bauman 1991) are similarly limited in multiple respects, but the few abnormalities observed may have important implications for understanding the timing of any CNS insult. On the other hand, the development of more effective pharmacological treatments, notably for the childhood psychoses, has encouraged more research that is more specifically focused on neurochemical systems.

Neurochemistry

The efficacy of specific pharmacological interventions for schizophrenia, mania, and psychotic depression is well established in adult psychiatry. As noted in this volume (Chapters 1 to 3), evidence on the efficacy of these agents in children is more limited. In schizophrenia of very early onset, pharmacological data are minimal; in children with mania or with major depression and psychosis the body of research is slightly larger.

In major depression with psychosis there has been some work on identifying more specific biological markers in children (see Chapter 2), although again available research is limited and the results somewhat contradictory; this may reflect possible differences in the child and adult forms of affective illness or biological heterogeneity (Goodyer et al. 1991). Such differences may also be related to the apparently decreased efficacy of the tricyclic antidepressants in this age group (Strober et al. 1990).

In autism, one of the most intriguing and well-replicated findings has been that of elevated blood levels of serotonin in individuals with the disorder (see Anderson and Hoshino 1987 for a review). Originally reported by Schain and Freedman (1961), subsequent research has consistently noted that group mean elevations in autism are markedly increased relative to various control groups, with a median increase of approximately 50% (Anderson and Hoshino 1987). The significance of this finding does, however, remain unclear. The finding is not specific to autism and is not uniformly observed with the condition. Various developmental correlates of peripheral serotonin level are observed, and the relationship of peripheral blood levels to central serotonergic activity remains unclear. Several alternative explanations are possible, such as decreased catabolism, increased synthesis of serotonin, or altered peripheral (blood platelet) mechanisms of binding serotonin (5-HT). However, the well-replicated nature of the finding and its possible implications for treatment (see McDougle et al. 1994) have added to interest in the nature of this phenomenon.

Studies of other neurotransmitter systems have not revealed the same robust findings as those related to serotonin. Plasma and urine measures of norepinephrine, epinephrine, and their metabolites have not consistently revealed significant group differences (Minderaa et al. 1989). Again, various confounding factors have complicated the interpretation of much of the available research.

In Rett's disorder, and beginning with Rett's (1966) original description, considerable interest has focused on the possibility that the condition may result from some abnormality in metabolism. Various potential deficiencies have been postulated focusing on elevated serum ammonia, cerebrospinal fluid (CSF) biogenic amines, and plasma glycosphingolipids, but no consistent abnormality has been identified (Tsai 1994).

Neurophysiology and Neuroimaging

Higher rates of abnormal or equivocal EEGs are observed in childhood-onset schizophrenia as well as in autism and other PDDs (King 1994; Volkmar and Nelson 1990). Both in autism and in childhood schizophrenia a growing body of work has focused on neurophysiological responses such as auditory-event-related potentials (Asarnow et al. 1991; Ervin et al. 1986; Ornitz 1987). This line of work is of particular interest given the report that problems in attention and information processing may be observed in individuals at risk for schizophrenia (Erlenmeyer-Kimling and Cornblatt 1987).

Studies using computed tomography or magnetic resonance imaging have yielded rather mixed results. Interpretation of the few available studies on childhood schizophrenia (e.g., Hendren et al. 1991; Reiss et al. 1983) is complicated by major methodological problems such as diagnostic heterogeneity, lack of appropriate controls, and so forth. Similarly in autism studies have produced conflicting results. Courchesne et al. (1988) reported a relatively specific abnormality in cerebellums of higher-functioning individuals with autism; this observation has not, however, proven to be readily replicable (Minshew 1992). Neuroimaging studies of Asperger's disorder may be of interest given the apparent similarity of this condition to Rourke's (1989) concept of nonverbal learning disability, which posits specific neuroanatomical correlates of the characteristic psychological profile. Only one MRI study has, to date, focused on patients with Asperger's disorder (Berthier et al. 1993), and its interpretation is hampered by small sample size.

Prenatal, Perinatal, and Genetic Factors

Studies of adults with schizophrenia have suggested that various prenatal and perinatal factors (including obstetrical complications and infections) may have some role in the pathogenesis of the condition, possibly in relation to some genetic vulnerability (Mednick et al. 1988). This observation has not yet been replicated with childhood-onset schizophrenia (King 1994). In autism a general increase in levels of obstetrical risk has been observed when children with autism are compared with siblings. It is possible that at least some of the apparent risk factors observed might relate to underlying genetic factors. Although autism has been associated with some extrinsic factors (e.g., congenital rubella and cytomegalovirus) such cases appear to be rather uncommon. The issue of possible interaction of some degree of genetic vulnerability with some environmental risk factor(s) remains open. Evidence regarding the operation of prenatal and perinatal factors in other psychotic and PDD conditions is highly limited.

A role of genetic factors in childhood schizophrenia is suggested by family and twin studies in which the concordance rate for twins, when one twin has childhood-onset schizophrenia, is even higher than concordance rates for adults (King 1994). As noted in Chapter 1, approximately 10% of parents of a child with schizophrenia themselves exhibit the disorder. In autism several different lines of evidence suggest an important role for genetic factors in syndrome pathogenesis. For example, both the relatively high rates of minor physical abnormalities and the few available neuropathological studies tend to suggest prenatal rather than postnatal insult, probably relatively early on in CNS morphogenesis. Early impressions that genetic factors had little role in pathogenesis of autism failed to consider the relative infrequency of the condition, the likelihood that patients would not reproduce, and the possibility that siblings might exhibit some alternative condition rather than autism. More recent genetic studies have clearly suggested the operation of some genetic factor or factors. This work included both twin and family studies and made it clear that siblings are at significantly increased risk both for autism and for other developmental disorders (August et al. 1984; Cohen et al. 1994; Folstein and Rutter 1977).

Treatment Studies

Given the severity of these conditions, essentially every conceivable treatment has been attempted—although, unfortunately, only rarely has this been done in a systematic way. For autism these treatments have included various pharmacological agents, somatic therapies (e.g., "patterning" or "holding"), ECT, auditory retraining, special education and behavior modification, and so forth. With a few exceptions, most notably studies of behavior modification techniques and some drug studies, the available literature on treatment evaluations is minimal. It does appear that intensive, special educational interventions are associated with better outcomes than are less structured approaches (Rutter and Bartak 1973). Given the poor prognosis of the condition and the lack of knowledge of fundamental aspects of pathogenesis it is probably not surprising that parents are readily interested in therapies that hold out the promise of either a "cure" or a marked amelioration in symptoms. Unfortunately, substantive evaluation data are lacking, particularly for the less orthodox treatments. In the absence of such data there is an understandable tendency on the part of parents and sometimes educators to rely on a sense of "feeling good" rather than on empirical data. This is clearly true regarding "facilitated communication," in which the available data consistently fail to support the validity of the method or the communications received (see Prior and Cummings 1992 for a discussion).

The report of an apparent cure in any single case must be treated with considerable skepticism, because it is clear that a small number of individuals with autism have a very good outcome. Often reports of cures or recovery provide very little diagnostic information—much less sufficient information to evaluate the putative treatment; it is not always clear that individuals with autism are being studied, nor is it clear that any changes observed necessarily reflect an effect of the intervention. Clearly, the most substantive data have emerged from drug and behavioral studies, although even here initial findings have not always been replicated and apparent positive results have proved to be neither sustained nor readily replicable. A relative lack of research support has compounded the difficulties of conducting research in this area. Marked geographic variations in terms of access to services, even in the United States, remain a problem even in the face of legal entitlements to services. For example, in at least one state, North Carolina, a statewide program—Treatment and Education of Autistic and Related Communications-handicapped Children (Division TEACCH)—is available to provide for the education and treatment of autistic children (Schopler 1994). This model program is, unfortunately, the exception rather than the rule. More typically, programs vary markedly from one education district to the other and involve treatments that are not systematically evaluated. The impact of the affected child on the family has often been underappreciated (Schopler and Mesibov 1984).

In adult-onset schizophrenia and major affective disorders, pharmacotherapy is a mainstay of treatment. Controlled studies of these agents in children are much less common, although major tranquilizers, antidepressants, lithium, and other agents clearly have importance as one aspect of what usually should be a somewhat broader biopsychosocial treatment program.

In autism, recent pharmacological work has tended to focus on the neuroleptics, which, in a number of carefully designed studies, have been noted to be more effective than placebo in decreasing hyperactivity, temper tantrums, irritability, stereotypies, and withdrawal in autistic children (McDougle et al. 1994). Although the potential usefulness of the neuroleptics is well established for the treatment of certain aspects of autism and for childhood schizophrenia, these agents have various disadvantages, including their clear potential for oversedation and for tardive dyskinesia and other movement problems.

An initial, preliminary study of fenfluramine, an indirect 5-HT agonist, was prompted by the observation of high peripheral serotonin levels in autism. The results of this preliminary study achieved considerable national recognition, and various replications, including a large multisite study, were undertaken. However, side effects of this agent were quickly noted and controlled studies have generally found fenfluramine to be no better than placebo in reducing levels of maladaptive behavior in children with autism (e.g., Campbell 1988; Schuster et al. 1986). Similarly, initial enthusiasm for use of the opiate receptor antagonist naltrexone was tempered by the results of a double-blind placebo-controlled study by Campbell et al. (1990). It is clear that controlled studies of these various agents are critically needed. Recent research suggests that agents such as fluoxetine and clomipramine, which facilitate serotonergic systems, may reduce certain symptoms in patients with autism (McDougle et al. 1994). Because of the limitations of other agents (Campbell et al. 1988), controlled studies of selective serotonin uptake inhibitors, such as fluvoxamine, are needed.

For childhood schizophrenia neuroleptics remain the mainstay of pharmacological treatment. As might be expected, the vast majority of drug studies have been conducted with adolescents and adults. It appears clear that with children sedation is a major problem and that lower doses of neuroleptics are apparently required to achieve the same antipsychotic effects (Caplan 1994). The presence of tardive dyskinesia in children and adolescents treated with these agents is a major concern (Campbell et al. 1988). The use of agents such as clozapine, an atypical neuroleptic, in childhood schizophrenia is an important area for future research (Blanz and Schmidt 1993).

Summary

Developmental factors clearly influence the expression (and detection) of all these disorders. As this review demonstrates, progress in research and clinical knowledge was initially impeded by overly quick assumptions of continuity between adult and childhood conditions. Differences in clinical phenomenology are observed even in conditions like schizophrenia and mania, in which similarities of the childhood-onset and adult-onset forms of the disorder are clearest.

With the possible exception of autism, studies of the other childhood psychoses and PDDs are limited in very important respects. The relative infrequency of all these disorders poses a significant obstacle for research. Partly because these conditions are so infrequent, clinicians may be more likely to fail to recognize them when they present in childhood. For purposes of research the relative infrequency of these conditions means that small samples are typically studied and variations in methods are the rule rather than the exception. These observations suggest the need for a more focused research strategy in which multicenter, collaborative studies may play a prominent role. Such studies will, however, bring their own special problems and will require methodological consistency and rigor in relation to standardization of diagnostic criteria used, not to mention a greater commitment of research funds.

Comparatively little systematic research has been conducted on children with borderline personality disorder. The stability of this diagnosis in children has also been questioned (Lofgren et al. 1991), although it must be noted that the potential overlap of this and phenomenologically similar conditions presents a substantial problem for research. Likewise, the similarities of children with dissociative disorders and with schizophrenia can, at least acutely, be a problem for differential diagnosis (Putnam 1991). The absence of detailed, developmentally appropriate definitions is particularly problematic. The absence of such definitions makes it difficult to conduct research and compare results. It also makes the use of other research strategies, such as longitudinal studies, markedly more difficult. For childhood disintegrative disorder the relative dearth of reported cases (which likely reflects both the infrequency of the condition and the lack of clinician familiarity with it) is a major obstacle for research. For Asperger's disorder, the areas of overlap with higher-functioning autism, on the one hand, and PDD NOS, on the other, should be helpful in clarifying aspects of syndrome boundaries. The lack, until now, of consistent definitions has been problematic, and the uniformity of the ICD-10 and DSM-IV definitions should facilitate research on this condition. Aspects of the phenomenology and epidemiology of all these conditions remain important areas for future research both on basic mechanisms of pathogenesis and for delivery of clinical care. For example, the explication of basic brain-behavior relationships in autism may help increase our knowledge of fundamental biological aspects of social and affective development.

References

Akiskal HS, Weller EB: Mood disorders in children and adolescents, in Comprehensive Textbook of Psychiatry, 5th Edition, Vol 1. Edited by Kaplan HI, Sadock BJ. Baltimore, MD, Williams & Wilkins, 1989, pp 1981–1993

American Psychiatric Association: Diagnostic and Statistical Manual of Mental Disorders, 3rd Edition. Washington, DC, American Psychiatric Association, 1980

American Psychiatric Association: Diagnostic and Statistical Manual of Mental Disorders, 3rd Edition, Revised. Washington, DC, American Psychiatric Association, 1987

American Psychiatric Association: Diagnostic and Statistical Manual of Mental Disorders, 4th Edition. Washington, DC, American Psychiatric Association, 1994

Anderson GM, Hoshino Y: Neurochemical studies of autism, in Handbook of Autism and Pervasive Developmental Disorders. Edited by Cohen DJ, Donnellan A. New York, Wiley, 1987, pp 166–191

Andreasen NC, Olsen S: Negative vs. positive schizophrenia: definition and validation. Arch Gen Psychiatry 39:789–794, 1982

Asarnow JR, Asarnow RF, Hornstein N, et al: Childhood-onset schizophrenia: developmental perspectives on schizophrenic disorders, in Schizophrenia Life Course Developmental Perspective. Edited by Walker EF. New York, Academic Press, 1991, pp 97–123

Asperger H: Die "autistischen psychopathen" in Kindesalter. Archiv für Psychiatrie und Nerven Krankheiten 117:76–136, 1944

August GJ, Stewart MA, Tsai L: The incidence of cognitive disabilities in the siblings of autistic children. Br J Psychiatry 138:416–422, 1984

Bailey A, Bolton P, Butler L, et al: Prevalence of the fragile X anomaly amongst autistic twins and singletons. J Child Psychol Psychiatry 34:673–688, 1993

Baron-Cohen S: The autistic child's theory of mind: a case of specific developmental delay. J Child Psychol Psychiatry 30:285–297, 1989

Bauman M: Microscopic neuroanatomic abnormalities in autism. Pediatrics 31:791–796, 1991

Bender L: Childhood schizophrenia: clinical study of 100 schizophrenic children. Am J Orthopsychiatry 17:40–56, 1947

Berthier ML, Bayes A, Tolosa ES: Magnetic resonance imaging in patients with concurrent Tourette's disorder and Asperger's syndrome. J Am Acad Child Adolesc Psychiatry 32:633–639, 1993

Bettelheim B: The Empty Fortress. New York, Free Press, 1967

Bettes BA, Walker E: Positive and negative symptoms in psychotic and other psychiatrically disturbed children. J Child Psychol Psychiatry 28:555–568, 1987

Bishop D: Autism, Asperger's syndrome, and pragmatic semantic disorder: where are the boundries? British Journal of Disorders in Communication 24:107–121, 1989

Blanz B, Schmidt MH: Clozapine for schizophrenia. J Am Acad Child Adolesc Psychiatry 32:223–224, 1993

Campbell M: Fenfluramine treatment of autism. J Child Psychol Psychiatry 29:1–10, 1988

Campbell M, Adams P, Perry R, et al: Tardive and withdrawal dyskinesia in autistic children: a prospective study. Psychopharmacol Bull 24:251–255, 1988

Campbell M, Anderson L, Small A: Naltrexone in autistic children: a double-blind and placebo-controlled study. Psychopharmacol Bull 26:130–135, 1990

Cantor S: Childhood Schizophrenia. New York, Guilford, 1988

Caplan R: Childhood schizophrenia: assessment and treatment. Child and Adolescent Psychiatric Clinics of North America 3:15–30, 1994

Caplan R, Guthrie D, Fish B, et al: The Kiddie Formal Thought Disorder Rating Scale (K-FTDS). Clinical assessment, reliability, and validity. J Am Acad Child Adolesc Psychiatry 28:208–216, 1989

Caplan R, Perdue S, Tanguay PE, et al: Formal thought disorder in childhood onset schizophenia and schizotypal personality disorder. J Child Psychol Psychiatry 31:1103–1114, 1990

Caplan R, Guthrie D, Foy JG: Communication deficits and formal thought disorder in schizophrenic children. J Am Acad Child Adolesc Psychiatry 31:151–159, 1992

Chess S, Fernandez P, Korn S: Behavioral consequences of congenital rubella. J Pediatr 93:699–712, 1974

Cohen DJ, Paul R, Volkmar FR: Issues in the classification of pervasive developmental disorders and associated conditions, in Handbook of Autism and Pervasive Developmental Disorders. Edited by Cohen DJ, Donnellan A. New York, Wiley, 1987, pp 20–40

Cohen DJ, Volkmar FR, Anderson G, et al: Integrating biological and behavioral perspectives in the study and care of autistic individuals: the future. Israel Journal of Psychiatry 30:15–32, 1993

Cohen DJ, Pauls D, Volkmar FR: Recent research in autism. Child and Adolescent Psychiatric Clinics of North America 3:161–172, 1994

Courchesne E, Yeung-Courchesne R, Press GA, et al: Hypoplasia of cerebellar vermal lobules VI and VII in autism. N Engl J Med 318:1349–1354, 1988

Curcio F: Sensorimotor functioning and communication in mute autistic children. Journal of Autism and Childhood Schizophrenia 8:281–292, 1976

Dahl EK, Cohen DJ, Provence S: Clinical and multivariate approaches to the nosology of pervasive developmental disorders. J Am Acad Child Adolesc Psychiatry 25:170–180, 1986

DeMyer MK, Hingtgen JN, Jackson RK: Infantile autism reviewed: a decade of research. Schizophr Bull 7:388–451, 1981

Despert JL: Some considerations relating to the genesis of autistic behavior in children. Am J Orthopsychiatry 21:335–350, 1951

Deykin EY, MacMahon B: The incidence of seizures among children with autistic symptoms. Am J Psychiatry 126:1310–1312, 1979

Eisenberg L: The course of childhood schizophrenia. Archives of Neurology and Psychiatry 78:69–83, 1957

Erlenmeyer-Kimling L, Cornblatt B: High risk research in schizophrenia: a summary of what has been learned. J Psychiatr Res 21:401–411, 1987

Ervin RJ, Edward R, Tanguay PE, et al: Abnormal P300 responses in schizophrenic children. J Am Acad Child Psychiatry 25:615–622, 1986

Folstein S, Rutter M: Infantile autism: a genetic study of 21 twin pairs. J Child Psychol Psychiatry 18:297–321, 1977

Frith U (ed): Autism and Asperger Syndrome. New York, Cambridge University Press, 1991

Frith U, Baron-Cohen S: Perception in autistic children, in Handbook of Autism and Pervasive Developmental Disorders. Edited by Cohen DJ, Donnellan A. New York, Wiley, 1987, pp 85–102

Garralda ME: Hallucinations in children with conduct and emotional disorders: I. The clinical phenomena. Psychol Med 14:589–596, 1984

Ghaziuddin M, Tsai LY, Ghaziuddin N: A comparison of the diagnostic criteria for Asperger syndrome. J Autism Dev Disord 22:643–649, 1992a

Ghaziuddin M, Tsai LY, Ghaziuddin N: A reappraisal of clumsiness as a diagnostic feature of Asperger syndrome. J Autism Dev Disord 22:651–656, 1992b

Gillberg C: Clinical and neurobiological aspects of Asperger syndrome in six family studies, in Autism and Asperger Syndrome. Edited by Frith U. Cambridge, Cambridge University Press, 1991a, pp 122–146

Gillberg C: Debate and argument: is autism a pervasive developmental disorder? J Child Psychol Psychiatry 32:1169–1170, 1991b

Gillberg C: Autism and autistic-like conditions: subclasses among disorders of empathy. J Child Psychol Psychiatry 33:813–842, 1992

Gillberg C: Debate and argument: having Rett syndrome in the ICD-10 PDD category does not make sense. J Child Psychol Psychiatry 33:377–378, 1994

Goodyer IM, Herbert J, Moor S, et al: Cortisol hyper-secretion in depressed school-aged children and adolescents. Psychiatry Res 37:237–244, 1991

Green WH, Campbell M, Hardesty AS, et al: A comparision of schizophrenic and autistic children. J Am Acad Child Psychiatry 23:399–409, 1984

Hagerman R, Jackson A, Levitas A, et al: An analysis of autism in 50 males with Fragile X syndrome. Am J Med Genet 23:359–374, 1986

Hendren R, Hodde-Varga J, Vargba L, et al: Magnetic resonance imaging of severely disturbed children—a preliminary study. J Am Acad Child Adolesc Psychiatry 30:466–470, 1991

Heller T: Dementia infantilis. Zeitschrift für die Erforschung un Behandlung des Jugendlichen Schwachsinns 2:141–165, 1908

Kanner L: Autistic disturbances of affective contact. Nervous Child 2:217–250, 1943

King RA: Childhood onset schizophrenia: development and pathogenesis. Child and Adolescent Psychiatric Clinics of North America 3:1–13, 1994

Klin A: Asperger Syndrome. Child and Adolescent Psychiatric Clinics of North America 3:131–148, 1994

Klin A, Shepherd B: Psychological assessment of autistic children. Child and Adolescent Psychiatric Clinics of North America 3: 53–70, 1994

Klin A, Volkmar FR, Sparrow SS: Autistic social dysfunction: some limitations of the theory of mind hypothesis. J Child Psychol Psychiatry 33:861–876, 1992

Kolvin I: Studies in the childhood psychoses, I: diagnostic criteria and classification. Br J Psychiatry 118:381–384, 1971

Kraepelin E: Dementia Praecox and Paraphrenia. Edinburgh, Churchill Livingstone, 1919

Lane J: The Wild Boy of Aveyron. London, Allen & Unwin, 1977

Le Couteur A, Rutter M, Lord C, et al: Autism diagnostic interview: a standardized investigator-based instrument. J Autism Dev Disord 19:363–388, 1989

Lofgren DP, Bemporad J, King J, et al: A prospective follow-up study of so-called borderline children. Am J Psychiatry 148:1541–1547, 1991

Lord C, Rutter M, Goode S, et al: Autism Diagnostic Observation Schedule: a standardized observation of communicative and social behavior. J Autism Dev Disord 19:185–212, 1989

Losche G: Sensorimotor and action development in autistic children from infancy to early childhood. J Child Psychol Psychiatry 31:749–761, 1990

Lovaas OI: Behavioral treatment and normal educational and intellectual functioning in young autistic children. J Consult Clin Psychol 55:3–9, 1987

Lovaas OI, Schreibman L, Koegel R, et al: Selective responding by autistic children to multiple sensory input. J Abnorm Psychol 77:211–222, 1971

Mahler M: On child psychoses and schizophrenia: autistic and symbiotic infantile psychoses. Psychoanal Study Child 7:286–305, 1952

Makita K: The age of onset of childhood schizophrenia. Folia Psychiatrica Neurologica Japonica 20:111–121, 1966

Maudsley H: The Physiology and Pathology of the Mind. London, Macmillan, 1867

Mayes LC, Volkmar FR, Hooks M, et al: Differentiating pervasive developmental disorder not otherwise specified from autism and language disorders. J Autism Dev Disord 23:79–90, 1993

McClellan JM, Werry JS: Schizophrenia. Psychiatr Clin North Am 15:131–148, 1991

McDougle CJ, Price LH, Volkmar FR: Recent advances in the pharmacotherapy of autism and related conditions. Child and Adolescent Psychiatric Clinics of North America 3:71–89, 1994

Mednick SA, Machon, RA, Huttunenen MOP, et al: Adult schiozphrenia following prenatal exposure to an influenza epidemic. Arch Gen Psychiatry 45:189-192, 1988

Minderaa RB, Volkmar FR, Hansen CR, et al: Snout and visual rooting reflex in infantile autism. J Autism Dev Disord 15:409–415, 1985

Minderaa RB, Anderson GM, Volkmar FR, et al: Neurochemical study of dopamine functioning in autistic and normal subjects. J Am Acad Child Adolesc Psychiatry 28:200–206, 1989

Minshew NH: Neurological localization in autism, in High-Functioning Individuals With Autism. Edited by Schopler E, Mesibov G. New York, Plenum, 1992, pp 65–89

O'Connor N, Hermelin B: Annotation: low intelligence and special abilities. J Child Psychol Psychiatry 29:391–396, 1988

Ornitz EM: Neurophysiological studies in infantile autism, in Handbook of Autism and Pervasive Developmental Disorders. Edited by Cohen DJ, Donnellan A. New York, Wiley, 1987, pp 148–165

Ornitz EM, Ritvo E: Perceptual inconstancy in early infantile autism. Arch Gen Psychiatry 18:76–98, 1968

Parks SL: The assessment of autistic children: a selective review of available instruments. J Autism Dev Disord 13:255–267, 1983

Petti TA, Vela RN: Borderline disorders of childhood: an overview. J Am Acad Child Adolesc Psychiatry 29:327–337, 1990

Piaget J: The Child's Construction of Reality. London, Routledge & Kegan Paul, 1955

Pomeroy JD: Autism and Asperger's: same or different? J Am Acad Child Adolesc Psychiatry 30:152–153, 1991

Potter HW: Schizophrenia in children. Am J Psychiatry 89:1253–1270, 1933

Prior M, Cummings R: Questions about facilitated communication and autism. J Autism Dev Disord 21:57–67, 1992

Putnam F: Dissociative disorders in children and adolescents: a developmental perspective. Psychiatr Clin North Am 14:519–531, 1991

Rank B: Adaptation of the psychoanalytic technique for the treatment of young children with atypical development. Am J Orthopsychiatry 19:130–139, 1949

Reiss D, Feinstein D, Weinberger D, et al: Ventricular enlargement in child psychiatric pateints: a controlled study with planimetric measurements. Am J Psychiatry 140:453–456, 1983

Rett A: Uber ein eigenartiges hirntophisces Syndrome bei Hyperammonie im Kindersalter. Wein Medizinische Wochenschrift 118:723–726, 1966

Riddle M: Individual and parental psychotherapy in autism, in Handbook of Autism and Pervasive Developmental Disorders. Edited by Cohen DJ, Donnellan A. New York, Wiley, 1987. pp 528–544

Rourke B: Nonverbal Learning Disabilities: The Syndrome and the Model. New York, Guilford, 1989

Rumsey JJ: Neuropsychological studies of high-level autism, in High-Functioning Individuals With Autism. Edited by Schopler E, Mesibov G. New York, Plenum, 1992, pp 42–64

Russel AT, Bott L, Sammons C: The phenomenology of schizophrenia occurring in childhood. J Am Acad Child Adolesc Psychiatry 28:399–407, 1989

Rutter M: Autistic children: infancy to adulthood. Seminars in Psychiatry 2:435–450, 1970

Rutter M: Diagnosis and definition, in Autism: A Reappraisal of Concepts and Treatment. Edited by Rutter M, Schopler E. New York, Plenum, 1978, pp 1–25

Rutter M: Debate and argument: there are connections between brain and mind and it is important that Rett syndrome be classified somewhere. J Child Psychol Psychiatry 35:379–381, 1994

Rutter M, Bartak L: Special educational treatment of autistic children: a comparative study, II: follow-up findings and implications for services. J Child Psychol Psychiatry 14:241–270, 1973

Rutter M, Schopler E: Classification of pervasive developmental disorders: some concepts and practical considerations. J Autism Dev Disord 22:459–482, 1992

Rutter M, Shaffer D, Shepherd M: A Multiaxial Classification of Child Psychiatric Disorders. Geneva, World Health Organization, 1975

Rutter M, Bailey A, Bolton P, et al: Autism and known medical conditions: myth and substance. J Child Psychol Psychiatry 35:311–322, 1994

Schain RJ, Freedman DK: Studies on 5-hydroxyindole metabolism in autistic and other mentally retarded children. J Pediatr 58:315–320, 1961

Schopler E, Andrews CE, Strupp K: Do autistic children come from upper-middle-class parents? J Autism Dev Disord 10:91–103, 1980

Schopler E: Convergence of learning disability, higher level autism, and Asperger's syndrome (editorial). J Autism Dev Disord 15:359, 1985

Schopler E: A statewide program for the treatment and education of autistic and related communication handicapped children (TEACCH). Child and Adolescent Psychiatric Clinics of North America 3: 91–103, 1994

Schopler E, Mesibov G (eds): The Effects of Autism on the Family. New York, Plenum, 1984

Schuster C, Lewis M, Seiden L: Fenfluramine: neurotoxicity. Psychopharmacol Bull 22:148–151, 1986

Schwab-Stone M, Towbin KE, Tarnoof GM: Systems of classification: ICD-10, DSM-III-R, and DSM-IV, in Child and Adolescent Psychiatry: A Comprehensive Textbook. Edited by Lewis M. Baltimore, MD, Williams & Wilkins, 1991, 422–434

Siegel B, Pliner C, Eschler J, et al: How autistic children are diagnosed: difficulties in identification of children with multiple developmental delays. J Dev Behav Pediatr 9:199–204, 1988

Stone WL, Lemanek KL, Fischel PT, et al: Play and imitation skills in the diagnosis of autism in young children. Pediatrics 86:267–272, 1990

Strober M, Freeman R, Riagli J: The pharmacotherapy of depressive illness in adolescence, I: an open label trial of imipramine. Psychopharmacol Bull 26:80–84, 1990

Szatmari P, Tuff L, Finlayson MA, et al: Asperger's syndrome and autism: neurocognitive aspects. J Am Acad Child Adolesc Psychiatry 29:130–136, 1990

Tager-Flusberg H: What language reveals about the understanding of minds in children with autism, in Understanding Other Minds: Perspectives From Autism. Edited by Baron-Cohen S, Tager-Flusberg H, Cohen DJ. Oxford, Oxford Medical Publications, 1993, pp 138–157

Tantam D: Asperger's syndrome. J Child Psychol Psychiatry 29:245–256, 1989

Towbin KE: Pervasive developmental disorder not otherwise specified: a review and guidelines for clinical care. Child and Adolescent Psychiatric Clinics of North America 3:149–160, 1994

Treffert DA : The idiot savant: a review of the syndrome. Am J Psychiatry 145:563–572, 1988

Tsai LY: Rett syndrome. Child and Adolescent Psychiatric Clinics of North America 3:105–118, 1994

Volkmar FR: Social development, in Handbook of Autism and Pervasive Developmental Disorders. Edited by Cohen DJ, Donnellan A. New York, Wiley, 1987, pp 41–60

Volkmar FR: Childhood disintegrative disorder. Child and Adolescent Psychiatric Clinics of North America 3:119–129, 1994

Volkmar FR, Cohen DJ: Co-morbid association of autism and schizophrenia. Am J Psychiatry 148:1705–1707, 1991a

Volkmar FR, Cohen DJ: Debate and argument: the utility of the term pervasive developmental disorder. J Child Psychol Psychiatry 32:1171–1172, 1991b

Volkmar FR, Nelson DS: Seizure disorders in autism. J Am Acad Child Adolesc Psychiatry 29:127–129, 1990

Volkmar FR, Cohen DJ, Hoshino Y, et al: Phenomenology and classification of the childhood psychoses. Psychol Med 18:191–201, 1988

Volkmar FR, Carter A, Sparow SS, et al: Quantifying social development in autism. J Am Acad Child Adolesc Psychiatry 32:626–632, 1993

Volkmar FR, Klin A, Siegel B, et al: Field trial for autistic disorder in DSM-IV. Am J Psychiatry 151:1361–1367, 1994

Volkmar FR, Becker DF, King RA, et al: Psychotic processes, in Handbook of Developmental Psychopathology. Edited by Cicchetti D, Cohen DJ. New York, Wiley, 1995, pp 512–534

Watson MS, Leckman JF, Annex B, et al: Fragile X in a survey of 75 autistic males (letter). N Engl J Med 310:1462, 1984

Weller RA, Weller EB, Tucker SG, et al: Mania in prepubertal children: has it been underdiagnosed? J Affect Disord 11:151–154, 1986

Werry JS: ICD 9 and DSM III classification for the clinician. J Child Psychol Psychiatry 26:1–6, 1985

Werry JS: Long-term outcome of pervasive developmental, psychotic, and allied disorders, in Do They Outgrow It? Long-Term Outcome of Childhood Disorders. Edited by Hechtman L. Washington, DC, American Psychiatric Press (in press)

Werry JS, McLellan JM, Chard L: Child and adolescent schizphrenia, bipolar and schizoaffective disorder: a clinical and outcome study. J Am Acad Child Adolesc Psychiatry 30:457–465, 1991

Wing L: Asperger's syndrome: a clinical account. Psychol Med 11:115–130, 1981

Wolff S: Schizoid personality in childhood and adult life, I: the vagaries of diagnostic labelling. Br J Psychiatry 159:615–620, 1991

World Health Organization: International Classification of Diseases, 10th Edition—Diagnostic Criteria for Research (draft). Geneva, World Health Organization, 1990

Yule W: Research methodology: what are the "correct controls"? In Autism: A Reappraisal of Concepts and Treatment. Edited by Rutter M, Schopler E. New York, Plenum, 1978, pp 155–162

Index

Page numbers printed in **boldface** *type refer to tables or figures.*

Adults *(continued)*
  thought disturbance in
    psychoses of, 258–259
Affective disorders. *See* Depression
Age at onset
  of autism, 143–145, 230–231, 239
  of bipolar disorder with
    psychosis, 78, 83
  of childhood disintegrative
    disorder, 230–231, **232,**
    239, 260, 261
  of cohort effect, 75
  of manic episodes, 74, 75–76
  of Rett's disorder, 230, 233,
    260–261
  of schizophrenia, 1, 7, 18, 19
  of seizure disorder in autism
    cases, 156, **157**
Aggression, and borderline
  personality disorder, 101
Altered consciousness, and
  dissociative hallucinosis, 111
Anna O. case, 108
Antidepressants
  dissociative hallucinosis and, 124
  major depression with psychosis
    and, 64
Antisocial personality disorder, 91,
  96
Anxiety. *See also* Anxiety disorders
  Asperger's disorder and, 199
  borderline personality disorder
    in children and, 101
  depression in children and
    adolescents and, 55
Anxiety disorders
  atypical pervasive
    developmental disorder
    and, 212

  borderline personality disorder
    and, 93, 94
  depression in adolescents and, 63
Apnea, and Rett's disorder, 235
Asperger, Hans, 192–193, 253, 254
Asperger's disorder
  assessment of, 201–202
  autism and, 170, 197–199
  case study of, 216–217
  clinical features of, 196–197,
    266, 268
  course and prognosis of,
    199–200, 262
  diagnostic definition of,
    193–195, 253
  differential diagnosis of, 36, 167,
    168, 197–199, 203–204,
    213, 214, 239
  etiology and pathogenesis of,
    200–201, 273
  overview of, 192–193
  prevalence and epidemiology of,
    195–196, 261
  research on, 214–216, 254–255,
    278
Assessment. *See also* Diagnosis;
  Differential diagnosis
  of Asperger's disorder, 201–202
  of atypical pervasive
    developmental disorder,
    212
  of autism, 158–166, 259
  of bipolar disorder with
    psychosis, 80–81
  of childhood disintegrative
    disorder, 237–239
  of major depression with
    psychosis, 57–63
  of schizophrenia, 30–32, 259